Arbatax

S. Priamo

THE
EASTERN
COAST

Nurallao

Quartu S. Elena

Fordongianus

Sanluri

Cagliari

THE
WESTERN
COAST

CAGLIARI AND
THE SOUTH

Pula

Oristano

Fluminimaggiore

Iglesias

Carbonia

Isola
San Pietro

S. Antioco

Isola di
Sant'Antioco

0 kilometres   20

0 miles   20

EYEWITNESS TRAVEL

SARDINIA

EYEWITNESS TRAVEL

SARDINIA

Main Contributor **Fabrizio Ardito**

DK | Penguin Random House

Produced by Fabio Ratti Editoria Libraria e Multimediale, Milano, Italy

Project Editor Diana Georgiacodis

Editors Anna Lia Deffenu, Giovanni Francesio, Renata Perego, Laura Recordati

Designers Paolo Gonzato, Stefania Testa, Studio Matra

Maps Paul Stafford

Picture Research Fabio De Angelis, Riccardo Villarosa

Dorling Kindersley Ltd

Project Editor Fiona Wild

Editor Francesca Machiavelli

DTP Cooling Brown

DTP Designer Ingrid Vienings

Main Contributor Fabrizio Ardito

Additional Contributors Patrizia Giovannetti, Raffaella Rizzo

Illustrators Giorgia Boli, Alberto Ipsilanti, Daniela Veluti, Nadia Viganò

English Translation Richard Pierce

Printed and bound in China

First published in Great Britain in 1998
by Dorling Kindersley Limited
80 Strand, London WC2R 0RL

17 18 19 20 10 9 8 7 6 5 4 3 2 1

**Reprinted with revisions 2000, 2001, 2002, 2003, 2006,
2008, 2011, 2014, 2017**

Copyright 1998, 2017 © Dorling Kindersley Limited, London

A Penguin Random House Company

A CIP catalogue record for this book is available from the British Libary.

ISBN 978-0-24127-385-2

Throughout this book, floors are referred to in accordance with
European usage, i.e. the "First Floor" is the floor above ground level.

MIX
Paper from
responsible sources
FSC
www.fsc.org   FSC™ C018179

**The information in this
DK Eyewitness Travel Guide is checked regularly.**
Every effort has been made to ensure that this book is as up to date as possible
at the time of going to press. Some details, however, such as telephone numbers,
opening hours, prices, gallery hanging arrangements and travel information are
liable to change. The publishers cannot accept responsibility for any consequences
arising from the use of this book, nor for any material on third-party websites, and
cannot guarantee that any website address in this book will be a suitable source of
travel information. We value the views and suggestions of our readers very highly.
Please write to: Publisher, DK Eyewitness Travel Guides, Dorling Kindersley,
80 Strand, London, WC2R 0RL, UK, or email: travelguides@dk.com.

Front cover main image: Rugged coastline surrounding Li Cossi beach, Costa Paradiso

◀ The 12th-century castle overlooking the village of Burgos

Contents

How to Use this Guide 6

Sand dunes at Capo Spartivento
near Cagliari

Introducing
Sardinia

Discovering
Sardinia 10

Putting Sardinia
on the Map
16

A Portrait
of Sardinia 18

Sardinia Through
the Year 30

The History
of Sardinia 34

A prehistoric tower of the Santu Antine
nuraghe at Torralba

The beach at Stintino on the tip of the northwestern coast

Knight on horseback during the Sa Sartiglia festival at Oristano

The museum-village of San Sperate, known for its sculptures

Illustrated view of the city of Alghero

HOW TO USE THIS GUIDE

This guide helps you get the most from your visit to Sardinia, providing comprehensive expert recommendations as well as detailed practical information. *Introducing Sardinia* sets the island in its geographical, historical and cultural context. The five area chapters in *Sardinia Area by Area* describe the main sights and monuments in detail, with maps, pictures and illustrations. *Travellers' Needs* offers recommendations for hotels, restaurants and bars, as well as features on what to eat and drink and where to shop. The *Survival Guide* contains practical information on everything from transport to safety.

Sardinia Area by Area

Sardinia has been divided into five main sightseeing areas, each coded with a coloured thumb tab for quick reference. A map illustrating how the island has been divided can be found on the inside front cover of this guide. The sights covered within the individual areas have been plotted and numbered on a *Regional Map*.

1 **Introduction** The landscape, history and character of each region is described here, showing how the area has developed over the centuries and what it has to offer visitors today.

Each area can be identified quickly by its colour coding.

A locator map shows the region in relation to the other areas of Sardinia.

2 **Regional Map** This gives an illustrated overview of the whole area. All the sights covered in the chapter are numbered and there are useful tips on getting around by car and public transport.

Features and story boxes highlight special or unique aspects of an area or sight.

3 **Detailed Information** All the important towns and other places of interest are described individually. They are listed in order, following the numbering on the *Regional Map*. Within each entry there are details on the important buildings and other major sights.

4 **Major Towns** All the important towns are described individually. Within each entry there is further detailed information on important buildings and other sites. The *Town Map* shows the location of the main sights.

A Visitors' Checklist gives you the practical details to plan your visit, including transport information, the address of the tourist office, market days and festivals.

The Town Map shows all major and minor roads. The key sights are plotted, along with train and bus stations, parking areas, churches and tourist information offices.

5 **Street-by-Street Map** Towns or districts of special interest to the visitor are given a bird's-eye view in detailed 3D with photographs and descriptions of the most important sights.

A suggested route for a walk covers the most interesting streets in the area.

Opening hours, telephone number and transport details for the sight are given in the Visitors' Checklist.

6 **The Top Sights** These are given two or more pages. Historic buildings are dissected to reveal their interiors, while the photographs highlight the most interesting features.

INTRODUCING SARDINIA

DISCOVERING SARDINIA

The following leisurely itineraries enable you to experience as many of Sardinia's highlights as possible. First comes a themed three-day tour, which delves into the island's archaeological heritage, revealing the rich legacy of the Phoenician, Carthaginian and Roman periods. Next comes a two-day tour of Sardinia's capital city, Cagliari, showcasing its rich artistic wealth and historical importance. Finally there are two seven-day tours. The first follows the

northern coast, taking in deluxe resorts and medieval towns, then swinging south to Catalan-flavoured Alghero and inland to the mountain town of Nuoro. The second explores the southwestern coast, with forays into the interior taking in major historical sites. These two seven-day tours can be combined to create a two-week itinerary. Or simply dip in and out of these itineraries and be inspired.

Archaeological Tour

- Visit the archaeological museum in **Cagliari**, which boasts the largest collection of artifacts on the island.

- Marvel at the remains of the ancient city of **Nora**, right by the sea.

- Relax in the bucolic surroundings of the **Temple of Antas**.

- Climb up to **Tiscali**, a nuraghic village located within a mountain.

- Seek out the scattered group of monuments around **Arzachena**.

Cagliari
The island's bustling capital, Cagliari, with its rich history, lies in a sheltered gulf on Sardinia's southwestern coast.

Arzachena
Situated at the centre of Sardinia's glitzy resort destination, the Costa Smeralda, Arzachena is famous for a clutch of prehistoric monuments nearby.

◀ Painting of *Sardinian Landscape* (1900–1910) by Guglielmo Micheli

Castelsardo

Sassari

Palmavera
Nuraghe

Grotta di
Nettuno

Alghero

Santissima
Trinità di
Saccargia

San Salvatore
San Giovanni di Sinis

Tharros

Oristano

Santa
Giusta

Golfo di Oristano

Gùspir

Temple of
Antas

Iglesias

Portovesme

Carloforte
San Pietro

Calasetta
Sant'Antioco

*Sant'
Antioco*

| 0 kilometres | 30 |
| 0 miles | 30 |

Key

A Week in Northern Sardinia

- Explore the spectacular northeastern coast, which includes the five-star hotels and beaches of the **Costa Smeralda** and the **Maddalena archipelago**.
- Wander the medieval lanes of **Castelsardo**, dominated by an impressive castle.
- Enjoy the shops, restaurants and beaches of **Alghero**.
- Savour the traditional atmosphere of **Nuoro**, an inland centre with rich cultural heritage.

Castelsardo
Overlooked by the ruined *castello* (castle) that sits atop a rocky volcanic headland, the town of Castelsardo lies not far from Sassari, Sardinia's second city.

A Week in Southern Sardinia

- Admire the archaeological and artistic treasures contained within the Antiquarium Arborense in **Oristano**.
- Spend a day soaking up the historical sites and unspoiled beaches of the **Sinis peninsula**.
- Get stuck into Sardinia's prehistory at **Su Nuraxi**, the island's most important nuraghic site.
- Get a taste of the charming offshore isles of **Sant'Antioco** and **San Pietro**, full of historical interest and boasting some excellent beaches.
- Drive along the Costa del Sud and **Baia Chia** for magnificent views, superlative swimming and interesting archaeological sites.

Archaeological Tour

- **Duration** Three days
- **Airports** Arrive at Cagliari's Elmas airport and depart from Olbia-Costa Smeralda.
- **Transport** You'll need your own transport to visit the places on this itinerary.

Day 1: The Southwest

Start off in Cagliari's **Museo Archeologico Nazionale** (p62), the most comprehensive collection of archaeological finds on the island. Head southwest to explore the Roman and Carthaginian ruins at **Nora** (pp78–9), then continue along the south coast to Chia, site of the Phoenician settlement of **Bithia** (p78), ending up in **Sant'Antioco** (pp76–7), with its extensive Punic remains.

Day 2: Tharros and Tiscali

Visit the well-preserved Carthaginian and Roman **Temple of Antas** (p72), en route to **Tharros** (pp136–7), another important Roman and Carthaginian site on the Sinis peninsula. Devote the afternoon to the mountain cave-village of **Tiscali** (pp108–9), preferably on a guided walk.

Day 3: Gallura

Maiori Nuraghe (p155), in the mountains of Gallura, is a fascinating relic of Sardinia's ancient nuraghic civilization, lying in dense woods outside

Ruins of the Carthaginian and Roman Temple of Antas, near Fluminimaggiore

Tempio Pausania. End the tour on the coast to see the cluster of nuraghic remains in the countryside around the village of **Arzachena** (p149).

Two Days in Cagliari

Sardinia's capital has a rich selection of sights, mostly located in the atmospheric old town.

- **Arriving** Cagliari's Elmas airport lies 6 km (4 miles) northwest of the city. You can reach the city centre in less than 10 minutes by train. Rail service is available from 9am–5pm and one ride costs €1.30.

- **Moving on** Situated in Piazza Matteotti, where taxis are also available, the station is close to the port for mainland ferry connections.

Day 1

Morning The best-preserved area of Cagliari is the **Castello** district (pp60–61), crowning the city and girdled by stout walls. Here, seek out the **Cathedral** (p59), which vividly displays its 12th-century Pisan origins.

An imposing gateway at the far end of Piazza Palazzo leads to the **Cittadella dei Musei** (p62), a complex of museums that include important archaeological finds, Renaissance art and Asian treasures.

Afternoon Climb up either of the two defensive towers that punctuate the old city walls: **Torre di San Pancrazio** (p60) and **Torre dell'Elefante** (p61), for some of the best views over the city and out to the sea. From here, saunter to the northern end of Castello for more sweeping vistas from

Vineyards surrounding the nuraghic village of Tiscali

the **Bastione San Remy**
(p58), a wide esplanade
constructed in the 19th
century and now furnished
with elegant bars. The view
over the port and Cagliari's salt
flats and marshes is especially
magnificent at sunset.

Day 2
Morning Head up Viale
Sant'Ignazio for the **Orto
Botanico** *(p59)*, a botanical
garden planted with more
than 500 exotic species.
A shady sanctuary from the
summer heat, it also contains
grottoes and Roman remains.
Just above it is the **Roman
Amphitheatre** *(p58)*, once
a grand arena for popular
entertainment. If the site is
closed (for ongoing restoration
work), you can still appreciate
the scale of the site from the
outside. Carry on over the
brow of the hill to visit the
Galleria Comunale *(p62)*, which
contains a fine collection of
modern Sardinian art.

Afternoon Visit the modern
Villanova district, where a
former slaughterhouse has
been converted into an arts
centre. The venue, **Exma** *(p63)*,
hosts exhibitions and has
a bookshop and café. A short
walk west, **San Saturnino**
(p63) is one of Sardinia's oldest
churches, dating from the
5th century. The building

Flamingoes in flight over the salt marshes
on the outskirts of Cagliari

The Costa Smeralda, known for its exclusive resorts

suffered bomb damage during
World War II, but retains some
Roman remnants. Buses pass
nearby that will take you to the
sands of **Poetto** *(p25)*, a seaside
resort that makes the perfect
place to unwind, with full
beach facilities available.

A Week in Northern Sardinia

- **Airports** Arrive at and
depart from Olbia-Costa
Smeralda airport, or use the
ferry service, with frequent
connections between Olbia
and the mainland.

- **Transport** A car is essential
for this trip.

Day 1: Costa Smeralda
Travel north out of Olbia
and turn off towards **Porto
Rotondo** *(pp146–7)* for your first
taste of the stretch of coast
known as the **Costa Smeralda**
(pp147–9). As well as a yacht
marina, chic boutiques and
pricey bars, it also boasts a
selection of granite-backed
sandy beaches. Continuing
along the coast with its
seductive vistas over creeks and
bays, you'll soon reach **Porto
Cervo** *(p148)*, the stylish centre
of the Costa Smeralda, where
you can indulge in leisurely
window-shopping among
the famous fashion outlets.
Inland **Arzachena** *(p149)* is
more down-to-earth and

worth a stop for the nearby
archaeological sites of Albucciu
Nuraghe, Tomba dei Giganti
Coddu Vecchju and Li
Muri Necropolis.

**Day 2: Maddalena
archipelago**
From Palau, board a ferry for
La Maddalena *(p152)*, the
main island of the Maddalena
archipelago, and wander
around the port's alleys and
squares. In the afternoon, take
a boat tour of the uninhabited
islands; these often include
swimming stops. Alternatively,
explore the **Compendio
Garibaldino** *(p153)*, a museum
dedicated to the life of the
Italian hero Giuseppe Garibaldi,
situated on the small island
of **Caprera** *(p152)*.

Day 3: Castelsardo
Head down Sardinia's
panoramic northwestern coast
to the town of **Castelsardo**
(p168), built on a promontory
that is capped by the remains
of a formidable stronghold.
Explore the town's steep lanes,
stopping at its ancient churches
and the castle, which houses a
museum displaying a collection
of typical basketwork. You can
find home-made examples for
sale in the town.

Day 4: Sassari
A short drive inland, Sardinia's
second city, **Sassari** *(pp164–7)*,
has most of its major sights

Watchtower at Alghero, with the azure Mediterranean Sea below

located within its medieval core. Seek out the flamboyant, Spanish-inspired Duomo and the graceful Fontana del Rosello, which was carved by Genoese craftsmen, before crossing the grandiose Piazza d'Italia to the Museo Archeologico on Via Roma, which contains a wealth of nuraghic and Roman finds.

Day 5: Alghero and environs
The port and resort of **Alghero** *(pp122–3)* has long attracted visitors for its pretty lanes, lively atmosphere and Catalan culture. In the morning, walk the stout city walls, browse the shops selling jewellery and visit the Cathedral. After a lunch al fresco, travel north out of town to enjoy gorgeous sandy beaches and explore the

archaeological remains at **Palmavera Nuraghe** *(p123)*. If there's time and the weather permits, take a boat tour to view the fascinating natural rock formations in the **Grotta di Nettuno** *(p127)*.

Day 6: Santissima Trinità di Saccargia to Nuoro
Located in open countryside southeast of the city of Sassari, the Romanesque church of **Santissima Trinità di Saccargia** *(pp162–3)* is striking, with its black-and-white design recalling its Tuscan workmanship. Look out for the carved animals, the ornate decoration of the façade and the frescoes in the apse. From here, head east, taking in the traditional villages of **Ozieri** *(p159)*, **Pattada** *(p158)* and **Bitti** *(p104)* on the road to Nuoro.

Day 7: Nuoro
On a hill in the centre of the island, **Nuoro** *(pp102–3)* provides fascinating insights into Sardinia's culture and traditional way of life. Explore the **Museo Etnografico**, a repository of traditional masks, costumes and objects relating to rural culture. A walk through the old town will bring you to the **Museo Deleddiano**, devoted to the town's literary star Grazia Deledda, and to the **Museo Archeologico**, both worth a visit.

A Week in Southern Sardinia

- **Airports** Arrive at Olbia-Costa Smeralda and leave from Cagliari's Elmas airport (both cities also have a ferry service to the mainland).

- **Transport** You'll need your own vehicle to explore this area.

Day 1: Oristano and Santa Giusta
On Sardinia's west coast, the town of **Oristano** *(pp138–9)* has a long and glorious history, championing the opposition to the Spanish in the Middle Ages. You can see evidence of its cultural wealth at the superb **Antiquarium**

The picturesque Grotta di Nettuno on the Capo Caccia promontory

Oristano's cathedral, with its unusual octagonal belltower

Arborense *(p139)*, one of the island's foremost museum collections, and in its **cathedral**, with its octagonal bell tower. Just south of town, the Romanesque cathedral and the nearby lake at **Santa Giusta** *(p140)* merit a stop.

Day 2: Tharros and the Sinis peninsula

West of Oristano, the **Sinis peninsula** *(pp134–5)* is a low-lying, sparsely populated area boasting a cluster of historic sites and some of Sardinia's finest beaches.

The ancient Punic and Roman site of **Tharros** *(pp136–7)* is the most prominent sight, best seen on a guided tour. Close by are **San Giovanni di Sinis** *(p135)*, one of the oldest churches on the island, and **San Salvatore** *(pp134–5)*, a double-level church surrounded by *cumbessias* –simple white-painted houses used as pilgrims' lodgings. Spend the rest of the day enjoying the secluded sandy beaches of Sinis.

Day 3: Su Nuraxi and Sanluri

Turn off the Carlo Felice highway (SS131) to reach the village of Barùmini, outside which lies Sardinia's largest nuraghic site, **Su Nuraxi** *(pp68–9)*, whose origins date to 1500 BC. Visit the museum for an overview before taking in this extensive complex of

Salt pans on Sant'Antioco, harvested since Roman times

palace, huts and fortifications on a guided tour. Heading south, you'll find yourself back on the SS131 at **Sanluri** *(p66)*, the site of a decisive battle in 1409 that led to the Aragonese takeover of the island. The castle still stands, and is now home to an entertaining collection of militaria and quirky historical items, including a museum of wax.

Day 4: Temple of Antas to San Pietro

Head west to **Gùspini** *(p71)*, then follow the S126 south to visit the **Temple of Antas** *(p72)*, which mixes nuraghic, Carthaginian and Roman elements. Further south, stop at **Iglesias** *(pp72–3)* if you have time, otherwise carry on to

Portovesme for the car ferry to **San Pietro** *(pp74–5)*, whose Ligurian origins can still be detected in the local dialect and cuisine.

Day 5: Sant'Antioco

A ferry crosses from San Pietro's only town, Carloforte, to **Calasetta** *(p75)* on the neighbouring, larger island of Sant' Antioco. The main town, also called **Sant'Antioco** *(pp76–7)*, was once the centre of the Carthaginan region of Sulki, and still holds a concentration of Phoenician and Punic finds, including a *tophet*, a type of pre-Christian shrine, and a necropolis. Save some time to see the museum here and the catacombs below the nearby basilica of Sant'Antioco.

Day 6: The Costa del Sud and Nora

Crossing the land causeway that connects Sant'Antioco with the Sardinian mainland, follow the southern coast road past scenic coves and rocky promontories, pausing for a dip at one of the beaches of **Baia Chia** *(p78)*. Continuing north from here, you'll come to **Nora** *(pp78–9)*, one of Sardinia's most important Carthaginian and Roman archaeological sites.

Day 7: Cagliari

Round off your tour with a day spent exploring the island's capital: pick a day from the two-day city itinerary on pp12–13.

The town of Sanluri on the Campidano plain, scene of a famous battle

Putting Sardinia on the Map

Sardinia lies west of the Italian mainland, surrounded by the Mediterranean Sea. The island is flanked by the Tyrrhenian Sea to the east and by the Sardinian Sea to the west. Sardinia's population of 1,700,000 lives in an area of 24,000 sq km (9,300 sq miles), divided into eight provinces: Cagliari (surrounding the island's capital city), Carbonia-Iglesias, Medio-Campidano, Oristano, Ogliastra, Nuoro, Olbia-Tempio and Sassari.

Key

- Area covered by this guide
- Motorway
- Major road
- Ferry routes
- International boundaries

See inside back cover

Europe

A PORTRAIT OF SARDINIA

The very isolation of this large island, set in the middle of the western Mediterranean, has shaped its unique character. For thousands of years Sardinia has stood on the sidelines of mainstream Mediterranean historical events, remaining a singular world to itself. Even the Romans found it a difficult place to subdue.

The experience of invasion from across the water over the centuries has left a legacy which is still evident today. The roads tend to follow valleys inland rather than tracing a scenic path along the beautiful coastline. There are yachting marinas and harbours, but fishing is not a mainstay of the economy and, even in peacetime, Sardinia has never really become a seafaring nation. Over the years Sardinia's shores have seen the arrival of Phoenicians, Romans, Genoans battling for supremacy with Pisans and Arabs, the Spanish, and finally the House of Savoy. The different cultures have all contributed to the art, architecture and cultural life of Sardinia and evidence is scattered throughout the island: prehistoric dwellings and fortresses from the earliest known inhabitants,

ancient rock-cut tombs, and Romanesque churches which resemble those of Pisa or Lucca. Introduced artistic styles were often taken up and developed with distinctive Sardinian character – the altar paintings in the Spanish *retablo* tradition, for instance. In 1848 this untamed island became part of the newly created nation of Italy.

The 20th century brought with it dreams of industrialization and newfound prosperity, as well as the beginnings of a tourist industry.

However, the Sardinia that attracts the visitors is a land of white beaches and deep blue sea, which does not really represent the essence of the place. The coastline is certainly beautiful, apart from some stretches where random building has spoilt the views.

People dressed in colourful costume for the horse ride during Cavalcata Sarda *(see p30)*

◀ Cala Gonone, a popular resort on the eastern coast of the island

But the interior is stunningly beautiful too, and deserves further exploration. The natural scenery is extremely varied, providing totally different environments and habitats for plants, animals and birds. In some areas there are fertile alluvial plains, in others steep mountains of granite and limestone, and flat landscapes drop suddenly into steep ravines within the space of a few kilometres.

People, Language and Music

Human settlements have existed in the interior for thousands of years, and Sardinia is studded with the traces of ancient pastoral civilizations, further proof that the people have always tended to prefer to live in the comparative safety of the mountainous interior rather than along the coasts. The passing of the seasons is still marked by the stages in the agricultural year, and by celebrations of successful harvests.

Ancient traditions – now deeply rooted in Catholicism but showing traces of far older religions – are manifested in numerous festivals, which are often based on the very close relationship between the people and their natural environment.

A number of very different dialects can be heard in the interior of the island,

Hand loom at the Museo Etnografico in Nuoro

and the Sardinian language still has a clear Latin base – the word *domus* is used to mean a house, for instance, instead of the Italian *casa*. Years of Spanish rule mean that in Alghero, on the west coast, you can still hear Catalan spoken on the streets, and, on the island of Sant'Antioco in the southwest, the traditions and the cooking reflect a Ligurian and Tunisian influence.

Music features strongly in Sardinian life, at feast days and weddings, and even everyday events, especially in the interior, are always celebrated with music. Musicologists and musicians – such as Peter Gabriel, who recorded the music of the Tenores di Bitti group in his world music series – have described traditional Sardinian music as unique in Europe. Today it is undergoing something of a revival. There is a great deal of vocal and instrumental variety; based on the sound of the *launeddas*, a cane wind instrument, and polyphonic music for four voices. The most well-known example is the *cantu a tenore*.

Economic Development

In an uneasy position between the past and the future, the economy of Sardinia is complex. Agriculture

Decanting ewes' milk after the morning milking

and shepherding used to be the key factors in the economy, and there was also a mining boom in certain areas after unification, particularly around Sulcis, an abundant source of both coal and metals. But the Sardinian mining industry declined, especially after World War II, and is unlikely to recover, despite some extraction of quartz and gold in the past decades. Attempts in the 1950s to eradicate malaria, by treating marshy areas with pesticides, produced impressive results: in a short space of time the coast became habitable. Meanwhile, Sardinia embraced the Internet revolution. In 1998, entrepreneur Renato Soru founded Tiscali, which soon emerged as one of Europe's main Internet service providers.

Traditional bread from the Sulcis region

Tourism in Sardinia Today

Sardinia possesses some of the most unspoilt scenery in Europe which, like its other special qualities, can only be fully appreciated by visiting the island. Interest in creating the facilities needed for tourism in Sardinia was initially subdued, and services were slow to take off. The gradual development of

tourism has, however, made the island famous, opening up Sardinia to the outside world, as well as increasing awareness of its history, local culture, arts and handicrafts.

The island's varied wildlife was perhaps bound to be affected by increasing numbers of visitors, and several wildlife and marine reserves have now been established to protect unique habitats and their flora and fauna. The vast, wild Gennargentu range is also now a protected National Park. The rare monk seal, previously thought to be extinct, has been sighted once again off Sardinia's western coast, an indication that it is possible for tourism and ecology to co-exist in comfort.

Limestone stacks rise from the sea off the headlands of the Masua and Nebida coastlines

Marine Life of Sardinia

The waters around Sardinia are considered to be the cleanest in Italy and are rich in flora and fauna. The generally healthy sea beds are havens for both scuba divers and naturalists. The sheer cliffs along the coast are home to dozens of species of nesting birds and birds of prey. Years of marine research in the Golfo di Orosei, on the eastern coast, have finally confirmed the return of the fabled monk seal, once so widespread in the area that caves and inlets were named after it. Dolphins and other large sea mammals, such as small whales, can occasionally be seen in the northwestern waters and the Straits of Bonifacio. The area has been declared an international marine reserve.

Neptune grass *(Posidonia oceanica)* is a sea plant with shaggy leaves that grows down to a depth of 30–35 m (100–115 ft). Sea grass, as it is also known, has flowers, which is unusual for a marine plant.

Rocks of volcanic origin

The striped sarago, quite a common fish in the Mediterranean, combs the sea bed in search of prey.

Rocks are covered with seaweed such as *Cystoseira*.

Sardinian coral can be various shades of red or white and lives on the rocky sea bed, at depths of 15–100 m (50–330ft) below sea level.

The lobster is a crustacean that lives mostly along the rocky shores, but can also be found at depths of up to 100 m (328 ft). The meat is a local delicacy.

The sea anemone attaches itself to rocks in shallow water. Its deceptively delicate tentacles contain stinging cells, enabling it to capture small fish and crustaceans.

Gorgonian coral survives because the water is so clean. The flexible branches may be white, yellow or red, and can grow to be 1m (3 ft) tall.

Birds of the Coastline

The cliffs along the Sardinian coastline provide an ideal habitat for birds. Wild pigeons build safe nests here and raise their young without being disturbed. Herring gulls, Audouin's gulls and cormorants perch on the rocks between bouts of fishing. Further up the cliff edge, birds of prey such as the peregrine falcon, the red kite and the rare griffon vulture, build their nests.

Cormorants on the cliff ledges

Audouin's gull

Herring gull

Peregrine falcon

Red kite

Underwater Mediterranean

The Mediterranean Sea has a rich and varied ecosystem, sustained by warm currents and clean waters. There is coral and myriad species of seaweed, a wide variety of fish, crustaceans and molluscs and marvellous rock formations for snorkellers and scuba divers to enjoy.

Cracks and crevices in the rocks make an ideal habitat for the moray eel.

Fronds

Brown meagres move in schools to defend themselves from predators by day. At night they hunt molluscs, small fish and prawns.

Dolphins are frequently seen riding the waves at the bow of a boat in the warm waters around Sardinia, particularly in the clear seas around Maddalena along the northern shore.

The moray eel has powerful teeth and poisonous mucus. It also has an excellent ability to camouflage itself, making it one of the most dangerous creatures in the Mediterranean Sea.

Monk seals, once thought to be extinct, have returned to the Golfo di Orosei where they live in grottoes and solitary caves.

The Sardinian Coastline

Washed by the clear blue waters of the Mediterranean, Sardinia offers a varied coastline of sculpted cliffs and coves. Secluded inlets alternate with golden sand dunes, where wild lilies and cistus bloom, or rugged cliffs that plummet into the sea. One of the most well-known resorts is the world-famous Costa Smeralda where visitors come to enjoy luxury villas and pretty, sandy beaches. Other popular areas are the coast south of Olbia, including the sheltered Cala Gonone, and the southeastern tip of the island, near Villasimius (easily accessible from Cagliari). Several stretches of coastline have remained untouched, such as the isolated coves between Orosei and Arbatax, and the southwestern area between Baia Chia and Oristano.

At Capo Caccia, sheer limestone cliffs, 186 m (610 ft) high, jut out from the sea.

Between Bosa and Alghero the spectacular coastline is punctuated by cliffs of volcanic origin, covered with mastic trees.

Around Piscinas the coast is known for its impressive wind-carved sand dunes. The sand is an ideal habitat for juniper and tamarisk.

Trinità d'Agultu

Golfo dell'Asinara

Porto Torres

THE NOR AND TH COSTA SMERAL

Sassari

Alghero

Mar di Sardegna

⑤ Bosa Marina   Macomer

Ottan

THE WESTERN COAST

Is Arutas
④   Oristano

Nural

S. Nicolo d'Arcidano

San

③ Piscinas

Vil

② Cala Domestica

Silíqua

Cagl

Carbonia   CAGLIARI AND THE SOUTH

San Pietro

S. Antioco

The cliffs on the island of San Pietro, eroded by sea and wind, are of pink and grey trachyte. Crevices and ledges offer useful shelter to rare birds like Eleonora's falcon.

The Costa Smeralda is characterized by granite cliffs shaped by wind and water erosion, and by inlets with clear water – paradise for scuba divers, snorkellers and surfers.

In the Golfo di Orosei the limestone cliffs plunge into the sea. Isolated coves can be reached only by boat or a long hike on foot through the maquis.

**Map labels:**

- to
- o
- ⑦ Isola di Budelli
- Porto Cervo
- achena
- Olbia
- La Cinta ⑧
- Budduso
- Siniscóla
- Berchida ⑨
- Orosei
- Nuoro
- ENTRAL ARDINIA AND RBAGIA
- ⑩ Cala Luna
- *Golfo di Orosei*
- Arbatax
- THE EASTERN COAST
- S. Priamo
- artu S. Elena
- oetto
- o di iari

0 kilometres 30
0 miles 30

The Arbatax coast is famous for the reddish colour of the porphyry rock and the steely grey colour of the older granite, jutting out in pinnacles from the sea.

Sardinia's Ten Best Beaches

① Most lively
Poetto, near Cagliari, is one of the liveliest beaches on the island. Locals throng here at weekends and through the summer.

② Most hidden beach
Cala Domestica, protected by a Saracen tower, is invisible from the sea. In World War II it was used as a German military base.

③ Best dunes
At Piscinas there are 7 km (4 miles) of sand dunes covered with maquis vegetation. Some are as high as 50 m (164 ft), the highest found in Europe.

④ Most tropical
The beach at Is Arutas is made of tiny "grains" of quartz. A forest of pine trees forms a green backdrop to the sand.

⑤ Cleanest sea
Bosa Marina, unchanged since the 1950s, has won medals for being the cleanest beach in Italy.

⑥ Best windsurfing
A strong and constant breeze from the mouth of the Liscia river makes Porto Pollo *(Porto Puddu* in Sardinian dialect) perfect for windsurfing.

⑦ Best coral beach
The beach on the island of Budelli consists of pieces of shells, coral and marine micro-organisms. Now, however, landing on the island is forbidden.

⑧ Best beach for young people
La Cinta, 4.5 km (3 miles) long, is a favourite with the trendy younger set. It is ideal for soaking up the sun and for windsurfing.

⑨ Most remote beach
Berchida, with its white beach and red rocks, can only be reached via a long sandy track through the shrubby maquis.

⑩ Most inaccessible beach
The secluded Cala Luna, with its white sand, pink oleanders and green mastic trees, is only accessible by boat or on foot.

The Flora and Fauna of Sardinia

From the rugged Gennargentu massif to the Campidano plains, and from the Nurra hills to the wind-eroded rocks of the Gallura area, Sardinia offers a great variety of natural habitats for wildlife. The forests, especially in the north, are dominated by cork oaks, for centuries a useful source of raw material. The Mediterranean maquis is permeated with the scents of lentiscus, cistus, myrtle and strawberry trees. Despite decades of farming, the fauna is still varied and interesting. Deer and wild boar abound in the scrub and forests and the rocks are home to the moufflon. The small Monte Arcosu reserve retains a tiny population of rare Sardinian deer, and the island of Asinara is the home of wild donkeys. In the spectacular Giara di Gesturi plateau, unbroken horses graze freely. Assorted reptiles can also be found, but no vipers.

The moufflon is an ancient inhabitant of the island. It has a thick coat and impressive curving horns.

Sardinian deer are stocky, with smaller horns than their mainland counterparts.

Foxes can be seen throughout all regions of Sardinia.

Mountain

Woods

Marshla

The Sardinian horse is a compact animal native to the island. The horses only roam on the Giara di Gesturi plateau.

The Kermes oak *(Quercus coccifera)* thrives mostly on the southern coastline.

The cork oak *(Quercus suber)*, important to the economy, dominates the forest of Gallura *(see p155)*.

Sardinian boar live in various parts of the island. They are smaller and stouter than species on mainland Italy.

The holm oak *(Quercus ilex)* predominates in almost all medium-altitude woods.

The Mediterranean Maquis

The thick, often impenetrable covering of shrubby vegetation known as maquis *(macchia* in Italian) thrives in the coastal and mountainous regions of Sardinia. The shrubs – including myrtle, arbutus (strawberry tree) and blackthorn – flower in spring, rest in summer and revive again in autumn. Even in winter the island looks green, with splashes of colour from berries. In recent years the area of maquis has increased, as a result of forest fires which encourage plenty of new growth.

Myrtle in flower

Strawberry tree

White cistus flowers

The kite's habitat is the wooded upland valleys.

The Sardinian Terrain

The southwestern corner of Sardinia began to emerge from the sea over 500 million years ago.

Turtles, which may grow up to as much as 1 m (3 ft) in length, are dying out because their eggs are highly prized.

Mastic trees *(Pistacia lentiscus)* grow on the coast, on Monte Limbara and the Gennargentu.

Plain

Prickly pears *(Opuntia)* are a characteristic feature every-where along the coastline.

The flamingo winters in the coastal marshes and lagoons, and now nests on Sardinia.

The white-headed duck, which nests among reeds, is quite a rare sight on Sardinian marshland.

The Nuraghi

There are over 7,000 nuraghi in Sardinia, their distinctive truncated cones a familiar part of the landscape. Little is known about their builders, a civilization that flourished on the island from 1800 to 500 BC (in some areas the nuraghic peoples resisted the Romans long after this date). Initially a nuraghe consisted of a single tower made of huge blocks of stone laid without mortar. Later, more towers were added, with connecting ramparts, resulting in more complex structures such as the Losa nuraghe at Abbasanta, the Santu Antine at Torralba and the Su Nuraxi at Barùmini. Nuraghi served as both dwelling and fortress, and the towers were often surrounded by a village and wall. There is no trace of any written language, but over 1,500 bronze figures have been found in tombs and near holy wells. The figures, and other finds, are now on display in Sardinia's archaeological museums.

Tribal chief
This bronze figure comes from the nuraghic village of Santa Vittoria, at Serri, one of the largest in Sardinia. It is a portrait of a prince at prayer.

Simple nuraghe
This is the most commonly seen and simplest form of nuraghe, consisting of a single tower with a chamber made of inwardly stepped circular tiers of stones. At times these nuraghi had more than one storey.

The central tower
is in the shape of a truncated cone.

The rampart
incorporates three defence towers.

Outer defence wall

• SASSARI

NUORO •

• ORISTANO

CAGLIARI •

• Principal Nuraghic Sites

The Losa Nuraghe at Abbasanta
This nuraghe is in three parts and is surrounded by a rampart with small towers. The oldest tower dates from before 1500 BC. There is a fine panoramic view of the Gennargentu mountains from the terrace.

Maiori Nuraghe at Tempio Pausania
This ground-floor room of the Maiori nuraghe in northern Sardinia could only be illuminated by light filtering in from the outside.

Nuraghic Burials

The nuraghic peoples built monumental tombs known as Tombe dei Giganti (Tombs of Giants) to bury their dead. Each tomb consisted of a long covered corridor constructed with huge slabs of stone. The shape represented the horn of the Bull God. A monolithic oval stele, with an opening at the base, formed the front face. Two rows of stones on either side, forming an arch, completed the burial chamber. The central, arched stele could sometimes be as much as 3 m (10 ft) tall. The area around a typical Tomba dei Giganti was often surrounded by long rows of menhirs.

The Tomb of Giants at Li Lolghi is one of the most famous prehistoric sites in Sardinia

The central tower
had three superimposed chambers.

The side towers
were built at a later stage, in the early Iron Age.

The rampart
created a solid defence system.

Santu Antine Nuraghe

The central tower of this roughly triangular nuraghe is surrounded by a three-sided rampart with three towers. It was built in different stages in the 9th–8th centuries BC. The huge complex was later dedicated to the Roman emperor Constantine.

This reconstruction
shows the original layout of Santu Antine. The central tower was the main fortress and dwelling, protected by the external towers.

Arrubiu Nuraghe
This consists of a massive fortress built in red stone at the edge of a plateau dominating the Flumendosa valley. Imposing external ramparts with five towers protected the inner courtyard and the central nuraghic construction, which was 16 m (52 ft) high.

SARDINIA THROUGH THE YEAR

Spring is by far the best season to visit Sardinia. Perfumed flowers are in bloom in the maquis thickets, the woods and meadows are still green and the temperatures have not reached the scorching heights of summer. Easter, with its colourful processions, marks the religious high point of the island. During the rest of the year, towns and villages organize festivals to commemorate the feast day of the local patron saint and sanctuaries are enlivened by celebrations and banquets. The summer months are dedicated to activities along the island's stunning coast, such as bathing, sailing and windsurfing. Inland, it can get stiflingly hot in summer, but the higher mountainous areas provide a cool retreat from the crowds and an ideal place for walking. Grape harvesting begins in the autumn, and in early winter there is heavy snowfall on the Mount Gennargentu massif. At times snow can even fall on the lower areas covering the rocky landscape of the Supramonte. It is advisable to check online or with the tourist information office *(see p200)* before attending festivals, as dates may vary.

Narcissus in bloom, a typical flower of the Mediterranean

Spring

Once the warm spring weather sets in, the sheep and goats grazing on the hillsides will be moved to higher pastures. The aromatic plants and strongly scented flowers of the maquis are in full bloom, and bees abound. They produce the rather bitter honey used in many traditional Sardinian cakes.

In the flatlands and on the hills of the Anglona and Montiferru regions the fruit trees are in blossom, while in the countryside young arti-chokes are almost ready to be picked. These are shipped to vegetable markets on mainland Italy and are traditionally the first on the market.

March and April

Holy Week and **Easter** *(Mar or Apr)* are a time of great religious celebrations, with colourful processions taking place throughout the island. In Cagliari there is an important procession through the streets on Good Friday. A representation of the *Iscravamentu* and *Incontru* mystery plays is performed at Iglesias. At Oliena the costume procession known as *S'Incontru* takes place on Easter Sunday. *Su Concordu* in the town of Santu Lussurgiu features 15th-century psalms sung in Gregorian chant. On Holy Monday at Castelsardo, there is the *Lunissanti*, a religious feast of Spanish origin.

Sagra del Riccio di Mare *(early Mar)*. A festival of the sea urchin in Alghero.

The **Fiera di San Marco** *(25 Apr)*, at Ollastra Simaxis, is a livestock festival held in honour of St Mark.

Festa Patronale *(2nd Sat after Easter)*. The island of Sant' Antioco celebrates its patron saint's feast day.

May

Sant'Efisio *(1–4 May)*, in Cagliari, offers a grand procession commemorating the end of the plague in 1656. The saint's statue is carried through the city and is then taken to Nora on an ox-drawn cart. During this splendid display of religious feeling the faithful cast flowers onto the street as the statue passes by.

San Francesco's feast day *(second Sun)*. Held at Lula, this is one of the most popular celebrations in the Baronie and Nuoro areas.

Festa dell'Annunziata *(third Sun)* at Bitti. A pastoral cele-bration of the Annunciation.

San Bachisio *(29 May)*. This feast day consists of three days of *Ballu Tundu* (round dance) in the squares of Onanì.

Cavalcata Sarda *(Ascension Day)*. A celebration of spring, the "Sardinian Horseride" has become one of the island's major folk festivals. Handicraft stalls and general festivities fill the streets of Sassari's old town centre. People from all over the

Women in colourful traditional costume during the festival of Sant'Efisio in Cagliari

Average Daily Hours of Sunshine

Sunshine Chart
Summer is the sunniest, as well as the hottest time, and June has the maximum hours of sunshine daily. The least sunny month is January, but the weather varies a great deal between inland and coastal regions, and in general, coastal areas will be brighter.

The Ardia horse race in front of the Sant'Antine sanctuary at Sedilo

island crowd into the town on horseback or dressed in colourful costumes to hear traditional songs and poetry from the different towns and regions of the island until the early hours of the morning.

Summer

The high temperatures and stunning coastline attract locals and visitors alike to the seashore during the summer months. The coastline is filled with bathers and windsurfers, and yachts and sailboats from all over Europe dock at the small, picturesque harbours. For snorkellers and scuba divers there are underwater beds of posidonia to explore. Sailing, windsurf and scuba diving clubs organize lessons throughout the summer months (see pp194–5). The cooler temperatures on the slopes of Gennargentu make it excellent for hikers, and the climb down the gorges of Su Gorroppu is also popular with experienced mountaineers.

This is the period of rural festivals, when small religious sanctuaries hidden among the valleys and hills come to life with pilgrimages and feasting. **Pani, Pisci, Pezza e Piricchittus** (Jun–Sep), meaning "bread, fish, meat and almond pastry", is a food festival held in the restaurants of Quartu. Cagliari offers a programme of music, theatre and cinema during the summer. At San Gavino Monreale there are concerts and other cultural events as well as sports activities at night.

June

Horse Festival (2 Jun). Santu Lussurgiu holds an important agricultural festival with a handicrafts exhibition.
Sagra delle Ciliegie (first Sun of month). Festival celebrating the cherry harvest at Villacidro, Bonarcado and Burcei.
San Leonardo (11 Jun). An evening of music, dance and food in Villanova Monteleone.

July

Ardia (5-8 Jul). This characteristic rural festival is held at San

Costantino a Sedilo in front of the Santu Antine sanctuary. A lively horse race accompanies celebrations honouring the saint.
Madonna of the Shipwrecked (third Sat in Jul) at Villasimius. A procession takes the Madonna from the church to the port, and there are festivities in the piazza.
Sagra delle Pesche (17 Jul), is a peach festival held at San Sperate on the feast day of the town's patron saint.
Estate Musicale (Jul–Aug), at Alghero, with concerts in the Chiostro di San Francesco.
International Folklore Festival (end of Jul), held in Tempio Pausania, during the summer Carnival.
Carpet Fair (two weeks in Jul or Aug) at Mogoro. This is one of the leading displays of Sardinian handicrafts, in particular carpets, tapestry and hand-made furniture.
Music in Antas Valley (Jul–Aug). Classical music concerts held in the splendid setting of the Temple of Antas at Fluminimaggiore (see p72).

Advanced sailing lessons off the Costa Smeralda

Average Monthly Rainfall

Rainfall Chart
In Sardinia most of the rainfall occurs in the autumn and winter. The rainfall is heavier in the mountainous regions of the interior, with precipitation as high as 1,000 mm (39 inches) per year. The driest season is during the summer months, particularly in the coastal regions.

August

Mauretanian Wedding
(1–15 Aug) at Santadi.
A ceremony dating back to the ancient traditions of the North Africans who inhabited the Sulcis region in Roman times.
Dieci Giorni Sulcitani
(1–15 Aug) in Sant'Antioco. This consists of ten evenings of traditional local entertainment, including plays in dialect, recitals of Sardinian poetry, traditional folk dances and local choral music.
Carpet Show *(first Sun of Aug)*. Traditional hand-made carpets and blankets are exhibited at Aggius.
Madonna della Neve feast day *(first Sun of Aug)*. The hardships of winter are exorcised in the Tascusì sanctuary at Desulo.
Sagra della Vernaccia *(first Sun of Aug)*. Festival of the local wine at Baratili San Pietro, near Oristano.
Sagra del Vino *(4 Aug)*. Wine festival at Jerzu with costume parades, dances, traditional songs and Cannonau wine.
Sagra del Pomodoro
(11 Aug). The tomato festival offers tomato-based dishes

Men and women parading in the Processione del Redentore in Nuoro

served outdoors at Zeddiani. There is also an exhibition of local farm produce.
Faradda de li Candareri
(14 Aug). Candles *(candelieri)*, weighing between 200–300 kg (440–660 lbs) are carried by members of the ancient guilds in Sassari. Each candle is decorated with the coat of arms of the guild and its patron saint.
Time in Jazz *(the week incorporating Ferragosto)*. Berchidda hosts an annual jazz festival.
Processione del Redentore *(29 Aug)*. Nuoro hosts one of Sardinia's most popular celebrations with a procession through the streets in honour

of Christ the Redeemer, and performances of local folklore.
Launeddas Festival *(fourth Sun)* at San Vito. This festival features performances by leading musicians of the traditional triple-piped wind instrument *(see p94)*. The music is accompanied by the *Ballu Tundu*, a circular dance.
Rassegna di Musica Leggera *(Aug–Sep)*. Performances of popular music and theatre in Piazza Peglia, Carloforte.
Regata Vela Latina *(end of Aug)*. A regatta for traditional Sardinian fishing boats held in Stintino *(see p124)*.
Mostra del Tappeto *(mid-Aug–late Sep)*. Carpet fair held at Nule.

Autumn

It is still possible to swim in the sea well into September, but the air becomes cooler in the evening. October is grape harvest time and autumn marks the beginning of the hunting season. The favourite game is wild boar, a tasty meat used in the strongly flavoured Sardinian cuisine. The chestnut harvest in the mountains often ends with lively festivals.

September

Pilgrimage to the Madonna di Gonare Sanctuary *(8 and 16 Sep)*. Departures to this hilltop church alternate between the centres of Sarule *(see p106)* and Orani.
Fiera del Bestiame *(third Sun of month)* at Serri. A livestock fair on the day of Santa Lucia.
San Cosimo *(27 Sep)*. The *Mamuthones (see p106)* parade through the streets of Mamoiada in sheepskins.

Traditional costumes worn for the Madonna della Neve festival at Desulo

Average Monthly Temperature

Temperature Chart
The summer months between June and September are hot and dry, with temperatures above 20° C (68° F), and at times reaching 30° C (86° F). In winter the temperatures are mild, rarely dipping below 5° C (41° F). January generally has sunny days and cold nights.

Locals dressed in sheepskin and bells during carnival at Ottana

October

Santa Vitalia Festival *(first Mon of month)*. A festival dedicated to agriculture held at Serrenti, with stalls selling local handicrafts.

Sagra delle Castagne e delle Nocciole *(last weekend)*. Festival to celebrate the harvest of chestnuts and hazelnuts at Aritzo. There is also a handicrafts fair.

November

Festa della Madonna dello Schiavo *(15 Nov)*. A statue of the Madonna is worshipped as it passes through the town of Carloforte. The statue is said to have been sculpted by citizens from Carloforte, who had been kidnapped by pirates and held in Tunis.

Santa Caterina *(25 Nov)*. The saint's feast day is celebrated in Abbasanta.

Winter

Winter is a fairly cold season throughout the island and snow covers the mountainous interior. Livestock is returned to its lower winter pastures and pens, and the chill wind puts an end to fishing activity along the coast.

As well as **Christmas**, which is very important in Sardinia, there are many other feast days and local festivals in the Carnival period before Lent.

December

Sagra delle Salsicce *(first Sun of month)* held at Siligo. After the pig slaughter, preparation and curing of the meat, the sausage festival is an opportunity to taste the year's new delicacies.

Christmas is celebrated at home with presents and by preparing traditional sweets.

January and February

Feast of Sant'Antonio Abate *(16–17 Jan)* is celebrated at Mamoiada and Fluminimaggiore *(see p72)* with huge bonfires.

Carnival *(the ten days before Shrove Tuesday)* is extremely popular in Sardinia, especially in the Barbagia region. Masked and costumed figures parade on Shrove Tuesday and the last Sunday of Lent. At Mamoiada, the *Mamuthones*, men dressed in sheepskins with heavy bells strapped to their backs, are driven through the town by the *Issohadores (see p106)*. Similar

festivals during carnival are the *Thurpos* at Orotelli, and the *Merdules* and *Boes* at Ottana *(see p105)*. At *Sa Sartiglia* in Oristano, masked horsemen spear a silver star hanging from a tree. There are cakes and free wine at Iglesias *(see p72)* and food is served in the main square at Perfugas. At Tempio Pausania an effigy of "King George" is burned and at Santu Lussurgiu *(see p132)* there is the *Sa Carrela 'e Nanti* horse race.

Processo a Su Conte *(Ash Wednesday)*. At Ovodda the stuffed figure of "Su Conte" is tried in the main square and burned at the stake.

Public Holidays

New Year's Day (1 Jan)
Epiphany (6 Jan)
Easter Sunday and Monday (Mar or Apr)
Liberation Day (25 Apr)
Labour Day (1 May)
Republic Day (2 Jun)
Ferragosto (Assumption Day, 15 Aug)
All Saints' Day (1 Nov)
Immaculate Conception (8 Dec)
Christmas Day (25 Dec)
Santo Stefano (26 Dec)

Snow-covered mountains of the Gennargentu in winter

THE HISTORY OF SARDINIA

The origins of Sardinian history go back thousands of years. The first people to settle are thought to have reached the island by crossing over a natural causeway which once linked Tuscany and Sardinia, perhaps between 450,000 and 150,000 years ago. A succession of different cultures led up to the rise of the nuraghic civilization. These tribes of shepherds and warriors lived in round stone dwellings called nuraghi, defended by walled fortresses, and their occupation left exceptional megalithic ruins across the island. Of the 7,000 nuraghi left in Sardinia, some are in an excellent state of preservation: the Su Nuraxi settlement at Barùmini, the Santu Antine complex and the nuraghi at Losa.

The Phoenicians arrived in 1000 BC, settling along the coastline at Tharros, Nora, Bithia and Cagliari and, after winning the Punic Wars, the Romans occupied the island. Roman dominion lasted 700 years despite strong resistance from Sardinians, and evidence can still be seen in the many ruins. When the Roman Empire fell, Sardinia again fell prey to various conquerors. For centuries the Vandals, Byzantines and Arabs fought for possession of the strategic harbours, until the maritime republics of Pisa and Genoa made their appearance on Sardinian waters. A golden age of Sardinian Romanesque architecture was introduced, which gave way to Gothic when the House of Aragon conquered the island. After 400 years of Spanish rule, control of the island passed to Austria, which ceded it to the House of Savoy in 1718. The Kingdom of Sardinia survived up to the unification of Italy. A long period of neglect was ended only after World War II, with the reclamation of the malarial marshes. The scheme's success opened up possibilities for a tourist industry and the development of an autonomous, modern Sardinia.

Calaris, modern-day Cagliari, in a print dating from 1590

◀ The Roman Temple of Antas at Fluminimaggiore, built over a 6th–5th century BC Phoenician temple

Prehistoric Sardinia

Although some stone tools found at Perfugas show that Sardinia was inhabited from the Paleolithic period (150,000 years ago), it was only around 9000 BC that the island began to be settled by populations from Asia Minor, the African coasts, the Iberian peninsula and Liguria. The fertile, mineral-rich land and the obsidian mines at Monte Arci were a major factor in the island's prosperity. By around 3000 BC the Sardinians had grouped into tribes. They lived in villages with thatched-roof huts and buried their dead in rock-cut tombs called *domus de janas* (house of fairies). By about 1800 BC this rural society had evolved into the warrior nuraghic civilization, who built thousands of circular stone towers *(nuraghi)* across the island. Many of these remarkable prehistoric constructions are still visible.

Necklace with Tusk
This ornament was found in a tomb dating from 2000–1800 BC, the bell-shaped pottery era.

Earthenware
These jugs and vases were everyday objects used to store water and grain.

The motifs on the prow have more to do with the land than the sea.

Monte d'Accoddi ruins
These traces reveal the ruins of a tiered, terraced construction, probably a temple, dating from the 3rd millennium BC. It looked remarkably similar to the famous ziggurat temples of Mesopotamia and the Aztec pyramids.

6000 BC Sardinian peoples make tools and weapons from the obsidian found at Monte Arci

Obsidian arrowhead

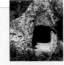

A typical example of domus de janas

6000 BC	5000 BC	4000 BC

Boar tusk, an ornament from the early Neolithic period

4000–3000 BC The age of the Bonu Ighinu culture – small communities living by raising sheep and goats. Distinctive, high-quality grey pottery with incised decoration is produced

Bronze Artifacts from Abini
These spears were part of a hoard of 100 kg (220 lb) of objects hidden in large clay vessels, perhaps to conceal them from the Roman invaders.

Candelabrum

These bronze figurines were made using the melted wax technique.

Ex Voto with Deer Motif
This ex voto lamp in the shape of a ship was one of 70 or so found at Is Argiolas near Bultei. It dates from the 8th–7th centuries BC, and is now in the Museo Archeologico Nazionale in Cagliari. In the nuraghic age, Sardinians had a love-hate relationship with the sea, which ended with the arrival of the Carthaginians, Romans and later conquerors, who forced the local inhabitants to live in the interior.

Where to see Prehistoric Sardinia

Pre-nuraghic ruins include a ziggurat at Monte d'Accoddi and rock-cut tombs (*domus de janas*) at Pranu Muteddu (Goni). Nuraghic villages survive at Su Nuraxi (*see pp68–9*), Serra Òrrios (*see p88*), Tiscali (*see pp108–9*) and Abini. Burial chambers, or "Tombs of Giants", can be seen at places such as Sa Ena 'e Thomes, and holy wells can be visited at Santa Cristina (Paulilàtino) and Santa Vittoria (Serri).

The nuraghic village of Serra Òrrios is one of the best preserved in Sardinia. It consisted of about 70 dwellings (*see p88*).

The Montessu necropolis houses *domus de janas* of the Ozieri pre-nuraghic era.

3000 BC Era of Ozieri or San Michele culture. Villages are established throughout the island and the dead are buried in the *domus de janas*

Replica of the goddess Mater Mediterranea of Senorbi

1800 BC Rise of nuraghic civilization, characterized by truncated cone-shaped buildings erected at the edges of upland plateaus

The Santa Barbara nuraghe at Macomer

3000 BC	2000 BC	1000 BC

Dolmen at Luras

2000–1800 BC Civilization known for its bell-shaped pottery. Rectangular or round dwellings constructed

1500 BC The first simple forms of nuraghe appear

1000 BC Phoenician ships moor along coast

The Phoenicians, Carthaginians and Romans

Around 1000 BC Phoenician ships began to use the inlets of the Sardinian coasts as harbours. When commerce intensified about 200 years later, they founded the cities of Nora, Sulcis, Tharros, Olbia and, later on, Bithia and Karalis (today's Cagliari). But good relationships with the local chiefs soon waned. After a brief period of peace, the nuraghic populations attacked the Phoenician settlements which, in 509 BC, asked Carthage for help. In 238 BC the Carthaginians, defeated in the first Punic War, ceded Sardinia to the Romans, who made it their province. For over a century the Sardinians put up fierce resistance, a situation which ended in 215 BC with the battle of Cornus *(see p133)*. The Romans never succeeded in subduing the entire island and rebellion in the interior continued for years. However, Roman civilization gave the island a network of roads, as well as baths, temples, aqueducts and amphitheatres.

Gold Bracelet
Decorated with palmettes, lotus flowers and a scarab beetle, this bracelet came from Tharros *(pp136–7)*.

This shape of nose is typical of the Phoenicians.

Glass Vase and Perfume Bottle
In Roman times glass was used to make ornamental vessels as well as practical objects like cups, bowls and bottles. Numerous glass pieces have been found in burial grounds and examples can be seen in the Museo Archeologico Nazionale in Cagliari *(p62)*.

Lines on the face imitate tattoos.

Carthaginian Necklace
Carthaginian jewellery was often quite elaborate, as shown by this necklace with pendants carrying human and animal symbols.

Grinning Mask
This mask dates from the 4th century BC, when the island was under Carthaginian rule. Masks like these were used to ward off evil, to protect children or ensure the sleep of the dead. This mask was found in the settlement beneath the town of San Sperate (see p66).

900 BC Nuraghic villages, bronze figures and stone sculptures

Phoenician ship

500–400 BC Sardinians flee to Barbagia after losing battles against Carthaginians

900 BC	750 BC	500 BC

730–700 BC
First Phoenician harbours built: the future Nora, Tharros, Bithia and Karalis

ca. 550 BC
The Carthaginians arrive and found the first Punic cities

509 BC The nuraghic peoples attack the coastal cities, who ask Carthage for help

**Statue of Drusus Junior
(13 BC–AD 23)**
The portrait of the Roman consul, son of the emperor Tiberius, was found at Sant'Antioco *(see p76)*, together with other busts from the early Empire.

The incisions show lotuses and rosettes.

Roman amphitheatre at Cagliari, 2nd century AD.

The Roman theatre at Nora is still used for summer cultural events.

Where to see Punic–Roman Sardinia

The best preserved Punic-Roman cities are Nora *(see pp78–9)* and Tharros *(see pp136–7)*. The ruins at Sulki, present-day Sant'Antioco *(see p76)*, are wholly Punic. Roman ruins include the amphitheatre in Cagliari *(see p58)*, near the Villa of Tigellio *(see p63)*, and baths at Fordongianus *(see pp140–41)*.

Punic Inscription
This inscription was engraved on the base of the pedestal of a 4th-century BC statuette, found in the Temple of Antas.

Glass Bowl with the Figure of Christ
This beautiful early Christian piece was found inside a tomb near Ittiri. Christ is depicted in the role of both legislator and emperor.

The nose-ring is shaped like a leech.

---

238 BC The Carthaginians lose the first Punic War

227 BC Sardinia, together with Corsica, becomes Roman province

Mosaic found at Nora

AD 200–300 Full of disease, Sardinia becomes a deportation site

| 250 BC | AD 1 | AD 250 |

Temple of Antas dedicated to Sardus Pater

27 BC Sardinia is divided from Corsica and becomes a senatorial province

AD 66 Roman Sardinia becomes an imperial province and is occupied by legions

The Middle Ages: from the Vandals to the Aragonese

In AD 456 the Vandals conquered Sardinia. Shortly afterwards, liberated by Byzantium, the island became one of the seven African provinces of the Eastern Roman Empire. The subsequent power vacuum, aggravated by Arab invasions, gave rise to the four autonomous *giudicati*, or principalities, of Torres, Gallura, Arborea and Cagliari. Around AD 1000 the Pisans and Genoese, after fierce campaigns against the Arabs, took over parts of the island. The long relationship with Aragon was formalized in 1295, when Pope Boniface VIII signed the papal bull naming James II of Aragon as King of Corsica and Sardinia. On 12 June 1323 the Infante Alfonso landed in Sardinia with his army.

The Castello quarter, Cagliari
Built during the era of Pisan rule, the fortified Castello quarter in Cagliari was the heart of the city until the 1800s.

Eleonora of Arborea
This remarkable woman inherited Arborea from her father Mariano IV in 1383. After two wars against the Aragonese, Eleonora gained control of most of Sardinia in 1394. Known as the Giudica, she remains a symbol of Sardinian independence.

Papal coat of arms

Benedetto Caetani was the real name of Pope Boniface.

66,
de
elet
po

Boniface VIII

In 1295, Pope Boniface VIII (depicted here while celebrating the Jubilee of 1300) signed the papal bull giving control of the Regnum Sardiniae et Corsicae *to James II of Aragon, in exchange for relinquishing Sicily. The Aragonese continued to annexe Sicily, ignoring the agreement.*

Barison I's seal
In 1038 the Pisans, after wresting Sardinia from the Arabs, helped Barison I of Arborea to take possession of its four *giudicati* (principalities).

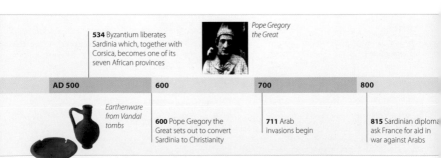

534 Byzantium liberates Sardinia which, together with Corsica, becomes one of its seven African provinces

Pope Gregory the Great

| AD 500 | 600 | 700 | 800 |

Earthenware from Vandal tombs

600 Pope Gregory the Great sets out to convert Sardinia to Christianity

711 Arab invasions begin

815 Sardinian diploma ask France for aid in war against Arabs

Capo Falcone
This tower was part of a defence system which finally put an end to barbarian raids on Sardinia in the 16th century.

Pope Boniface VIII

Where to see Medieval Sardinia

The medieval conquerors often infiltrated the interior, influencing local architecture. San Saturnino in Cagliari *(see p63)* and San Gavino at Porto Torres *(see p124)* are two of the earliest medieval churches in Sardinia. Evidence of artistic contact with the mainland can be seen in the Romanesque churches of Logudoro *(see pp160–61)*, the cathedral of Oristano *(see pp138–9)* and the cathedral of Santa Maria in Cagliari *(see p59)*. Some castles remain: the Rocca at Castelsardo *(see p168)* and the Castello complex in Cagliari *(see pp60–61)*.

Santissima Trinità di Saccargia is Pisan Romanesque *(see pp162–3)*.

Boniface VIII, despite this serene pose, was a highly controversial pope.

Alghero city walls
The massive walls and their towers date from the 14th-century period of Catalan rule.

The Castello Malaspina dominates the town of Bosa *(see pp130–31)*.

1016 Pope Benedict VIII asks Pisa and Genoa to intervene in Sardinia

1087 Guglielmo di Massa, in Cagliari, becomes the first non-Sardinian ruler

1164 Frederick Barbarossa makes Sardinia a kingdom

1257–9 Last years of the Cagliari and Torres principalities

James II of Aragon

| 900 | 1000 | 1100 | 1200 | 1300 |

Frederick I Barbarossa

1243 Frederick II crowns his son Enzo King of Sardinia

1323 12 June: Alfonso of Aragon lands in Sardinia

Spanish Rule

The Spanish conquest of Sardinia was slow: the rulers of Arborea waged a lengthy war against the invaders, there were determined revolts in Alghero and, in 1355, the Spanish crown was forced to grant a form of parliament to the six largest cities. The Aragonese took power definitively only in 1409, when the principality of Arborea was eliminated after the bloody battle of Sanluri and replaced by the marquisate of Oristano. Spanish domination of Sardinia was strengthened in 1479, with the marriage of Ferdinand of Aragon and Isabella I of Castile and Leon. The Spanish era also saw the founding of the first universities: Sassari in 1562 and Cagliari in 1620. Following the Peace of Utrecht in 1714, the island was ceded to Austria who then, in the Treaty of London, passed it over to King Vittorio Amedeo II of the House of Savoy.

The upper part shows scenes from the life of St Peter; below are the saints with St Peter in the centre.

Vittorio Amedeo II of Savoy
Vittorio Amedeo became king in 1718 when Austria gave Sardinia to him in exchange for Sicily. The Cagliari parliament swore allegiance to the new king on 2 August 1720.

VICTOR AMÉDÉE.

Decorated border

Four Moors Coat of Arms
Of Catalan origin, the coat of arms with four Moors first appeared in Sardinia after the arrival of Alfonso of Aragon in 1323. It has become one of the symbols of the island.

The Four Evangelists are depicted in the elaborately bordered predella. Sardinian artists put their own stamp on the Catalan *retablo* style.

1355 Sardinian parliament established

1409 Battle of Sanluri; end of Arborea as a principality

1541 On his way to Tu... Charles V stops at Alghe...

1350

1400

1500

1402 *Anno de Sa Mortagia Manna*, the year of the great plague

1509–1520 Repeated Arab pirate raids on Sardinia

Ferdinand of Aragon and Isabella of Castile

Alghero Cathedral
The interior of the cathedral of Santa Maria, begun in the 16th century, is a splendid example of the Catalan Gothic style in Sardinia.

Where to see Spanish Sardinia

The first Spanish building in Sardinia was the Gothic-Aragonese chapel in the cathedral in Cagliari (*see p59*), followed by San Francesco in Iglesias, San Giorgio in Perfugas, and San Francesco and the cathedral in Alghero (*see p122*). The cathedral in Sassari was built in the style known as "Colonial Baroque". Baroque influence is also evident in Àles cathedral. A notable school of *retablo* painting developed. There are 15th- and 16th-century paintings in the Art Gallery in Cagliari.

The St Peter *Retablo*

The retablo *is a religious panel painting that was quite often used as an altarpiece. It was one of the most important artistic genres in 16th-century Sardinia under Spanish rule. This work,* Madonna and Child with Saints Peter, Paul and George of Suelli, *is by Pietro and Michele Cavaro (1533–5). It is now in the church of San Giorgio at Suelli (Cagliari). The elaborate frame and wealth of decorative elements reveal its Flemish derivation.*

Retablos often combined painting, sculpture and carved decoration.

This Aragonese house at Fordongianus was built in the 15th–16th centuries.

San Francesco in Alghero (14th century) was rebuilt in the Gothic-Aragonese style.

Philip V (1683–1746)
Forced to relinquish France and Sardinia, Philip tried to reconquer Sardinia in 1717 with the help of his chief minister Alberoni.

Charles V

1620 Under Philip III the University of Cagliari is founded

1688 Discontent and uprisings: the Spanish viceroy is assassinated

1600

1700

Cardinal Alberoni, Philip V's chief minister

1717 Philip V of Spain tries to reconquer Sardinia and Naples

1718 Treaty of London: Sardinia ceded to the House of Savoy

The Kingdom of Sardinia

One of the first acts of the Savoyard government was to reinstate the island's universities. However, a serious economic and social crisis led to unrest and the spread of banditry. After the Revolution of 1789, France made vain attempts to conquer Sardinia, but, by 1795, the island was overwhelmed by revolutionary fervour of its own and a "Sardinian revolution" broke out in Cagliari. In 1799 the Savoys took refuge on the island after losing their other territories to Napoleon. In 1847, in Cagliari and Sassari, huge crowds persuaded the Savoys to link the kingdom of Sardinia with Piedmont in "*fusione perfetta*". In 1861 both became part of the Kingdom of Italy.

The Harbour at Cagliari
The port was developed after the arrival of the Savoy rulers. Together with Porto Torres it became the island's principal harbour.

The University of Cagliari
The university was founded as part of a cultural reorganization and development policy adopted by Carlo Emanuele III (1730–73), who set up a committee for Sardinian affairs in Turin.

Carlo Emanuele IV
King of Sardinia from 1796 to 1802, Carlo Emanuele took refuge here after losing his mainland territories to Napoleon in 1798. His brother Vittorio Emanuele I became King of Savoy.

The Absolutist Viceroy
Carlo Felice, seen here receiving the keys of Cagliari, was viceroy of Sardinia from 1799 to 1821, when he became king. Unchallenged, he nonetheless governed the island as an absolute monarch.

1720 Filippo Pallavicino becomes the first Savoyard viceroy of Sardinia

Throne of the Kingdom of Sardinia in Turin

1793 Anti-Savoy rebellion

| 1720 | 1740 | 1760 | 1780 |

1764–5 Re-establishment of Cagliari and Sassari universities

1788 The court of the House of Savoy flees Turin and remains in Cagliari until 1815

Memorial Tablet
This tablet, embedded in Palazzo Viceregio in Cagliari, was dedicated to Carlo Felice by Vittorio Emanuele I, his brother, who abdicated in his favour in 1821.

Where to see Savoyard Sardinia

Important Savoy buildings are the theatres in Cagliari, Sassari and Alghero, the provincial administration buildings and Cagliari Town Hall (see p58). Many of Sardinia's railway lines were laid down in this era. Statues of prominent Savoy figures, like the one of Garibaldi at Caprera, were put up everywhere. The Villa Aymerich at Làconi was one of many country houses to be rebuilt.

Giuseppe Garibaldi
After years in exile because of his republican ideas, Garibaldi came to Caprera in 1857. He settled here permanently after conquering the Kingdom of Two Sicilies for the House of Savoy with his army of 1,000 volunteer soldiers, the Redshirts (see p152).

The Galleria Comunale d'Arte di Cagliari, the capital's art gallery.

Monument to Carlo Emanuele III at Carloforte, the town he founded.

House of Savoy Coat of Arms
Dating back to the 11th century, the dynasty first ruled Savoy and Piedmont, then the Kingdom of Sardinia and finally the Kingdom of Italy.

Vittorio Amedeo III, king of Sardinia (1773–89)

1847 Sardinia and Piedmont join forces

1857 Garibaldi settles on Caprera and then buys part of the island

| 1800 | 1820 | 1840 | 1860 |

Tomb of Carlo Emanuele IV of Savoy, Cagliari

1826 Alberto La Marmora's *Voyage to Sardinia* published

Alberto La Marmora

1861 Sardinia, together with Piedmont, becomes part of the Kingdom of Italy

Sardinia and a United Italy

Industrialization in Sardinia began to make progress after unification: in 1871 the first railway line was built and the mines in Sulcis and Iglesiente became fully operational. The first daily newspapers were founded and Nuoro became the centre of a cultural movement that included the Nobel Prize-winning novelist Grazia Deledda. In World War I the heroism of the Brigata Sassari emerged as a symbol of the island's new confidence, and led to the foundation of the Partito Sardo d'Azione political party in 1921. Between the wars the mining industry continued to develop, and the town of Carbonia was founded in 1938. A wide-ranging programme of land reclamation and artificial lakes – such as Lake Omodeo, created by a dam on the Tirso river – was carried out, significantly altering the health of previously malarial areas. On 31 January 1948 the island became an autonomous region of Italy.

The Monteponi mine
A 19th-century print shows the huge plant at this important Sardinian lead and zinc mine.

The crowd consisted of the social groups suffering most from the high cost of living.

Carbonia
In 1938 Mussolini himself inaugurated the newly built town of Carbonia (see p75). The town was meant to become the leading mining centre in Sardinia.

Brigata Sassari
The brigade consisted entirely of Sardinians. They distinguished themselves in World War I by their heroism, winning two gold medals of honour.

Emilio Lussu (1890–1975) This author recorded his World War I experiences in the Brigata Sassari in Un anno sull'altopiano (One Year on the Plateau).

1871 Writer Grazia Deledda is born

1889–1899 Arrival of army task force to combat rampant banditry in Sardinia

1897 First ever special restrictive laws passed in Sardinia

| 1870 | 1880 | 1890 | 1900 |

1889 The first daily newspaper in Sardinia, Unione Sarda, is founded

Quintino Sella, Minister of Finance in 1862, 1865, 1869–73

1891 Political writer Antonio Gramsci born in Ales

Antonio Gramsci

The Cagliari-Arbatax Railway

As part of a unified Italy, Sardinia embarked on a programme of modernization. The first railway lines were laid in 1871; by 1881 Cagliari and Sassari were linked by rail. The line connecting Cagliari and Arbatax passes through lovely scenery and is now an attractive tourist route *(see pp96–7)*.

The strikers attacking the customs and excise office to protest against the bread tax.

The Dam on the Tirso River

This dam, 70 m (230 ft) high, with a 40-m (130-ft) drop, was begun in 1918, creating Lake Omodeo. At 20 km (12 miles) long, it was the largest artificial lake in Europe of its time.

The Cabras Marsh

The marsh is one example of the wide-ranging land reclamation schemes carried out in Sardinia. These public works freed the island from malaria, paving the way for the development of a tourist industry.

The Strike In Cagliari

At the turn of the century, social conflict and tensions were so strong in Sardinia that the first special restrictive laws were enacted. The unrest of miners at the Buggerru mine on 3 September 1904 led to the first general strike in Italy. In 1906, distress at the high cost of living led to a wave of riots in Cagliari which were brutally repressed; ten people died and many others were injured.

1915–18 The Sardinians make a significant contribution to the war effort

1924 The "billion lira law" finances vast public works programme in Sardinia

Flag of the Region of Sardinia

1943 Allied bombings seriously damage Cagliari

| 1910 | 1920 | 1930 | 1940 |

1921 Partito Sardo d'Azione founded

1926 The Sardinian writer Grazia Deledda wins a Nobel Prize

1938 Mussolini founds mining town of Carbonia

1948 Sardinia declared an Autonomous Region

Modern Sardinia

The reclamation of Sardinia's coastal marshes was crucial to the modern development of the island. Sardinia's lovely coastline, abandoned and shunned for millennia, could now be developed and seaside resorts built. New luxury villas and holiday villages sprang up, and the Costa Smeralda, or Emerald Coast, became world-famous as an exclusive holiday area. Reclaimed land could also be used for agriculture for the first time, and market gardens and orchards could be planted. The economy has started to shift as a result. Sheep-rearing is on the decline, while industry and services are developing, sometimes adversely affecting the environment. Sardinia at present appears to be at a crossroads, modern life competing with the most precious resource: unspoilt nature and habitat diversity.

1972 The first mines are abandoned, signalling the decline of the Sardinian mining industry

1979 Revolt of terrorists in maximum security prison on island of Asinara

1980 The Caprera National Park is founded

1970 The Cagliari football team of star striker Gigi Riva wins the Italian championship for the first time

1962 Antonio Segni, a Christian Democrat from Sassari, is elected President of the Italian Republic

1950	1960	1970	1980
1950	1960	1970	1980

1956 Sardinia starts receiving television broadcasts from RAI, the Italian state TV

1970 Pope Paul VI visits Sardinia

1971 Industrial workers outnumber farmers for the first time

1979 Cases of kidnapping increase: well-known Italian singer/songwriter Fabrizio De André and his wife Dori Ghezzi kidnapped

1953 First island kidnapping at Orgósolo, marking the beginning of one of Sardinia's most serious postwar problems, one which has fortunately decreased in recent years. Vittorio de Seta's film on Sardinian banditry was awarded a prize at the 1961 Venice Film Festival

1962 Creation of the Costa Smeralda syndicate, promoted by Karim Aga Khan (above), which triggers development in the Costa Smeralda and a consequent tourist boom in north-eastern Sardinia. That same year a law is passed with the aim of stimulating all business sectors

1985 Francesco Cossiga from Sassari, former Prime Minister and Home Secretary, is elected President of the Italian Republic

1950 No Sardinian cases of malaria, for the first time. The American Rockefeller Foundation's public health programme eliminates the *Anopheles maculipennis* mosquito, which transmits the disease

1972 Enrico Berlinguer from Sassari (centre) elected secretary of the Italian Communist Party, a post he holds until his death (1983), promoting a "third way to socialism" and the "historic compromise" between Communists and Christian Democrats

1989 Fires, mostly cases of arson, kill ten tourists on the northeastern coast

2000 Together with tourism, the livestock industry (cattle breeding, dairies, tanning) is the leading force in the island's present-day economy

2001 Gold Mines of Sardinia and the Home-stake Mining Company of California agree to open up Sardinia's gold deposits. The metal was first detected in the 1980s, when traces were discovered in streams

2002 The euro replaces the lira, becoming Italy's new currency

2011 The Italian president, Giorgio Napolitano, visits Sardinia as part of the celebrations of 150 years since the unification of Italy

2013 Benedict XVI steps down from papacy. Francis I is elected as the pope in April. He visits Sardinia in September

1990	2000	2010	2020
1990	2000	2010	2020

1990 Sardinia struck by a terrible drought

1995 The mining industry crisis worsens; the Sulcis coal mines are put up for sale

1998 Renato Soru founds Tiscali. Based in Cagliari, the company becomes one of the biggest Internet service providers in Europe

2009 Ugo Cappellacci is elected president of Sardinia, defeating Renato Soru

2005 UNESCO hails Sardinian polyphonic music, cantu a tenore, as "intangible world heritage"

2004 Renato Soru, founder of successful ISP Tiscali SpA, is elected president of Sardinia

2000 The island's marinas, especially those at Porto Cervo, are rated among the best in the entire Mediterranean

SARDINIA AREA BY AREA

Sardinia at a Glance

Famous mostly for its sea and coastline, Sardinia also abounds in spectacular natural scenery and numerous archaeological ruins. Prehistoric nuraghi are scattered throughout the island, from Su Nuraxi to Orroli, Santu Antine and Silanus. Besides the Costa Smeralda, northern Sardinia is dotted with Romanesque churches in the Logudoro and Gallura countryside. In the Barbagia region and the eastern coast, which are dominated by the large Gennargentu National Park *(see pp86–7)*, the maquis vegetation reigns in the isolated valleys and on inaccessible hilltops. The south and west have interesting Punic ruins (Nora, Sant'Antioco, Tharros), as well as a relatively wild and undiscovered western coastline.

Ardara's Romanesque church, Santa Maria del Regno *(see p160)*

Tr
d'Ag

Porto Torres

Sassari

Alghero

Bosa

Mac

THE
WESTERN COA
(See pp116–41)

Flamingoes wintering in the marshes around Oristano *(see pp138–9)*

Tramatza

Oristano

The impressive ruins of Tharros *(see pp136–7)*

S. Nicolo
d'Arcidano

Sanl

CAGLIARI A
THE SOUT
(See pp54–7)

Iglesias

Villamassárgia

Carbonia

S. Antíoco

0 kilometres   20

0 miles   20

The rugged coast near Buggerru *(see p72)*

◀ The cityscape of Cagliari on a bright summer day

Capo Testa lighthouse near Santa Teresa di Gallura, on the north coast *(see pp148–9)*

Porto Cervo

Arzachena

Golfo Aranci

Olbia

THE NORTH AND
THE COSTA SMERALDA
(See pp142–69)

Oschiri

Alà dei Sardi

Siniscola

Wild moufflon in the woods of central Sardinia *(see pp26–7)*

Nuoro

Orosei

Ottana

CENTRAL
SARDINIA AND
BARBAGIA
(See pp98–115)

Arbatax

Part of the route around the island followed by the *Trenino Verde* (little green train, *see pp96–7*)

Nurallao

THE EASTERN
COAST
(See pp80–97)

S. Priamo

Sestu

Cagliari

Cagliari, the ancient Roman city of Kàralis, capital of the region of Sardinia *(see pp58–65)*

CAGLIARI AND THE SOUTH

Southern Sardinia has a varied landscape, with tall sand dunes along the coast, marshland where pink flamingoes build their nests and abundant maquis where rare Sardinian deer still survive. It is also an area of interesting prehistoric sites, such as Nora and Su Nuraxi, and it was once the mining heartland of the island.

The mining history of the area dates back to 5000 BC, when the island's inhabitants discovered how to extract and smelt copper and silver. The Phoenicians used the area as a base for trade and shipped local ores across the Mediterranean. In the Middle Ages the Pisans brought new wealth to the region with expansion of the silver mines. During the Fascist era, Mussolini exploited the island's coal in an attempt to make Italy self-sufficient.

Today, after years of decline, the industrial buildings of the Sulcis and Iglesiente areas are being converted into tourist attractions with mines and museums to visit. The area's natural beauty merges with the 19th-century mining buildings, which look like Gothic castles among the maquis.

The island's capital, Cagliari, was founded by Phoenician sailors, but it was the Aragonese who left the most enduring mark. The Spanish fortification, or Castello district, still dominates today's city. North of Cagliari lies the Campidano plain, bordered by prickly pears and eucalyptus. This has long been Sardinia's "bread-basket", but farm labour now combines with factory work, especially around Cagliari. In the uplands to the east are the ruins of Sardinia's largest prehistoric site, Su Nuraxi, chosen for its vantage point over the surrounding plains.

The islands of San Pietro and Sant' Antioco are separate from the mainland culturally as well as geographically: the towns of Calasetta and Carloforte are inhabited by the descendants of Ligurian coral fishermen who were held hostage in North Africa by Muslim pirates and, once freed, were offered a home on the islands. Today, their dialect, cuisine and traditions remain little changed.

Ruins of nuraghe at Su Nuraxi

◀ The ramparts of Bastione San Remy in old Cagliari

Exploring Cagliari and the South

The southwestern coast is one of the most unspoiled on the island, with undisturbed coves and beaches. Few roads run along the coast, so the best way to explore is by sea or on foot. Inland, the wild maquis of the rugged Iglesiente and Sulcis terrain contrasts with the derelict 19th-century industrial buildings of this former mining area. In the north, excavations at Su Nuraxi have revealed a complex nuraghic settlement. Cagliari offers the city's sights and a wildlife sanctuary in the salt flats, and is also a good base for the ancient site of Nora.

18th-century walls at Carloforte on the island of San Pietro

Key

═══ Major road
──── Secondary road
═══ Minor road
──── Scenic route
┈┈┈ Main railway
──── Minor railway
△ Summit

0 kilometres   10
0 miles   10

For keys to symbols *see back flap*

Las Plassas hill with its castle

Cagliari's tourist marina at Poetto, at the foot of the Sella del Diavolo (Devil's Saddle)

Getting Around

The state railway (Trenitalia) offers services to towns in the Campidano plain along the Cagliari-Oristano line. The local railway, ARST, connects Cagliari to Isili. Coaches will take you almost everywhere. The roads are usually winding, except for those in the Campidano plain and the dual carriageways *(statali)* SS130 and SS131.

❶ Cagliari

The city's sheltered position, tucked into the Golfo di Cagliari, has long made Cagliari an important harbour. The Phoenicians chose the eastern shore of Santa Gilla lagoon in the 8th–6th centuries BC, as a stopover for trade ships en route between the Lebanon and the Iberian peninsula. Kàralis ("rocky city") soon became one of the leading Mediterranean centres of trade. The city's present appearance was the work of the Pisans, who developed the Castello district. Local inhabitants, who could only enter the city during the day, lived in the walled villages of Stampace and Villanova. These fortifications were demolished in 1862 and the areas are now part of the city. Modern-day Cagliari, capital of the region, is flanked on three sides by sea and marshes and has only expanded northwards.

Arcaded 19th-century buildings on Via Roma

Exploring Cagliari

For those arriving by sea, the elegant boulevard of Via Roma, parallel to the quay and lined with 19th-century buildings and long arcades, is the first view of the city. During the day crowds throng along this busy shopping street, stopping at the cafés to relax and chat. Stretching out behind are the narrow streets and alleys of the old Marina district. Formerly inhabited by fishermen and merchants, this area is now filled with trattorias and rustic taverns as well as shops selling antiques and local food and handicrafts. Heading northeast from Via Roma, Largo Carlo Felice is a wide, tree-lined avenue dating from the mid-1800s, with a statue of Carlo Felice, the viceroy of Sardinia (see pp44–5).

City's coat of arms

🏛 Palazzo Comunale

Via Roma. **Tel** 070 67 71.
📞 Call 070 677 72 35/6.

At the corner of Via Roma and Largo Carlo Felice is the Palazzo Comunale (town hall). Built in the early 20th century in Neo-Gothic style, the building was restored after World War II. Its façade is decorated with double lancet windows and turrets. Paintings by Filippo Figari and Giovanni Marghinotti hang in the Sala della Rappresentanza, and in the Sala del Consiglio Comunale depicting key moments in Sardinian history.

🏛 Bastione San Remy

Terrazza Umberto I.
Closed for restoration.

Built in the late 19th century over the Spanish ramparts, the bastions can be reached from Piazza

Sala del Consiglio Comunale, Palazzo Comunale

Costituzione up a stairway that leads to a wide terrace, Terrazza Umberto I (also accessible from Porta dei Leoni if the stairway is closed). From here, there is a magnificent view over the seafront to the surrounding marshes.

🏛 Roman Amphitheatre

Viale Sant'Ignazio da Láconi.
Tel 070 231 00 22. **Closed** for restoration; check the website for details of reopening.
🌐 **anfiteatroromano.it**

Northwest of the city centre is the most significant evidence of Roman Cagliari. The 2nd-century AD amphitheatre was hewn out of the rock, in the style of Greek theatres. Circus acts with wild beasts were performed here, as well as *naumachiae*, popular recreations of naval battles. A canal system made it possible to fill the arena with water.

Much of the brick masonry collapsed during the Middle Ages and stone was taken from the tiers to build the Castello district. Of what remains, still visible are the *cavea*, the pit that held the wild beasts, the corridors behind the tiers and underground passageways, as well as some of the tiers where the spectators sat.

The ruins of the 2nd-century AD Roman amphitheatre

Orto Botanico

Viale Sant'Ignazio 13. **Tel** 070 675 35 12. **Open** Apr–Oct: 9am–6pm Mon–Fri; Nov–Mar: 9am–1:30pm Mon–Fri. (070 675 35 12).

South of the amphitheatre is the Orto Botanico. Founded in 1865, the botanic gardens contain over 500 species of tropical plants from the Americas, Africa, Asia and the Pacific, as well as from the Mediterranean region.

The Orto Botanico is full of small caves such as the Grotta Gennari, used to cultivate ferns because of its ideal temperature and high levels of humidity. There are also remains of Roman tunnels, constructed to improve the water supply to the gardens, a Roman gallery and a well.

Cathedral

Piazza Palazzo. **Open** 8am–noon, 4–7pm daily. Museo del Duomo: Via Fossario 5. **Tel** 070 68 02 44. **Open** 4:30–7:30pm Tue–Fri, 10am–1pm & 4:30–7:30pm Sat & Sun.
W museoduomodicagliari.it

Cagliari's Cathedral of Santa Maria was built by the Pisans in the 11th and 12th centuries. Gradually transformed over the

The Baroque marble interior of the Cathedral of Santa Maria

Holy water basin detail

centuries, particularly with 17th-century additions, today's façade is the result of radical restoration in the 1930s, which reinstated the original Romanesque style. Four lions guarding the entrance date from this period. Inside, Santa Maria retains much Baroque decoration, as well as some original detail. Close to the entrance are two pulpits by Mastro Guglielmo, sculpted in 1162 for the cathedral of Pisa and donated to Cagliari by the Tuscan city. A marble basin for holy water is decorated with the image of an angel.

A crypt under the altar houses the tombs of the princes of the House of Savoy. In the chapterhouse, paintings include a *Flagellation of Christ* attributed to Guido Reni. The **Museo del Duomo** (Treasury) displays precious church items such as chalices and amphoras, as well as a large gilded silver cross.

VISITORS' CHECKLIST

Practical Information
Road map C6. 177,000.
Via Roma 145 (070 677 81 73).
Sun, Sant'Elia district (general). 1 May: Sant'Efisio Feast Day. **W** cagliariturismo.it

Cagliari Town Centre

1. Roman Amphitheatre
2. Orto Botánico
3. Villa di Tigellio
4. Bastione San Remy
5. Cathedral
6. Cittadella dei Musei
7. Torre dell'Elefante
8. Exma
9. San Saturnino
10. Palazzo Comunale

For keys to symbols *see back flap*

Street-by-Street: Castello

The Castello district, the oldest part of Cagliari, was built by the Pisans and Aragonese. Positioned at the top of a hill, and protected by ancient city walls, it consisted of aristocratic mansions and the city's Cathedral. With time its function as a centre of power waned, and the elegant buildings gradually deteriorated. At the centre of the district is Piazza Palazzo with the Palazzo Arcivescovile (Archbishop's Palace) and the Cathedral. Surrounding the ancient citadel, imposing watchtowers dominate the entrance gates, and parts of the fortifications have been transformed into a museum complex and an esplanade.

★ **Cathedral**
Santa Maria Cathedral, rebuilt several times, combines Pisan, Aragonese and Baroque features. The multi-coloured marble interior has fine sculptures *(see p59).*

★ **Cittadella dei Musei**
This modern complex, converted from the former Savoyard arsenal, houses the city's most important museums *(see p62).*

Palazzo Arcivescovile

PIAZZA PALAZZO

VIA MARTINI

PIAZZA ARSENALE

VIA

Torre di San Pancrazio
The northern gate of the Castello district was built in 1305 by Giovanni Capula. It is dressed on three sides with limestone ashlar, while the inner face is open, exposing the stairs and wooden balconies of the interior.

Via La Marmora
A number of craft workshops and antique shops line the characteristic Via La Marmora.

★ Bastione San Remy
In the early 1900s the Spanish defensive walls were transformed into the bastions of San Remy, opening out onto a wide esplanade with spectacular views.

Porta dei Leoni
The gate that leads into the lower Marina district owes its name to the two Romanesque lions' heads (leoni) above the arch.

Palazzo Boyl
Overlooking the bastions of San Remy, this palazzo was built in 1840. It incorporates the remains of the Torre dell'Aquila (Eagle's Tower), one of the large Pisan towers that stood over the entrance gates of the ancient city.

Key

— Suggested route

Torre dell'Elefante
The "Elephant's Tower" was built by local architect Giovanni Capula in 1307. The mechanism for opening the gates is still visible and an elephant statue, after which the tower was named, can be seen on the façade.

Cittadella dei Musei, the modern complex in the Castello district

Cittadella dei Musei

Piazza Arsenale. **Tel** 070 67 57 627.

At the northern end of the Castello district is this modern museum complex. Fashioned from the former royal arsenal which had been built on the site of the Spanish citadel, the complex houses the Museo Archeologico Nazionale, the Museo Civico d'Arte Siamese Stefano Cardu and the Pinacoteca Nazionale.

🏛 Museo Archeologico Nazionale

Cittadella dei Musei, Piazza Arsenale. **Tel** 070 65 59 11. **Open** 9am–8pm Tue–Sun.

The National Archaeological Museum is devoted to the history of Sardinia. The ground-floor exhibits are arranged in chronological order, from the Neolithic era to the Middle Ages; the other floors are organized by archaeological site. In the Neolithic hall are fine alabaster statues of female divinities, including one in the shape of a cross from Senorbì. Objects from the late Bronze Age include axes with raised edges. There is an exceptional collection of nuraghic bronze figurines (see pp36–7), found in the Tempio di Teti at Abini. The collection includes votive swords decorated with the head of a deer, a tribal chief or a warrior. In the third hall is a statuette of a musician playing the Sardinian flute, the launeddas (see p94).

The Phoenician and Roman periods are represented by objects found mostly at sites around Cagliari, Tharros and Nora. These include jewellery

and amulets, small coloured glass heads and terracotta votive statuettes. Among the loveliest pieces of jewellery are an embossed golden bracelet and gold earrings from Tharros.

The Early Christian pieces, such as jugs, lamps and gold jewellery, give an insight into the island's medieval culture, and influences from Byzantine, Vandal and Moorish invaders.

🏛 Museo Civico d'Arte Siamese Stefano Cardu

Cittadella dei Musei. **Tel** 070 65 18 88. **Open** 10am–6pm Tue–Sun (to 9pm mid-Jun–mid-Sep).

The Museum of Oriental Art exhibits most of the 1,300 objects donated to the city in 1917 by Stefano Cardu, a Sardinian who served at the court of the King of Siam. The collection includes imperial gold and silver objects, ivory statues and vases, mostly dating from the 11th century.

🏛 Pinacoteca Nazionale

Cittadella dei Musei. **Tel** 070 67 40 54. **Open** 9am–7:15pm Tue–Sun. (buy ticket at the Museo Archeologico).

The entrance to this three-storey gallery is on the upper floor. Here, 15th- and 16th-century

paintings include Catalan and Sardinian altarpieces, like the *Annunciation* by Juan Mates (1391–1431), *Sant'Eligio* by the Master of Sanluri (early 16th century), and *Nostra Signora della Neve* (1568) by Michele Cavaro.

The middle floor houses 17th- and 18th-century paintings and reveals the original Spanish fortification wall (1552–63). The lower floor features the restored *Retablo di San Cristoforo*, rescued from the Chiesa di San Francesco di Stampace, which was damaged by lightning in 1871.

🏛 Galleria Comunale d'Arte

Giardini Pubblici, Viale Regina Elena. **Tel** 070 67 77 598. **Open** 10am–9pm Mon, Wed–Sun (to 6pm mid-Jun–mid-Sep).

The Municipal Art Gallery has a collection of significant works by Sardinian artists from the late 19th century to the 1970s. On the ground floor are works by Francesco Ciusa. The first floor features contemporary art.

🏯 Necropoli Tuvixeddu

Via Falzarego. **Open** Mar–Sep: 8am–sunset.

The hundreds of underground burial chambers of the Punic necropolis, west of the Botanical Gardens, are overgrown with brambles. The funerary paintings on the tombs, however, are worth a visit, especially the *Tomba del Guerriero* (Warrior's Tomb) and the *Tomba dell'Ureo*.

🏯 Grotta della Vipera

Viale Sant'Avendrace. **Tel** 070 41 108 or 070 6771. **Open** 9am–5pm Tue–Sun.

One of the tombs in the necropolis is that of Atilia Pomptilla, wife of Cassius Philippus, exiled here in the 1st century AD. Two snakes adorn the façade of the "viper's cave" and on the walls are inscriptions in Greek and Latin.

Marble sarcophagus (4th century AD) from the Archaeological Museum

The early Christian church dedicated to San Saturnino, patron saint of Cagliari

🔼 Subterranean Cagliari

Viale Sant'Ignazio. **Tel** 070 66 30 52.
Open for conducted tours only; see website. 🅦 **cagliaritour.com**

In the area below the Roman amphitheatre, the hospital and the Orto Botanico there are underground chambers and passageways cut out of the rock by the Phoenicians. The most spectacular of these is the vast chamber named after King Vittorio Emanuele II. From the Casa di Riposo in Viale Fra Ignazio, it is accessed via a dingy stairway which leads into the eerie chamber. The walls, around 2,500 sq m (26,900 sq ft), are covered with thick facing to protect them from the humidity.

The Phoenician underground chamber, "Vittorio Emanuele II"

🏛 Villa di Tigellio

Via Carbonazzi. **Tel** 070 40 92 306.
Open summer: 10am–2pm, 3–7pm; winter: 9am–5pm.

Situated southeast of the Botanical Gardens, Villa di Tigellio is a group of three aristocratic Roman villas and baths dating from the Imperial era. The first house has a *tablinum*, the room used to receive guests, which opens onto the central atrium.

🏛 Exma

Via San Lucifero 71. **Tel** 070 66 63 99.
Open 9am–8pm Tue–Sun (Jun–Sep: 10am–9pm). 🅿 ♿ 🖥

On the eastern side of the Castello district stands the former municipal slaughterhouse, built in the mid-19th century and closed in 1964. The dark red building, decorated with sculpted heads of cows, has been restructured to house the city's arts centre.

The centre's cultural calendar offers temporary exhibitions of photography, painting and sculpture, as well as courses for children and adults. Classical music concerts are held in the courtyard in the summer and in the auditorium in the winter.

A cow's head on the Exma building

🔼 San Saturnino

Piazza San Cosimo. **Tel** 070 201 03 01.
Open for Mass (11am Sun) and by arrangement May–Oct. ♿

East of the Exma building is the church of San Saturnino, also known as Santi Cosma e Damiano. Reopened after 18 years of restoration, and still not completely refurbished, this simple church is one of the oldest Christian buildings on the island. It was begun in the 5th century to commemorate the martyrdom of Saturno, the city's patron saint.

In the Middle Ages, San Saturnino, together with its adjacent monastery, became an important religious and cultural centre. The Greek cross plan of the church was enlarged in the 11th century by French Victorine friars from Marseille, who built three aisles with barrel vaults. Inside, a marble ex voto holds the oldest representation of San Saturno.

Glass windows have been placed in the sturdy tufa construction to prevent further damage and decay from humidity and air, and this has given the church a rather modern appearance. Nonetheless, it is still a fascinating place to visit.

The Marshes and Salt Flats

A network of marshes and lakes extends around the outskirts of Cagliari, particularly along the western shore of the bay. The vast lagoon of the Santa Gilla marsh stretches over 40 sq km (15 sq miles), including the ancient Macchiareddu salt flats. These saltworks are now the only ones in operation in the area. After years of neglect and environmental deterioration, the marshy areas around Cagliari have finally become reserves, and the area once again has a rich and varied fauna. To the east of the city, the Molentargius marsh is a favourite refuge for migratory birds. At least 170 species have been identified here, which is one-third of the entire bird population of Europe. Between August and March, flamingoes attract dozens of naturalists. Since 1993 these creatures have begun once again to nest along the banks of the Molentargius marsh.

A Naturalist's Paradise
In autumn the marshes are filled with migratory birds and are a favourite with bird-watchers.

The Saltworks
Of the numerous saltworks that once operated around Cagliari, only those in the Macchiareddu industrial area are still active.

Macchiareddu Salt Flat

130

195

Fishing port of Giorgino

Stagno di Santa Gilla

Nesting Grounds
In recent years, flamingoes have begun to use the marshes as a nesting ground again.

Key

━━ Major road
━━ Minor road
▨ Salt flat
▦ Marsh

For hotels and restaurants in this region see p176 and p186

Wildlife of the Marshlands

Many migratory and endemic bird species populate the marshes around Cagliari. These feed upon the small creatures, such as the brine shrimp *Artemia salina*, which thrive in the salt-rich water. As well as the colony of flamingoes, which sometimes exceeds 10,000, you will also see many other species of water birds such as blackwinged stilts, avocets, cormorants and teals. The waters of Macchiareddu salt flats, on the other hand, are populated by mallards, coots and pintail ducks, which hunt peacefully among the islets and inlets.

Flamingo

Blackwinged Stilt

Avocet

Cormorant

Teal

Cat's-tail flowers

554

Torre dell'Elefante, Cagliari

Stagno di Molentargius

Stagno di Simbirizzi

125

Stagno di Quartu

Quartu Salt Flat

Poetto beach

GOLFO DI CAGLIARI

Golfo degli Angeli

GOLFO DI CAGLIARI

Capo Sant'Elia

0 kilometres   2
0 miles   2

Molentargius Marsh
This is an ideal stopping place for migratory birds from Africa.

VISITORS' CHECKLIST

Practical Information
Road map C6. *i* Molo Sanità (070 37 91 92 16).
The best period for bird-watching is August–March.

Transport
P from Via Roma for Poetto; 8 for Santa Gilla.

The Romanesque church of Santa Maria at Uta

❷ Uta

Road map C6. 🏔 7,000. 🚌 🚉
ℹ️ Via Umberto I (345 80 12 482).
📅 26–31 Aug: Santa Lucia.
🌐 **prolocouta.it**

The flourishing agricultural town of Uta is situated at the edge of the Campidano plain, a vast fertile corridor that stretches northwards from Cagliari to Oristano. On the outskirts of town is the church of **Santa Maria**, built in 1140 by French Victorine friars from Marseille. The façade is made of light-coloured stone, with blocks of a darker hue, and is decorated with blind arches and a small bell gable. Sculptures of human heads, deer, calves and geometric patterns adorn the arches.

Environs:
The village of **San Sperate**, 8 km (5 miles) northeast of Uta, is a living museum with murals, and sculptures by local artist Pinuccio Sciola.

🏠 **Santa Maria**
Via Santa Maria. **Tel** 070 96 82 16.
Open by appt only.

❸ Sanluri

Road map C5. 🏔 9,000. 🚌 🚉
ℹ️ Via Mazzini 74 (070 937 05 05).
📅 10 Aug: San Lorenzo.
🌐 **facebook.com/proloco.sanluri**

An important town in the Campidano plain, Sanluri grew up around the 14th-century castle of Eleonora d'Arborea (see p40). This stronghold changed hands several times before it was taken by the Aragonese in 1409. The massive

square structure has towers on its four corners and an ornate wrought-iron gate.

Today the castle is owned by the Villasanta family and houses the **Museo Risorgimentale Duca d'Aosta**. The historical exhibits include fine furniture such as a 16th-century bed. A sculpture of San Michele (St Michael) stands in the entrance hall. On the upper floor is the **Museo della Ceroplastiche** in which there are 343 pieces of wax from 1500 to 1800.

In the restored 16th-century Convento dei Cappuccini (still a working monastery), on a hill overlooking the town, the **Museo Storico Etnografico** displays a collection of tools and archaeological finds.

Wax statue in Sanluri's
Museo della Ceroplastica

🏛 **Museo Risorgimentale Duca d'Aosta**
Castello di Eleonora d'Arborea. **Tel** 070 930 71 84. **Open** May–Sep: 10am–1pm, 4:30–9pm daily; Oct–Apr: 9:30am–1pm, 3–7pm daily. 🗺 🎥

🏛 **Museo Storico Etnografico**
Via San Rocco 6. **Tel** 070 930 71 07.
Open by appt only. 🗺 🎥 ♿

❹ Serri

Road map C4. 🏔 810. 🚌 🚉
ℹ️ Via Municipio 1 (0782 80 50 09);
Pro Loco, Via Roma 36 (0782 80 51 42).
📅 Third Sun of Sep: Santa Lucia.

This sheep-farming centre lies on the edge of a rocky plateau dominating the Trexenta hills. Right on the spur of the promontory is the **Santuario Nuragico di Santa Vittoria**, one of Sardinia's most fascinating nuraghic sites. The archaeological ruins here have yielded some important bronze votive statuettes, now housed in the Museo Archeologico Nazionale in Cagliari (see p62).

Pilgrims came here to worship the God of Water at the sacred well. The temple well, which is in an excellent state of preservation, is reached via 13 amazingly precise basalt steps. A short walk from the entrance leads to the Recinto delle Feste (festivities area). This elliptical building has a porticoed courtyard surrounded by rooms for the pilgrims. This is possibly a predecessor of the many rural sanctuaries (cumbessias or muristeni) found today in Sardinia's country churches.

🏠 **Santuario Nuragico di Santa Vittoria**
7 km (4 miles) NW. **Tel** 0782 84 72 69.
Open summer: 9:30am–8:30pm; winter: 9am–1pm, 2–6pm.

A modern mural in the village of San Sperate

The 16th-century parish church of the Beata Vergine Assunta at Sàrdara

➎ Sàrdara

Road map C5. 🚗 5,000. 🚌
🛈 Town Hall (070 93 45 02 00).
🎉 22 Sep: Santa Maria is Acquas.

Situated at the northern edge of the Campidano plain, the town of Sàrdara lay on the border between the medieval principalities of Arborea and Cagliari *(see pp40–41)*. Stone houses from this period, with large arched doorways, have been preserved in the district around **San Gregorio**. This Romanesque church was built in the 6th century. Its tall, narrow façade, however, shows the initial influence of Gothic architecture. On the western outskirts of town is the 16th-century parish church of **Beata Vergine Assunta**, interesting for its sculpted columns and arches, and vault patterned with stars.

Near the Assunta church are the remains of a nuraghic well-temple. This underground chamber, from the 9th–10th centuries BC, has walls of basalt and limestone and a domed

ceiling. Also known as the *Funtana de is Dolus* (fountain of pain), it is where worshippers came to take the curative spring waters. The source of the temple water was an ancient underground well, and a canal carried the mineral water from the spring to the temple. Decorated earthenware votive objects found in the temple are now in the Museo Archeologico Nazionale in Cagliari *(see p62)*.

Sàrdara is also famous for its carpet-weaving and woollen and cotton tapestries. These are colourfully embroidered with traditional animal and floral decorative motifs.

Environs
Ruins of the medieval **Castello di Monreale**, a fortification of the principality of Arborea, stand on a hill 1 km (half a mile) southwest of town. A little further west are the remains of the **Aquae Neapolitanae**, Roman baths, and nearby is the Gothic church of **Santa Maria is Acquas**, where a festival takes place in September.

➏ Villanovaforru

Road map: C5. 🚗 730. 🚌
🛈 Piazza Costituzione (070 93 45 1220). 🎉 15 Jul: Santa Marina.
🌐 comune.villanovaforru.ca.it

This agricultural centre was founded in the 1600s by the Spanish and has retained much of its original layout. Many houses have kept their decorative features. Today, the Monte Granatico building (formerly a grain store), in the town's central square, houses a small but well-run **Museo Archeologico**. Finds from the nearby nuraghic site of Genna Maria are on display, including bronze, iron and ceramic objects from the 9th century BC on the ground floor. On the first floor are votive items dedicated to Demeter and Persephone from the Roman era.

Environs
On the road to Collinas, 1 km (half a mile) west of the town, is the nuraghic village of **Genna Maria**. Discovered in 1977, the site, which is still being excavated, is on a prominent hilltop. This nuraghe has a typical design *(see pp40–41)*. Thick walls with three towers form a triangle which encloses a central tower and courtyard with a well. Another wall with six corner towers surrounds the entire village area.

🏛 **Museo Archeologico**
Piazza Costituzione. **Tel** 070 930 00 50.
Open 9:30am–1pm, 3:30–6pm (Apr–Sep: to 7pm) Tue–Sun. 🅿 ♿

🏰 **Genna Maria**
1 km (half a mile) W. **Tel** 070 930 02 32.
Open 9:30am–1pm, 3:30–7pm (to 6pm in winter) Tue–Sun. 🅿 📷 call in advance. 📷

The Saffron of Sardinia

Saffron

The production of Sardinian saffron, prized throughout Europe, is based around San Gavino in the Campidano plain. Saffron is obtained by drying the dark red stigma of *Crocus sativus*, a purple flower that carpets the barren fields in autumn. The harvest, however, is very brief as the stigmas must be collected the day the flower comes into bloom. Saffron, once considered as precious as gold, was used to make dyestuff for fabrics and rugs, as a colouring agent for sweets and as a spice for savoury dishes. It is still used in today's cooking *(see p182)*.

Crocus flowers

❼ Su Nuraxi

Excavations east of Barùmini have brought to light the largest nuraghic fortress in Sardinia, Su Nuraxi. The original settlement dates from 1500 BC, during the Middle Bronze Age. Built on a hill, the 19 m (62 ft) high fortress occupied an excellent vantage point, with clear views over the surrounding plains. In the 7th century BC, with the threat of Phoenician invasion, the central section of the fortress, consisting of a tower connected to four external nuraghi, was further protected by a thick outer wall with turrets and a sentinel's walkway. The village gradually developed outside the main fortifications with single- and multi-room dwellings, including a flour mill and bakery. The area was inhabited for almost 2,000 years although, after the Carthaginian conquest, the upper parts of the fort were demolished and the site lost its strategic importance.

Single dwellings
The oldest living quarters were circular with a single room.

Defences
In order to defend themselves from Carthaginian invasions, the Nuraghic inhabitants built an outer bulwark. This consisted of seven towers connected by a wall with a walkway for sentinel patrols.

KEY

① **The circular assembly hall** was built against the outer wall. During meetings the elders sat on a long stone bench that ran along the inside of the wall. Objects found here are held in Cagliari's archaeological museum *(see p62)*.

② **The outer wall** was added in the 7th century BC.

③ **The "keep"**, or central section, was the highest part and the centre of military operations.

④ **The four main towers** were connected by a central courtyard.

⑤ **Sentinel's walkway**

Multi-room Dwellings
These living areas were made up of seven or eight square or trapezoidal rooms which opened onto a courtyard or vestibule, often with a well.

Building Techniques
Huge irregular blocks of stone, laid in "dovetail" fashion without mortar, were used to build the nuraghi. The inner walls of the towers were often reinforced by another wall of stone.

Northeastern Tower
The outer corner towers of the fortress were pierced by a double row of radially arranged fissures through which light could penetrate.

The Village
The dwellings were built outside the fortress walls between the 8th and 6th centuries BC. There were about 200 circular houses with roofs made from wooden beams and branches.

❽ The Piscinas Dunes

The hills of sand at Piscinas and Is Arenas ("the sands" in Sardinian) are "moving" dunes, sometimes as much as 50 m (164 ft) high, that rise up around the estuary of the River Piscinas. Wind erosion by the mistral, the cold north wind that blows in from France, continually changes the landscape, while strongly rooted pioneer plants work their way across the sand. The robust roots of marram grass (*Ammophila arenaria*) gradually stabilize the dune slopes, which are then covered by other salt-resistant plants such as juniper and lentiscus. This unique ecological niche is also the habitat for many animals, and footprints of foxes, wild cats, partridges and rabbits are a common sight on the sand. Remains of the 19th-century mines that were once the mainstay of the Sulcis regional economy are also still visible.

Piscinas beach
The sandy beach at Piscinas is 7 km (4 miles) long. Exposed to the strong mistral wind in winter, the shape of the beach is continually changing.

Marine turtles
The isolated position of Piscinas makes it an ideal spot for loggerhead turtles to lay their eggs.

The Sardinian partridge favours sunny habitats. It was introduced from North Africa by the Romans.

Le Dune di Ingurtosu Hotel
This hotel overlooking the sea shore occupies an old restructured mine building (*see p176*).

The wild lily, though slim and delicate, manages to bloom and survive even in arid environments.

The sand, shaped by the wind, is an ever-changing landscape.

Tracks of wild animals can often be seen in the sand, particularly in the morning.

Mine railway
A section of the 19th-century narrow-gauge railway, once used to transport material from the mines to the sea, has been reopened near the beach.

Marram grass
This strongly rooted, perennial plant, *Ammophila arenaria*, is typical of sandy environments.

Wild rabbits are a common sight on the dunes. You may also come across other small animals such as foxes and lizards.

The sand dunes
Areas of the dunes are covered in thick maquis vegetation.

Exterior of San Nicola di Mira, at Gùspini, with its large rose window

❾ Gùspini

Road map: B5. 🏔 14,000. 🚌
ℹ️ Town Hall, Via Don Minzoni 10 (070 97 60). 🎫 15–31 Aug: Santa Maria. **W comune.guspini.vs.it**

Overlooking the flat and fertile Campidano plain, Gùspini is surrounded by olive groves and backed by the gradually rising foothills of Monte Arcuentu. The 17th-century church of **San Nicola di Mira**, in the main square, boasts a large rose window and is the hub of local life. The feast day of Santa Maria is celebrated with a procession and horse race.

The rose window of San Nicola di Mira

The **Montevecchio mine**, 8 km (5 miles) west, was one of the largest in Europe until the 1950s. Despite the state of abandon, the miners' houses, headquarters, church, school and hospital are worth a visit. There are guided tours of the mine and the office building as well as an exhibition on the life of the miners in the past.

🏛 Montevecchio mine
8 km (5 miles) W of Gùspini. **Tel** 070 97 31 73. **Open** days vary with season; check website. 🚻 🍴 every 30 mins from Piazzetta di Montevecchio.
W minieramontevecchio.it

❿ Arbus

Road map: B5. 🏔 8,000. 🚌
ℹ️ Via Repubblica 40 (328 708 09 34). 🎫 13 Jun: Sant' Antonio; 21 Aug: Santo Lussorio Palio (horse race). **W proloco.arbus.it**

Granite houses characterize the village of Arbus, set on the slopes of Monte Linas. Arbus is known for the production of traditional knives with curved blades, *arrasoias*.

Southwest down the N126 for 7 km (4 miles), then due west across a winding mountain road, is the mining village of **Ingurtosu**, built by the French firm Pertusola. Once home to over 1,000 mine workers, the houses, office building and church are now abandoned. The pine forest surrounding the dilapidated buildings was planted by the mine workers.

A dirt road runs among the old mines, abandoned buildings and former dumping area as far as Naracauli, where there are ruins of a more modern mine complex built shortly after World War I. A train once transported the extracted lead and zinc to the sea, where it was loaded onto ships. Certain sections of the narrow-gauge track and some carriages can be seen on the Piscinas beach.

Stretching northwards from the dune beach of Piscinas is a maquis-covered coast aptly called the Costa Verde. A quiet, scenic road follows the coastline, offering spectacular views of the sea. The road goes as far as the resort of Marina di Arbus, with easy access to sandy beaches.

The large tanks at the Montevecchio mine

⓫ Temple of Antas

Road map B5. **Open** 9:30am–7:30pm daily (to 4:30pm in winter). 🚌 to Fluminimaggiore. 🛈 Via Vittorio Emanuele 225 (0781 58 09 90).

First discovered in 1966, the ancient Temple of Antas is believed to have been a sacred nuraghic site. It was adopted by the Carthaginians in the 4th century BC and dedicated to the deity Sid Addir Babài. A century later the Carthaginians restructured the building with an atrium and a central chamber. The temple was decorated with Egyptian and Ionic symbols.

In the 3rd century AD, the Romans rebuilt the temple using some of the existing material, such as the Ionic capitals of the columns. This temple was dedicated to the god and "creator of Sardinians", Sardus Pater. Although only six of the columns remain standing today, the temple's isolated position amid the wild maquis makes it an enchanting place to visit.

Environs
In the fertile valley of the River Mannu, 9 km (5 miles) north, is the small agricultural village of **Fluminimaggiore**, founded in the 18th century. Turning west towards the sea for 9 km (5 miles), the road proceeds to **Portixeddu beach**, protected by extensive sand dunes. The headland of Capo Pecora offers stunning views of the coast.

The old mining community of Buggerru, now a tourist resort

⓬ Buggerru

Road map B5. 🔼 1,500. 🚌

Situated in a valley opening out onto the sea, Buggerru was founded in the mid-18th century in an area rich in mineral deposits. It soon became a flourishing mining town with a small theatre where opera singers used to perform, and the headquarters of the French *Société Anonyme des Mines de Malfidano*. In the lower part of the town, a sculpture by Pinuccio Sciola *(see p66)* is dedicated to the miners who died in the strikes of 1904. The mines are now closed, but some of the abandoned tunnels and caves can still be seen.

Today, the town has been reclaimed as a harbour for pleasure boats, the only one between Carloforte and Oristano. The docks, where boats were once loaded with local minerals for export, now serve as a port for visitors to the wild western coast of the island and its long stretches of sandy, sheltered beaches. To the south is the long and secluded **Cala Domestica**, a rocky bay over-looked by a Spanish watchtower.

⓭ Iglesias

Road map B5. 🔼 30,000. 🚌 🚉 🎭 Easter Week. 🖥 **comune.iglesias. ca.it**

Iglesias, or Villa Ecclesiae, was founded in the 13th century by Count Ugolino della Gherardesca (mentioned in Dante's *Inferno* XXXIII). The Pisans had conquered the area in 1257 and reopened mines abandoned in Roman times. Silver was extracted, and the city had the right to mint its own coins. In the

---

Temple of Antas

This plan shows how the later Roman temple incorporated the 3rd-century BC Carthaginian temple. The rectangular plan and six columns of the pronaos, the enclosed portico leading to the temple chamber, are still visible. An architrave above the entrance supported a triangular pediment and steps led up to the temple.

The columns, 8 m (26 ft) high, were made of smooth limestone blocks placed on bases about 1 m (3 ft) wide.

The capitals were in the Ionic style but are atypical, lacking the abacus and volutes.

Pronaos

Columns

Steps

The Roman temple was built over the Carthaginian temple.

The Easter procession during Holy Week at Iglesias

mid-19th century Iglesias grew into an important mining centre.

Today, the ruins of the mine buildings, most of which have been abandoned, create a striking contrast with the well-preserved historic centre. The elegant pedestrian shopping street, Corso Matteotti, leads to Piazza del Municipio and the Palazzo Vescovile (Bishop's Palace), built in 1785. On the west side is the 19th-century Palazzo del Comune (Town Hall) and opposite is the cathedral of **Santa Chiara**. Completed in the late 17th century, the cathedral has a Romanesque façade dating from 1288.

The narrow, winding streets around the cathedral are

Romanesque portal of Santa Chiara, Iglesias

lined with two-storey buildings adorned with wrought-iron balconies. **San Francesco** on Via Don Minzoni was built between the 14th and 16th centuries and has side chapels dedicated to noble families. Half an hour's walk from Piazza Sella is the **Castello di Salvaterra**, built in 1284 as part of the city's medieval defensive walls. A part of these walls is also visible in Via Eleonora d'Arborea.

During Easter week, holy processions and performances of mystery plays take place in the town (see p30).

The Sulcis Mines

The history of Sardinia's mines is inextricably linked with the island's economic development. Ancient rock formations, particularly in the southwestern region of the island known as Sulcis, have left rich mineral deposits of silver, copper, lead, iron and zinc. Nuraghic people are known to have had metalworking skills and there is evidence of Phoenician and Roman mines. In the short-lived boom of

Entrance to an abandoned mine

19th-century industrialization, the mines stood like citadels in a predominantly agricultural country. Today, the dream of prosperity through mining is vanishing, and all that remains is a rich heritage of mining architecture and culture.

The area around Iglesias is the mining heart of Sardinia, and the landscape descending to the sea has been deeply scarred by mine working. At Monteponi the industrial plants, mine shafts and miners' houses look as though they were only recently abandoned, while at Masua, tunnels and railways are still visible. At Buggerru, the Malfidano mine, exploited for eight centuries, opens onto the sea front.

Environs

At Case Marganai, 10 km (6 miles) northeast of Iglesias, the **Linasia Botanical Gardens** extend over an area of 9 sq km (3 sq miles) with several examples of plants from the maquis. The **Museo Casa Natura** here also has a collection of local plants and an exhibit of pieces from the local mine shafts. Guided tours of local mines are organized by the **Società Igea**. One tour takes in the lead and zinc Monteponi mine, with the elegant Bellavista building and Sella shaft. The Santa Barbara mine is also worth visiting; the shaft has unusual crenellated walls, which give it the appearance of a medieval castle.

🏡 Linasia Botanical Gardens
Località Marganai. **Tel** 0781 220 97. **Open** 9am–noon, 4:30–7:30pm Tue, Thu, Sat & Sun. 🅿 🚻 Museo Casa Natura: **Tel** 0781 220 97. **Open** 9am–noon, 4:30–7:30pm Tue, Thu, Sat & Sun.

🚻 Società Igea
Località Campo Pisano. **Tel** 0781 49 13 00 or 348 154 95 56. 🅿 🚻 phone in advance. 🆆 igeaspa.it

⓮ Costa di Masua

Road map B5. 🚹 (0781 311 70).

The corniche road between Fontanamare and Masua, 12 km (7 miles) north, follows a wild and splendid coastline. At Masua, the little beach of Porto Flavia is overlooked by pillars of eroded limestone and, offshore, the unmistakable profile of Pan di Zucchero ("sugarloaf") island. This sheer rock rises 132 m (433 ft) from the sea. At Nebida you can see the abandoned mines of the industrial archaeological area.

A panoramic path along the coast leads to the abandoned remains of La Marmora mine buildings and shafts.

The craggy limestone mass of Pan di Zucchero, jutting out from the sea

⑮ Island of San Pietro

Named after the apostle Peter, who is said to have taken refuge here during a storm, the island of San Pietro was virtually uninhabited until 1736, when Carlo Emanuele III offered it to a community of Ligurian coral fishermen whose ancestors had been exiled to the island of Tabarca, off the Tunisian coast. San Pietro's Ligurian origins can be seen in the architecture, dialect and cuisine, which also bears traces of North African influences. The rugged coast, inhabited by the rare Eleonora's falcon, has spectacular coves that can be reached only by sea. The island is covered in thick maquis vegetation.

VISITORS' CHECKLIST

Practical Information
Road map B6. 🚹 7,000.
ℹ️ Corso Tagliafico 1, Carloforte
(0781 85 40 09). In August book
a ferry. The Laguna and Sir
Lawrence motor boats at
Carloforte offer trips around the
island. 🎭 end Apr: Sagra del
Couscous; 29 Jun: San Pietro.
W prolococarloforte.it

Transport
🚢 Saremar from Calasetta or
Portovesme. **W** saremar.it

Cala Fico
Walls of silver rock on one side and brown rock on the other enclose this sheltered inlet.

Capo Sandalo
The westernmost point of the island, dominated by a lighthouse, is frequently exposed to the mistral wind.

Cala Vinagra

Montagna di Ravenna

Monte di Gasparro

La Caletta

0 kilometres   2
0 miles   2

La Caletta
Protected from rough seas by Punta Spalmatore, the sheltered bay of La Caletta has a white, sandy beach.

Punta delle Colonne
The name, Cape of Columns, refers to the trachytic stacks that jut out from the sea.

Eleonora's falcon, so named because Eleonora d'Arborea (*see p40*) passed a law forbidding falcon hunting, is protected in this reserve. The conservation area has observation points and marked footpaths.

Isola Piana

La Punta In September, for a couple of days only, local fishermen open their homes and feed visitors.

rloforte

Carloforte
The only town on the island, Carloforte overlooks the port, with alleys and stairways descending to the water. The centre of social life is Piazza Carlo Emanuele III. The San Pietro feast day procession of boats is also worth watching.

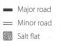

Salt flats on the outskirts of Carloforte attract a large number of migratory birds.

Key

— Major road

= Minor road

▨ Salt flat

– River

Carbonia's Piazza Roma, a typical example of Fascist architecture

⓰ Carbonia

Road map B6. 🚶 34,000. 🚌
ℹ Town Hall, Piazza Roma (0781 69 42 11). 🇼 **comune.carbonia.ci.it**

Carbonia, located in the mining region of Sulcis, was founded by Mussolini in 1936. The town has retained its Fascist town planning and architectural conception, with imposing buildings and broad streets that converge at the central Piazza Roma. The town's most important public buildings are found here, including the Town Hall, the Torre Civica tower and the parish church of San Ponziano.

Villa Sulcis, the former residence of the director of the mines, has become the **Museo Archeologico**. On display are earthenware and bronze statuettes and jewels from local *domus de janas*, and finds from the archaeological sites at Monte Sirai.

The **Museo Martel** has a collection of fossils dating back 600 million years.

Environs
West of Carbonia along the SS126, a signposted road leads to the imposing hill occupied by the Monte Sirai archaeological site. The stunning view alone is worth the visit, as you can see the islands of Sant'Antioco and San Pietro. The fortified **Parco Archeologico Monte Sirai** was built by the Phoenicians in 750 BC. The thick outer wall protected the acropolis and the surrounding garrison town, which could house 500 foot soldiers and 100 mounted soldiers. The ruins of this ancient military camp were discovered in 1963 and excavations are still under way.

The necropolis, northwest of the main citadel, is mainly · Carthaginian, but there is a

Phoenician section with common graves, as well as an area of Punic tombs.

🏛 **Museo Archeologico**
Villa Sulcis, Viale Arsia. **Tel** 0781 63 512. **Open** Apr–Sep: 10am–7pm Tue–Sun; Oct–Mar: 10am–3pm Wed–Sun.
▨ ▨ ▨

🏛 **Museo Martel**
Grande Miniera di Serbariu. **Tel** 0781 66 21 99. **Open** Apr–Sep: 10am–2pm, 3–7pm Tue–Sun; Oct–Mar: 10am–3pm Wed–Sun. ▨ ▨

🏛 **Parco Archeologico Monte Sirai**
3 km (2 miles) S of Carbonia. **Tel** 0781 626 65. **Open** Apr–Sep: 10am–7pm Tue–Sun; Oct–Mar: 10am–3pm Wed–Sun. ▨ ▨ ▨

Underground burial chambers in the necropolis of Monte Sirai

⓱ Calasetta

Road map B6. 🚶 2,800. 🚌 🚌
ℹ 0781 885 34.

The second largest village on the island of Sant'Antioco (*see p76*) and a trading port for Carloforte, Calasetta was founded in 1769 to house the Ligurian fishermen arriving from the Tunisian island of Tabarca. The straight streets with their two-storey houses lead to the main square. Here, the parish church has a bell tower of Arab derivation. The road heading south along the western coast offers a panoramic view of alternating cliffs, coves and beaches.

Urns that held the ashes of babies in the Tophet outside Sant'Antioco

⓲ Sant'Antioco

Road map B6. 13,000.
Town Hall (0781 80 301); Pro Loco,
Piazza Repubblica 41 (0781 84 05 92).
2nd Mon after Easter: Sant'Antioco;
29 Jun: San Pietro. **proloco
santantioco.it**

Sant'Antioco is the main
town on the island of the same
name. The island is connected
to Sardinia by a causeway and
remains of a Roman bridge
are still visible from the road.
The *faraglioni*, two large
menhirs, stand on one side.
According to legend these are
the petrified figures of a nun
and a monk, turned to stone
as they tried to elope.

The town was founded by the
Phoenicians in the 8th century
BC and named Sulki. It soon
became a major port in the
Mediterranean, due to the
trade in minerals, including
gold, extracted from the area.
Ptolemy, the Greek astronomer,
gave it the name of *insula
plumbaria* (island of lead). The
Carthaginians used the port
during the second Punic War
(see p38), but this alliance
was harshly punished by the
victorious Romans. Under the
Roman Empire the town
flourished, until continuous
pirate raids during the Middle
Ages led to its gradual decline.

The picturesque town centre
climbs away from the sea and
its characteristic houses have
small wrought-iron balconies.
The main street, **Corso Vittorio
Emanuele**, is shaded by an
avenue of trees. Above the
town is the church of

Sant'Antioco, built in the 6th
century with a Greek cross
plan and central dome, but
modified in the 11th century.
According to tradition the
remains of the island's patron
saint, Sant'Antioco, are buried
in the catacombs, reached via
the transept. The body of the
martyr is said to have floated
here after he was killed by
the Romans in Africa.
Some catacombs are
open to the public.
The chambers are less
than 2 m (6 ft) high and
some are decorated
with frescoes.

The **Museo
Archeologico** contains
Phoenician and Roman
earthenware, jewels
and other objects found
in the area, including
urns from the nearby
Tophet necropolis.

The **Museo Etnografico** is
housed in a former winemaking
plant. The large central hall
contains kitchen equipment
used to make cheese and
cultivate grapevines. The
weaving section has spindles

and looms on show, once
used for the processing of
wool and *byssus*, a fine filament
taken from the *Pinna nobilis*,
the largest bivalve mollusc
in the Mediterranean. Under
the arcade outside, original
wine-making equipment and
implements used for raising
livestock are on display.

Dominating the town is the
red stone **Castello Sabaudo**,
rebuilt by the Aragonese in the
16th century. Just outside the
town, on a cliff overlooking
the sea, the bleak **Tophet** is
a Phoenician sanctuary and
necropolis. This burial ground
was used for the ashes of still-
born babies, or those who died
shortly after birth. Nearby is the
Carthaginian **Necropolis** with
about 40 underground family
tombs. This area was later used
by the Romans for the ashes of
their dead. The tombs occupy
the upper part of town and
were used as catacombs during
the Early Christian period.

Fresco in the catacombs of Sant'Antioco

**🏠 Sant'Antioco Catacombs
and Necropolis**
Via Necropoli. **Tel** 0781 830 44.
Catacombs: **Open** 9am–noon, 3–8pm
Mon–Sat, 10–11am, 4–8pm Sun;
Necropolis: by reservation only.

Cala Domestica, north of Sant'Antioco *(see p72)*

Ⅲ Museo Archeologico
Piazza Sabatino Moscati. **Tel** 0781 821
05. **Open** 9am–7pm daily. 🚫 📷 ♿
W archeotur.it

Ⅲ Museo Etnografico
Via Necropoli. **Open** 9:30am–1pm,
3–6pm daily (summer: 9am–8pm).
🚫 ♿ **W** archeotur.it

♨ Tophet
Piazza Sabatini Moscati. **i** Archeotur
(0781 800 596). **Open** 9am–7pm
daily. 🚫

⑲ Tratalìas

Road map B6. 🏘 1,182. 🚌
W comune.tratalias.ca.it

This village in the Sulcis region
was the seat of the diocese
until 1413. The façade of the
Pisan Romanesque cathedral
of **Santa Maria**, consecrated
in 1213, is divided horizontally
by a row of little arches
surmounted by a rose window.
The tympanum is curious,
in that the last section
of a stairway juts out
from it.
The sides and apse
are decorated
with pilasters
and blind
arches. Inside,
the three naves
are separated
by large,
octagonal
pillars. An altar-
piece from

Cathedral of Santa Maria, Tratalìas

1596 depicts St John the Baptist
and St John the Evangelist with
the Madonna and Child.

⑳ Santadi

Road map C6. 🏘 4,100. 🚌
i 0781 95 51 78. 🎭 first Sun in
Aug: Matrimonio Mauritano.
W comune.santadi.ci.it

Built on the banks of the River
Mannu, Santadi's old town sits
on the higher, north side. Some
traditional architecture made
from rough volcanic rock is still
visible in the medieval centre.
Evidence that the area has been
inhabited since the nuraghic
age can be seen in the copper,
bronze, gold and earthenware
objects found here, which are
now on display in the Museo
Archeologico in Cagliari *(see
p62)*. Local tools and furniture
can be seen at the **Museo
Etnografico Sa Domu Antiga**.
The shop here sells typical
Sulcis handicrafts.

Environs
On a plateau southwest of the
town is the 7th-century BC
Phoenician fortress, **Pani
Loriga**. Continuing south
for 5 km (3 miles) are
two caves,
Grotte Is Zuddas,
with splendid
formations of
stalagmites and
stalactites, and
Grotta Pirosu
(now closed)
where archaeo-
logical finds
such as a votive lamp and a
Cypriot style tripod were found.
North of Villaperuccio, the

Domus de janas (tomb of giants) at the
necropolis at Montessu

Montessu Necropolis has
typical *domus de janas (see p37)*
tombs, some of which still have
traces of the original yellow and
red wall facing. Other tombs
were probably used for worship.
The August festival, Matrimonio Mauritano (Mauretanian
Wedding), is a ceremony that
may have started with the
North Africans who settled
here during the Roman era.

**Ⅲ Museo Etnografico Sa
Domu Antiga**
Via Mazzini 37. **Tel** 0781 94 10 10.
Open 9am–1pm, 5–7pm (3–5pm
winter) Tue–Sun.

🐾 Grotte Is Zuddas
Benatzu. **i** Cooperativa Monte
Meana (0781 95 57 41). **Open** Apr–
Jun: 11am–12:15pm, 3–7:30pm daily;
Jul–Sep: 10am–2:15pm, 2:30–6pm;
Oct & Mar: tours only, noon & 4pm
daily. 🚫 📷 compulsory.
W grotteiszuddas.com

♨ Montessu Necropolis
Villa Peruccio, Località Montessu.
i 0781 640 40. **Open** summer:
9am–1pm, 3–8pm; winter: 9am–1pm,
3–5pm. 🚫 📷

Monte Arcosu

The mountains in the Sulcis region are covered with forests of
cork oak, holm oak, strawberry trees and heather, from which
the granite peaks seem to emerge. This area extends for about
70 sq km (27 sq miles), interrupted only by a rough road
that connects Santadi and Capoterra along the Mannu and
Gutturu Mannu river valleys. There are plans to make the area
into a National Park: the World Wide Fund for Nature (WWF)
has purchased 2.5 sq km (1 sq mile) of land on the slopes
of Monte Arcosu to protect the Sardinian deer, which roamed
the entire island until 1900, but is now restricted to a few isolated
areas. Other forest mammals include fallow deer, wild cats, boar
and martens. Among the birds found here are the golden eagle,

Stag in the Monte Arcosu reserve

peregrine falcon and goshawk. This nature reserve is open all year and visitors can stay overnight
in refuges. There are well-marked nature trails as well as unmarked wild walks, although an official
WWF guide is obligatory in some areas. The Cagliari-based Cooperativa Quadrifoglio (070 96 87 14)
has information regarding accommodation and trekking. To reach the reserve, take the road east
from Santadi along the Gutturu river.

The sheltered beach at Baia Chia

❷❶ Baia Chia

Road map C6. **ℹ** 070 923 62 93.

The Southern Coast (Costa del Sud) is an area of high sand dunes and white beaches that extend as far as the Capo Spartivento headland. Junipers grow in the sand and there is marshland frequented by egrets, purple herons, grebes and other migratory aquatic birds. There are plans to turn the area into the centre of a regional nature reserve.

Along the coastal road, the hamlet of Chia is a popular tourist destination set among orchards and fig trees. A rough road leads to the sheltered bay of Chia, flanked on one side by the 17th-century **Torre di Chia**, and on the other by red cliffs covered with maquis vegetation. At the foot of the tower it is possible to visit the remains of Phoenician **Bithia**. This ancient city, mentioned in the writings of Ptolemy and Pliny the Elder, had been covered by the sea for centuries and has not yet been completely excavated.

Remains of a Punic and Roman necropolis are visible, as are the ruins of a temple probably dedicated to the god Bes. Earthenware pots and amphorae from the 7th century BC have been discovered in the sand, and traces of Roman wall paintings and mosaics decorate porticoed houses. Ancient Punic fortifications can be seen near the base of the watchtower and an elliptical cistern has also been found.

🏛 Bithia
Domus de Maria, Località Chia.
Open at all times.

Environs
Along the coast as far as the promontory of Capo Spartivento, where there are spectacular views, is a series of bays, dunes and pine forests that can be reached on foot.

The Roman theatre at Nora dating from the 2nd century AD

❷❷ Nora

Road map C6. **ℹ** 070 920 91 38. **Open** 9am–sunset daily. 🎫 combined ticket with Museo Archeologico. 🎧 ♿ 📱 **W** coptur.net

Founded under Phoenician rule in the 9th–8th centuries BC, the ancient city of Nora was built on a spit of land jutting out to sea. The town became the island's main city, a role it continued to enjoy under the Romans.

Repeated Saracen raids and the lack of fertile land finally forced the inhabitants to abandon the city in the Middle Ages; the three ports were gradually covered up by the incoming sea, resulting in the legend of the submerged city.

The promontory of Capo Spartivento overlooking the southern coastline

The ruins extend to the headland of Capo di Pula, dominated by the Spanish **Torre del Coltelazzo**. An impressive vestige of the Carthaginian city is the Temple of Tanit, goddess of fertility. Little else remains of the Punic period, although rich findings in the tombs testify to active trading.

Left of the entrance are the 2nd–3rd-century AD Terme di Levante, Roman baths decorated with mosaics. Nearby is a 2nd-century AD theatre, the only one in Sardinia, and the large rectangular Forum behind it. South of the theatre, the mosaics in the *frigidarium* and *caldarium* of the baths are decorated with white, black and ochre tesserae. Paved roads and the city's sewage system are also still visible.

Many finds, including Punic inscriptions in which the name of the island of Sardinia is first mentioned, are kept in Cagliari's Museo Archeologico Nazionale *(see p62)*.

Some earthenware objects found at the site are on display in the small **Museo Archeologico Patroni**. The nearby Romanesque church of **Sant'Efisio**, built by French Victorine monks in the 11th century, is the site of an annual procession from Cagliari *(see p30)*.

🏛 Museo Archeologico Patroni
Corso Vittorio Emanuele 67.
Tel 070 920 96 10. **Open** Apr–Oct: 9am– 7:30pm daily; Nov–Mar: 9am–dusk daily. 🚶 combined ticket with Nora. (No flash photography). 📷

The tower of Poetto, between Quartu Sant'Elena and Cagliari

㉓ Quartu Sant'Elena

Road map C5. 🏛 66,000. 🚌 🚆 Cagliari. ✈ Elmas. 🛈 Via Cavour 56, 070 233 46 57. 🎉 14 Sep: Sant'Elena.

Situated on the outskirts of Cagliari, Quartu Sant'Elena has grown to become one of the island's largest cities. It lies at the edge of the salt flats and marsh of the same name which are a favourite breeding and nesting ground for flamingoes.

The medieval church of **Sant'Agata** stands in the town's main square, Piazza Azuni. From here Via Porcu leads to the **Casa Museo Sa Dom 'e Farra**, literally "the house of flour". This large country house, converted into a museum, features over 14,000 traditional farm and domestic tools and equipment collected over the years by Gianni Musiu, a former shepherd. Each of the museum's rooms is dedicated to different farm activities: displaying saddles and leather harnesses to wagons and blacksmiths' bellows. One of the more curious objects is the snow-cooled icebox. Gathered in the Barbagia region, the snow was taken to Cagliari on muleback and kept cold in large straw-lined containers stored underground.

The farmstead consisted of the owner's home and living quarters for farm labourers. Other rooms around a large courtyard were used for various domestic and farm activities such as milling, bread-making and tool repair.

A bus ride southwest of Quartu Sant'Elena brings you to the beach resort of Poetto, a favourite with local people.

🏛 Casa Museo Sa Dom 'e Farra
Via Eligiu Porcu 143. **Tel** 070 81 23 40. **Closed** for restoration.

Foresta dei Sette Fratelli

The Forest of the "Seven Brothers" was named after the seven peaks that can be seen from Cagliari and which tower over the holm oak forests and maquis. Run by Ente Foreste Sardegna (070 279 91), the forest covers an area of 40 sq km (15 sq miles), replanted with pine, eucalyptus and cypress trees, and reaching an altitude of 1,023 m (3,355 ft). It is also one of the few areas inhabited by the rare Sardinian deer, now almost extinct. The mountain has many mule trails, once used by coal merchants; one of these footpaths begins at the forest headquarters at Campu Omo on the SS125. To drive into the mountains take a right turn past the Arcu 'e Tidu pass on the SS125.

Densely wooded Foresta dei Sette Fratelli, which extends over seven hills

THE EASTERN COAST

Mile after mile of pastures and rocks characterize the interior of eastern Sardinia, falling away to inaccessible cliffs on the coast, refuge for the rare monk seal. The coastline of the Golfo di Orosei is now part of the Parco Nazionale del Gennargentu, a vast nature reserve founded to protect golden eagles and moufflon.

There are no towns of any great size along the eastern coast but there are some good seaside resorts around Arbatax and Villasimius. Except for a few stretches, the road runs inland, so that most of the beaches can be reached only after walking a long way or by driving on dirt roads. The largest towns are Orosei, Muravera and Dorgali, also situated in the interior at a certain distance from the coast. The historical reasons for this go back to the endemic malaria that afflicted the island until after World War II and, before that, the constant pirate raids which plagued the coasts for centuries. This is still unknown Sardinia, the interior the domain of shepherds and their flocks, and the southeast yet to be discovered by tourism. The region of Sarrabus used to be isolated because of the absence of negotiable roads. The only way of reaching it was via a narrow-gauge railway from Cagliari, which followed the contours of the valleys. It is still in operation, and offers a delightful opportunity to take a trip back into the past. Sarrabus today attracts visitors who prefer to stray from the beaten track. Further north, the Ogliastra region, with its sandy beaches which vary from pearly grey to a startling reddish colour, has rugged mountains and hills where time seems to have stood still, pastoral life has not been invaded by the 21st century and strong traditions survive. The Baronie region, in contrast, has the towns of Siniscola and Orosei, with good public transport systems and a fast modern motorway, making the area more accessible.

The alluvial plain around Posada, seen from the Castello della Fava

◀ Hikers in Su Gorroppu gorge in Gennargentu National Park, Nuoro

Exploring the Eastern Coast

Splendid natural scenery and prehistoric archaeological sites around Dorgali and Orroli are the main attractions of the eastern coast. The cliffs along the coast are steep, and the most secluded coves in the Golfo di Orosei (Cala Sisine, Cala Luna, Cala Goloritze) are most easily reached by boat. The alternative is a lengthy walk, best tackled in hiking boots, and the trek rewarding. The countryside is marvellous however, and the main road winding through the region is the Orientale Sarda. There is a proposal – supported by the local people but vehemently opposed by environmentalists – to widen this road into a fast access motorway.

Olbia

11 POSADA

Torpè

Sant Lucia

10 SINISCOLA

Lago di Posada

Lodè

Liberò

Mamone

Monte Albo

MONTE ALBO TOUR

Monti Remule

9

Mar di Oro

Lula

S131d

OROSEI 7

Bitti

GALTELLI 8

Isalle

S129

Nuoro

Serra Orrios

Cala Gonone

DORGALI 5

S125

THE ORIENTALE SARDA ROAD 1

CODULA DI L

Genna Silana 1017m

GENNARGENTU

Urzulei

Talana

4

NATIONAL PARK

Seui

S198

TRENINO VERDE

11

ORROLI 18

Serri

Mandas

S128

A glimpse of the Golfo di Orosei, near Baunei

0 kilometres 10
0 miles 10

Sights at a Glance

2 Arbatax
3 Santa Maria Navarrese
4 *Gennargentu National Park pp86–7*
5 Dorgali
7 Orosei
8 Galtellì
10 Siniscola
11 Posada
12 Lanusei
13 Jerzu
14 Gairo

15 Bari Sardo
16 Muravera
17 Villasimius
18 Orroli
19 Perdasdefogu

Tours

1 The Orientale Sarda Road
6 Codula di Luna
9 Monte Albo Tour
20 *A Trip on the Trenino Verde pp96–7*

Key

— Major road
— Secondary road
---- Minor road
— Scenic route
-+- Main railway
— Minor railway
△ Summit

For keys to symbols *see back flap*

Meadows at Gennargentu National Park

Rocky outcrops of reddish granite at Arbatax

Pisan tower at Orosei

Golfo Orosei

Capo di Monte Santu

Baunei

🚉 **SANTA MARIA NAVARRESE** ③

otzorai

ARBATAX ②

Tortolì

S125

S198

BARI SARDO

LANUSEI ⑫ ⑮ *Torre di Barì*

Cardedu

GAIRO

Ulassai Marina di Gairo

JERZU ⑬

Capo Sferracavallo

Tertenia Melisenda

PERDASDEFOGU ⑲

Salto di Quirra

Quirra

Escalaplano Quirra

Flumendosa

S125

Ballao Villaputzu

Porto Corallo

Villasalto **MURAVERA** ⑯

San Priamo

Capo Ferrato

Camisa

Costa Rei

Cagliari

Castiadas Casa della Marina

Cala Sinzias

Isola Serpentara

Solánas **VILLASIMIUS** ⑰

Capo Carbonara

Getting Around

The Orientale Sarda road (SS125) was once famous for being winding and slow to drive. In 2007, works totalling nearly €50 million were completed. There is now a direct dual-carriageway link from Cagliari to Arbatax/Tortolì. There is also a north–south coach service. The Ogliastra plain (Tortolì and Arbatax) is connected to Cagliari by the Ferrovie Complementari della Sardegna narrow-gauge train; the trip takes about eight hours. It is slow, but the line goes through wonderful scenery.

One of the rocky coves on the eastern coast near Cala Luna

❶ The Orientale Sarda Road

Along the eastern peaks of the Gennargentu National Park *(see pp86–7)*, the SS125, or the "Orientale Sarda" route, connects Olbia to Cagliari. The most spectacular stretch is between Dorgali and Baunei, 63 km (39 miles) of winding road hewn out of the rock by Piedmontese coal merchants during the mid-1800s. These "foreigners" carved a road through the remote mountain valleys and felled trees that were sent to the mainland. The deforestation that resulted has proved irreversible.

② Flumineddu River Valley
This stretch of the SS125 road goes through rugged terrain with cliffs and a fine view of the Flumineddu river valley under the peaks of Monte Tiscali. There are many places where you can stop to enjoy the wonderful scenery.

③ Genna Silana Pass
This is the highest point of the tour at 1,017 m (3,336 ft). Stop here to get a dramatic view of the Gorroppu ravine. A footpath from Pischina Urtaddalà descends to the Flumineddu river bed.

④ Urzulei
Built on different levels on the slopes of Punta Is Gruttas, Urzulei was once an isolated town difficult to reach. The stone church of San Giorgio di Suelli dates from the 15th century.

Dorgali

Grotta Del Bue Marino

Golfo Di Orosei

Flumineddu

(Orientale Sarda)

SS125

Codula di Luna

Codula di S. ine

Gennargentu National Park

⑤ Baunei
The white houses of this mountain village stand out under the limestone crags.

Key
- ▬ Major road
- ═ Minor road
- ─ River

Tips for Drivers

Tour length: 63 km (39 miles).
Stopping-off points: at Dorgali, Genna Silana, San Pietro and Santa Maria Navarrese there are cafés and restaurants. Allow a full day to take into account the winding roads and opportunities to stop.

① Cala Gonone

A 400-m (1,300-ft) tunnel cut out of the limestone rock leads to the popular seaside resort of Cala Gonone. A winding road, with fabulous views of the sea, white rocks and the maquis, continues to the Grotta del Bue Marino where there have been sightings of the rare monk seal (see p23).

```
0 kilometres          4
0 miles               4
```

⑥ San Pietro

A rough track with precipitous hairpin bends climbs to a wooded plateau where wild pigs graze. At the end is the Golgo ravine, 295 m (967 ft) deep. A little further along is the 18th-century church of San Pietro. Shepherds still make offerings here and a rural festival takes place on 28–29 June.

The holiday resort of Cala Moresca, at Arbatax

❷ Arbatax

Road map D4. 🏔 1,100. ✈ 🚊 🚌
ℹ Pro Loco (0782 62 28 24). 📅 2nd Sun in Jul: Madonna di Stella Maris.

The small town of Arbatax lies on the northern tip of the Bellavista promontory, a red porphyry cliff that plunges into the sea. The port, guarded by a Spanish tower, is the terminus for the narrow-gauge trains arriving from Cagliari. Ferries from Cagliari, Olbia and the Italian mainland also dock here.

This stretch of coast has clear, clean water and enticing coves such as **Cala Moresca**, south of Arbatax. Several tourist resorts now cover this small promontory, such as the popular *Vacanze Club* village, built to resemble a typical Mediterranean village. The solid wood doors and wrought-iron grilles on the windows were taken from the abandoned

The Aragonese tower at Santa Maria Navarrese

village of Gairo (see p93). Further to the south is Porto Frailis, also protected by a Spanish tower, and the long, sandy Orrì beach. From Arbatax footpaths lead up to the lighthouse high on the Bellavista promontory.

❸ Santa Maria Navarrese

Road map D4. 🏔 1,500. ✈ 🚊
ℹ 0782 61 08 23. 📅 15 Aug: Festa dell'Assunta. 🅦 **turismo.ogliastra.it**

This seaside resort was named after the lovely country church around which it developed.

It is said that this three-aisle construction, with a semicircular apse, was built in the 11th century by the daughter of the king of Navarra after she had been saved from a shipwreck.

In the church courtyard is a gigantic wild olive tree that is reputed to be over a thousand years old.

The beautiful beach at Santa Maria Navarrese is bordered by a pine forest and protected by a Spanish watchtower. Opposite this is the huge Agugliastra (or Sa Pedra Longa) rock, a slim limestone pinnacle that rises up 128 m (420 ft) from the sea. Boat services from the little port of Santa Maria Navarrese will take visitors to the stack, as well as to Cala Luna, Cala Sisine and Cala Goloritzè, further up the coast.

The rocky Ogliastra island viewed from Capo Bellavista

❹ Gennargentu National Park

The park extends over 590 sq km (228 sq miles) of some of the wildest, most mountainous landscape in Sardinia, and includes the island's highest peak, Punta La Marmora. Established in 1989, most of the park lies in the province of Nuoro. There are 14 towns in this protected area, but few tarmac roads, and the steep-sided valleys and bare peaks give the area an isolated air. The unspoilt nature of the park makes it fascinating for walkers, geologists and naturalists alike. The climb up Punta La Marmora (1,834 m, 6,015 ft) is rewarding, and the limestone desert of Supramonte is one of Italy's spectacular sights. Monte Tiscali hides the prehistoric rock village of Tiscali *(see pp108–9)*, and the ravines of Su Gorroppu and the Su Gologone spring are unmissable. The coast to the east, home to the endangered monk seal, is one of Europe's loveliest. When walking, it is advisable to take an up-to-date map and plenty of water.

The Wild Cat
Larger than the domestic cat, the wild cat lives on Gennargentu and Supramonte.

The Mount Gennargentu Massif
In winter the barren peaks and the lower slopes, carpeted in oak and chestnut trees, are sometimes covered by snow.

The Highest Peak in Sardinia: Punta La Marmora

The massif of Gennargentu, whose name means "door of silver", reaches its peak in Punta La Marmora which, at 1,834 m (6,015 ft) above sea level, is the highest point on the island. The landscape here is quite barren and wild. The sky is populated by raptors circling around in search of prey and with a bit of luck you might be able to see, in the distance, small groups of moufflons, or mountain sheep.

Hikers on the top of Punta La Marmora

Refuge
Orgo
Fonni
Baunei
SS128
Desulo
Aritzo
Flumendosa
Se

0 kilometres 15
0 miles 15

The Crests of Supramonte
The peaks rise to the east of Gennargentu and their slopes descend towards the sea.

VISITORS' CHECKLIST

Practical Information
Road map D4. 🛈 0784 323 07 or 0784 23 88 78; Dorgali Pro Loco, Via La Marmora 108 (0784 962 43); Desulo Town Hall (0784 61 92 11); WWF Cagliari (070 67 03 08).
🔟 **wwf.it/sardegna**

Refuge

Dorgali

The Monk Seal
The monk seal (*Monachus albiventer*), once thought to be extinct, has been sighted again in the Golfo di Orosei. Tourism had been blamed for the fall in population.

Codula Di Luna

Urzulei

Key

━━━ Major road
═══ Minor road
▬▬▬ River

SS125

Baunei

SS389

Lago Alto Flumendosa

Arzana

Tips for Drivers

Ascending Punta La Marmora
From Desulo, follow the road to Fonni for about 5 km (3 miles) until you come to the S'Arcu de Tascusí pass, then take the asphalt road on the right until you reach a fork. Follow the dirt road on the right for 100 m (328 ft) and then take the right-hand road leading to the Girgini holiday farm. Skirt around it by keeping to the left. In a little less than 4 km (2 miles), take the right-hand fork and continue for 5 km (3 miles) until you reach the control cabin for an aqueduct. Leave your car here and follow the road on the right on foot until you reach the end, then proceed up the valley floor on the left until you reach the crest. From here you can continue up to the summit (an hour and a half on foot).

Su Gorroppu
This wild gorge, with its steep sides, can only be scaled by expert climbers.

Displays of exhibits at the Museo Archeologico in Dorgali

❺ Dorgali

Road map D3. 🏛 8,500. 🛈 Pro Loco
(0784 962 43). 🎭 16–17 Jan: Sant'
Antonio Abate. 🅦 **dorgali.it**

The charming town of Dorgali
lies on a ridge that descends
from Monte Bardia and is 30 km
(19 miles) from Nuoro and a
little less than 10 km (6 miles)
from the sea at Cala Gonone.
Dorgali is predominantly an
agricultural centre, but it is also
important for locally produced

Nuraghic dwelling at Serra Òrrios

crafts such as leather, ceramics
and filigree jewellery, as well
as rug- and carpet-weaving.
In the old part of town the
buildings are made of dark
volcanic stone. These include
several churches: Madonna
d'Itria, San Lussorio and the
Maddalena. The central square,
Piazza Vittorio Emanuele, is
dominated by the façade of the
parish church, Santa Caterina,
home to a large carved altar.
Dorgali's **Museo Archeologico**
contains objects from nuraghic
sites, as well as finds from sites
dating back to Punic and Roman
times. Some of the finest nuraghic
pieces come from the nearby
site of **Serra Òrrios**. The museum
also provides information on
visits to the rock village of Tiscali,
another major nuraghic site
(*see pp108–9*). The town is
known for its wine, and the
local wine-making cooperative
can be visited. The local dairy
is also of interest.

Environs

The **Parco Museo S'Abba Frisca**,
located about 6 km (4 miles)
north of Dorgali, shows how
rural people once lived. Guided
tours take visitors through the
indoor and outdoor displays,
including a working blacksmith's
forge and a shepherds' hut.
Visitors can also learn about the
flora and fauna of the region.

🏛 **Museo Archeologico di Dorgali**
Cooperativa Ghivina, Scuola Elemen-
tare, Via La Marmora. 🛈 338 834
16 18. **Closed** for restoration.
Check website for details. 🎭 ♿
🅦 **museoarcheologicodorgali.it**

🛈 **Serra Òrrios**
🛈 338 834 16 18. **Open** daily
9am–1pm, afternoon hours vary.
🎫 compulsory, on the hour. 🎭

🏛 **Parco Museo S'Abba Frisca**
Strada Cartoe. **Tel** 338 238 00 89.
Open 9am–1pm, afternoon hours
vary. 🎫 summer: 9am–noon &
3pm–7pm; winter: by reservation.
🎭 🅦 **sabbafrisca.com**

The Nuraghic Village of Serra Òrrios

At Serra Òrrios – about 10km
(6 miles) to the northwest of
Dorgali and 23 km (14 miles) east
of Nuoro – lies one of Sardinia's
best preserved nuraghic villages,
which dates from the 12th–
10th centuries BC. The 70 round
dwellings, each with a central
hearth, are arranged in at least
six groups around large central
spaces with a well. Small places
of worship have also been found
in the village.

Main Temple

Group of
Dwellings

❻ Codula di Luna

A 4-hour walk down the "Valley of the Moon" will take hikers from the Supramonte to the sea. The path is straightforward but strenuous, with little shade. The track runs through aromatic maquis scrub, and passes shepherds' huts, as well as the entrances to enormous caves, many of which have not yet been fully explored. It is highly advised that you do not attempt this walk without a local guide.

The beautiful, secluded beach of Cala Luna, backed by a small lake

Exploring the Grotta Su Palu

② Grotta Su Palu
This is one of the largest and most extensive caves in Sardinia. It was only discovered in 1980.

③ Cala Luna
Access is possible on foot from the valley (except after heavy rains), or by sea.

Key
- ▪ ▪ Tour route
- ▬ Major road
- ═ Minor road
- — River

SS125

③ Cala Luna

②

Cala Sisine

Coast near the Grotta del Bue Marino

0 km   2
0 miles   2

Genna Silana

Genna Cruxi

①

Urzulei

Genna Sarbene

Tips for Travellers
From the SS125 main road, also known as Orientale Sarda (at the Giustizieri fork, not far from the turn-off for Urzulei), take the road down the Codula valley and leave your car where the tarmac ends. Cross the river bed to begin the hike. About one hour's walk brings you to the entrance to Su Palu cave (on the right, for experienced cavers). Further along, the valley widens and opens out onto Cala Luna bay (a further two to four hours' walk). This walk is for experienced hikers only. In good weather the bay is accessible by boat from Cala Gonone *(see p85)*; boats also go to the **Grotta del Bue Marino** (mooring facilities). Bring plenty of drinking water.
Grotta del Bue Marino
🛈 347 720 96 96. **Open** 1 Apr–15 Oct. 🎟 book a boat trip to the Grotta from the website. 📶
🌐 excursionscalagonone.com

The Solluli nuraghe, strategically built on a ridge with views around

① Nuraghe Solluli
Before joining the Codula road you will see the Solluli nuraghe to the right.

The Chiesa delle Anime at Orosei

⑦ Orosei

Road map D3. 🏛 6,000. 🚌
ℹ Pro Loco (0784 99 83 67).
🎉 Easter Week, 26 Jul, San Giacomo.
🌐 orosei-proloco.com.

The historic capital of the Baronia region is situated about 5 km (3 miles) inland, and has a bustling, well-kept historic centre with churches, archways and small, white-washed stone buildings overlooking flowered courtyards.

The town of Orosei was probably founded in the early Middle Ages and its golden age occurred under Pisan domination, when it was ruled by the barons of the Guiso family. Orosei developed into an important harbour with moorings alongside the Cedrino river. After yielding to Aragonese rule, the town began to decline as a result of malarial disease, repeated pirate raids and the gradual silting up of

The portal of Santa Maria 'e Mare

the river. A labyrinth of alleys leads to the central Piazza del Popolo, where three churches stand. At the top of a flight of steps is **San Giacomo Maggiore** with an 18th-century façade and terracotta-tiled domes. Opposite is the **Chiesa del Rosario**, with a Baroque façade, and the **Chiesa delle Anime**, founded by the brotherhood of monks that participates in the Easter Week ceremonies.

Sant'Antonio Abate, once an isolated rural sanctuary, is now surrounded by the expanding town. Local handicrafts are on display in the Pisan tower inside the precincts of Sant'Antonio. The 17th-century Sanctuary of the Madonna del Rimedio, also once isolated, is now part of the outskirts and is surrounded by *cumbessias*, the houses used by pilgrims each September.

⑨ Monte Albo Tour

The massive white limestone ridge that gave this mountain its name (*albo* means white) extends like a bastion between the Barbagia and Baronia regions. There are magnificent panoramic views from the maquis-covered slopes of the mountain. The area is destined to become a reserve to protect 650 plant species as well as moufflons, wild boar and raptors. Part of this tour follows a narrow road along the base of the limestone cliffs.

② **Lodè**
This small town amid olive trees and maquis is the home of the Annunziata sanctuary, with its whitewashed, red-roofed *cumbessias*. On 22–23 May the sanctuary becomes a pilgrimage site.

③ **Bitti**
This lively town (*see p104*) lies in pretty countryside surrounded by clusters of oak and wild olive trees.

The Annunziata Sanctuary, Lodè

Key

━ Tour route
═ Other roads
━ River

0 kilometres 4
0 miles 4

Environs

Near the mouth of the Cedrino river is **Santa Maria 'e Mare**, founded in the 13th century by Pisan merchants. The church is full of ex votos, and on the last Sunday in May it is the focus of a pilgrimage, when a statue of the Madonna is taken down the river on a boat, followed by a flotilla of boats.

At the mouth of the estuary the river divides into two. The northern part flows into an artificial canal, the southern half feeds the Su Petrosu marsh. This is where to find coots, moorhens, mallards and purple gallinules. The shallows are home to avocets, stilts, grey heron and egrets.

❽ Galtellì

Road map D3. 🏔 2,400. 🚌
ℹ️ 0784 90 150; Pro Loco, Via Garibaldi 2 (0784 904 72). 🎭 16–17 Jan, Sant'Antonio Abate; 2nd Sat in Aug, Festa dell'Immigrato/Turista.

Lying on the slopes of Monte Tuttavista, Galtellì was the most important town in the region during the Middle Ages. Until 1496 it was the regional bishopric, as can be seen in Romanesque San Pietro, the former cathedral built in the 12th century. After this era the town began to decline thanks to the ravages of malaria and frequent pirate raids, but traces of its glorious past have been preserved in the parish church of Santissimo Crocifisso.

The historic centre is pretty, with its whitewashed buildings and well-kept houses. In August, the town throws a party for all foreigners and tourists living or staying there.

Environs

One of the most interesting sights in this area is Monte Tuttavista. A dirt road and then a footpath take you to Sa Pedra Istampada ("the perforated rock"), a wind-sculpted arch 30 m (98 ft) high. There are splendid views from the summit.

Near the village of La Traversa, 12 km (8 miles) from Galtellì, is the Tomba di Giganti (giants' tomb) of **Sa Ena 'e Thomes**, a very impressive prehistoric monument with a 3-m (10-ft) stele hewn out of a single block of granite.

The Sa Ena 'e Thomes "giants' tomb" near La Traversa

---

① Sant'Anna
This pass is 624 m (2,050 ft) above sea level, and offers splendid scenic views. The road winds up among cliffs, euphorbia bushes and cluster pines.

Tips for Drivers

Tour length: 76 km (47 miles). This tour takes about two hours by car, but allow half a day to include the stops.
Stopping-off points: the Sant'Anna roadman's house and the town of Bitti *(see p104)*.

Slopes of Monte Albo

④ Lula
This town in Barbagia has a famous sanctuary, which is dedicated to St Francis. Thousands of worshippers participate in the saint's feast day celebrations from 1–10 May, events described by Grazia Deledda in *Elias Portolu*.

⑤ The road leading up Monte Albo
The 20 km (12 miles) of this hillside road run along the northern slope of the mountain through pastures and maquis. On the right are steep limestone walls streaked with pink.

⑩ Siniscola

Road map D2. ⚐ 11,000. ▦
ℹ 0784 87 08 00. ⚑ 18 Aug:
Sant'Elena. ⓦ **comune.siniscola.
nu.it**

Set at the foot of Monte Albo,
the once agricultural town of
Siniscola was an important
trading centre in the 14th
century under the principality of
Gallura *(see p40)*. Since then, the
town has grown in a haphazard
manner around the medieval
centre. On the lively main street,
Via Sassari, the 18th-century
parish church of **San Giovanni
Battista** is decorated with a
fresco cycle representing the
life of St John the Baptist. The
town is also well known for its
local pottery studios.

Environs
A straight road
northeast from
Siniscola leads to
La Caletta, a small
tourist port with a
wide sandy beach,
4 km (2 miles) long.
Heading south-
wards, the SS125
passes the fishing
village of **Santa
Lucia**. Probably
founded by
emigrants from
the island of
Ponza, the
village is guarded by a Spanish
watchtower. Today Santa Lucia
is a popular summer resort, with
a pine forest that extends
behind the beach. Continuing
southwards, a long walk along

The church at Santa Lucia

the shore will take you to the
white sand dunes and juniper
bushes of **Capo Comino** (also
accessible from the SS125).
The headland of Capo
Comino consists of rounded
rocks and pebble beaches and
is overlooked by a lighthouse.
A two-hour walk along the
seashore and pine forest will
take you to **Berchida beach**,
where there is a huge rock
called *S'incollu de
sa Marchesa* (The
Marquise's Throat).
Eels and grey mullet
populate an area
of marshland here.
An alternative
excursion is to take
the rough track
that turns right
from the SS125
after the
Berchida river.
Winding
through the maquis it leads
to a splendid white sand beach
and clear blue sea. On the way,
the road passes the remains
of the nuraghic settlement of
Conca Umosa.

Spanish tower at Santa Lucia

⑪ Posada

Road map D2. ⚐ 2,600. ▦
ℹ Via Giuseppe Garibaldi 4 (0784 87
05 00). ⓦ **comune.posada.nu.it**

Perched on top of a limestone
bank covered with euphorbia
and lentiscus, this village is
dominated by the ruins of
Castello della Fava. The castle
was built in the 12th century
by the rulers of Gallura, who
were later conquered by the
principality of Arborea before
passing under Aragonese
dominion *(see p40)*. In the
Carthaginian era this place was
known as the colony of Feronia.
The town still retains its
medieval character, with winding
alleyways connected by steep
stairways, arches and tiny
squares. The castle has had a
face-lift, and wooden steps lead
to the top of its square tower,
where there is a panoramic view
of the sea, the mouth of the
Posada river and the surrounding
plain, covered with fruit orchards.

Environs
Inland, 9 km (5 miles) west of
Posada, is the artificial lake of
Posada. The pine forests and fine
views make this a popular spot.

⑫ Lanusei

Road map D4. ⚐ 5,800. ✈ 🚌 ▦
🍽 ℹ Via Roma 98 (0782 47 311).
⚑ 22 Jul. Santa Maria Maddalena.
ⓦ **comunedilanusei.it**

This large, austere-looking
town, situated on a hillside at
600 m (1,926 ft), overlooks the

The white sand dunes at Capo Comino

The village of Posada and the Castello della Fava

plain that descends to the sea. It was once a health retreat due to its excellent climate, high altitude and the many walking trails in the forest that surrounds it. The town was built on various levels and still has some aristocratic buildings of interest.

⓭ Jerzu

Road map D4. 🗻 3,600. 🚍 🚹
0782 713 11. 🎐 13 Jun: Sant'Antonio; 25 Jul: San Giacomo; 4 Aug: Sagra del Vino. 🆆 **prolocojerzu.it**

Tall, sharp pinnacles of rock, known locally as *tacchi* (high heels), are an impressive sight as they emerge from the maquis on the approach to Jerzu. This modern town is built on several levels up the hillside with houses of two storeys or more overlooking the main street. Steep side streets in the lower quarter lead to older houses that retain many of their original features.

Jerzu's economy is based mainly on viticulture and small vineyards cling to the steep slopes around the town. The area produces about 10,000 tonnes of grapes from which the local wine cooperative makes the good red wine Cannonau DOC, one of the most famous in Sardinia.

The most important holiday is the feast day of Sant'Antonio da Padova, on 13 June. One of the town's churches is dedicated to the saint.

Environs

At Ulassai, 7 km (4 miles) north-west of Jerzu, is the

limestone **Grotta Su Màrmuri**. Steps descend to reveal spectacular pools and stalagmites. Wear warm clothes and sturdy shoes.

🏞 **Grotta Su Màrmuri**
🚹 Piazzale Grotta Su Marmuri (0782 798 59). **Open** Apr–Oct. 🎐 🎐 compulsory: 11am, 2:30pm (& more in summer). 🖥

⓮ Gairo

Road map D4. 🗻 2,000. 🚍 🚍
🚹 0782 76 00 00. 🎐 third Sun in Sep: Nostra Signora del Buoncammino. 🆆 **comune. gairo.og.it**

Gairo Sant'Elena lies in the Pardu river valley, a deep ravine with limestone walls. The present-day village was built after 1951, when Gairo Vecchio had to be evacuated after excessive rain caused a series of landslides. All that remains of the abandoned village are gutted houses without doors and windows. The entire area has spectacular scenery.

Environs

On the coast, the bay of Gairo is protected by a headland covered with maquis. From here you can go to Coccorocci, the only beach with black sand in Sardinia. The coast road runs along the seashore, which is characterized by sandy inlets and cliffs of pink rock.

⓯ Bari Sardo

Road map D4. 🗻 4,500. 🚍
🚹 0782 29 523. 🎐 29 Aug: San Giovanni Battista; 8 Sep: Nostra Signora di Monserrato.
🆆 **comunedibarisardo.gov.it**

This agricultural centre is set in fertile countryside filled with vineyards and orchards. The name of the town is derived from the Sardinian word for marshes, *abbari*. In the oldest part of town, around the district of San Leonardo to the southwest, original stone houses are still visible. Here, the parish church, **Beata Vergine del Monserrato**, has a Rococo bell tower dated 1813. The town is also known for its textiles: tapestries, rugs and linen cushions and bedcovers.

Environs

On the coast, east of Bari Sardo, **Torre di Bari** is a pleasant seaside resort that developed around the 17th-century Spanish tower built to defend the town from pirates. It has a sandy beach and small pine forest. During the festivities for San Giovanni Battista, known here as *Su Nenneri*, grain and vegetable seedlings are cast into the sea to encourage a good harvest.

The vineyards at Jerzu produce Cannonau, Sardinia's best-known wine

The basalt rock promontory at Capo Ferrato, south of Muravera

⑯ Muravera

Road map D5. 🏔 4,500. 🛈 070 99
00 01. 🎉 14–15 Aug: l'Assunta.
🆆 visitmuravera.it

Muravera lies at the mouth of
the Flumendosa river, in the
middle of an area of fruit
orchards. It is a modern tourist
town, catering to the resort
complexes that have grown up
along the coast. In ancient times
this was the Phoenician city of
Sarcapos. Today, the only
building of any historical
interest is the church of **San
Nicola**, off the main street,
which retains its original
15th-century chapels.

Environs

Muravera is an ideal starting
point for trips along the coast
and into the valleys of the
interior. To the east, the beach
around **Porto Corallo** is long
and sandy, interrupted by small
rocky headlands. Near this

tourist port is another **Spanish
tower** which, in 1812, was used
as a stronghold in one of the
rare victories of the Sardinians
over the Muslim pirates.

Northwards, 11 km (7 miles)
along the SS125, also known as
the Orientale Sarda road (see
p84), are the remains of the
Castello di Quirra and the small
Romanesque church of **San
Nicola**, the only church in
Sardinia built of brick.

To the south, the coast
around **Capo Ferrato** is also
beautiful, with basalt rocks,
small white sandy coves and
pine trees. Past the headland of
Capo Ferrato is the **Costa Rei**, a
stretch of straight coastline with
beaches and tourist villages.
The sea bed at the bay of **Cala
Sinzias** further to the south
consists of long slabs of rock,
giving the water a strikingly
clean and transparent look.
Inland, the route towards
Cagliari along the SS125 offers

spectacular scenery, with red
rock among myrtle, juniper and
strawberry trees. A trip down
the Flumendosa river valley,
beyond San Vito, also offers
spectacular scenery.

Castiadas is a hamlet behind
the Costa Rei, set around a
19th-century prison amid vineyards and citrus trees. From the
late 19th century to the 1950s
the area was occupied by a
prison farm, where prisoners
worked on the land.

⑰ Villasimius

Road map D6. 🏔 3,000. 🚌
🛈 070 793 02 71. 🎉 Jul: Madonna
del Naufrago. 🆆 **comune.**
villasimius.ca.it

With its hotels, residences
and second homes, this modern
town is the leading seaside
resort on the southeastern
coast. Villasimius lies
on the northern edge of a
promontory that extends to
Capo Carbonara. At the centre
of the headland is the **Notteri
marsh**, separated from the sea
by Simìus beach, a long stretch
of sand. In the winter the marsh
is a popular stopping-off point
for migratory flamingoes. On
the very tip of the promontory
the lighthouse offers a
sweeping view of the coast and
the tiny islands of **Serpentara**
and **Cavoli** in the distance. The
stretch of water between the
two islands is shallow and has
witnessed many shipwrecks
over the years. Off the island of

The Town of the Launeddas

Northeast of Muravera is San Vito, an
agricultural town that thrived in past
centuries thanks to the silver mines on
Monte Narba. In the centre of town,
the parish church with its twin bell
towers over the façade is worth a visit.
San Vito is known for its tradition of
craftmanship, in particular the flute-like
instrument, the *launeddas*, which was
originally played by shepherds (see p29).
Luigi Lai, Sardinia's most famous player
of this ancient instrument, lives here and
makes the instrument himself. Other crafts
at San Vito include fine embroidery and
basketweaving with juniper twigs.

Luigi Lai, one of Sardinia's most famous *launeddas* players

The long beach separating the sea from Notteri marsh, south of Villasimius

Cavoli, at a depth of 10 m (33 ft), is the statue of the *Madonna dei Fondali* (Our Lady of the Sea Floor) by local sculptor Pinuccio Sciola. Excursions by glass-bottomed boat leave from the quay at Porto Giunco to view the submerged statue. This port is protected by the **Fortezza Vecchia**, a star-shaped fortress built in the 17th century. The sea around the headland is rich in fauna and flora and is popular with scuba divers.

⓲ Orroli

Road map D4. 🗺 3,300. 🚌
ℹ 0782 84 70 06. 🎟 30 Jun: Santa Caterina. 🖥 **comune.orroli.ca.it**

The town of Orroli lies in the rather barren Pranemuru plateau, at the edge of the Flumendosa valley. The area is dotted with archaeological sites, such as the necropolis of

View from the headland of Capo Carbonara, south of Villasimius

Su Motti where *domus de janas* tombs are cut out of the rock.

Other archaeological sites in the area include the ruins of the **Arrubiu Nuraghe**, 3 km (1.8 miles) southeast of Orroli. This complicated, pentagonal site is larger than the one at Su Nuraxi *(see pp68–9)*. The complex, made of red stone, was built around a 14th century BC central tower which, according to experts, was 27 m (88 ft) high. Five towers, probably dating from the 7th century BC, connected by tall bastions, were built around the complex, and an outer defensive wall was added in the 6th century BC. The ruins of the nuraghic village, consisting of round and rectangular dwellings, lie around the nuraghe.

Another interesting site is the nearby **Su Putzu** nuraghe, which has numerous dwellings in excellent condition.

🏛 **Su Motti**
4 km (2 miles) SE of Orroli. **Tel** 0782 84 72 69. **Open** by appt for groups of 25 or more. 🛗 🎫

🏛 **Arrubiu Nuraghe**
Tel 0782 84 72 69. **Open** 9:30am–8:30pm (Oct–Apr: 9:30am–5pm). 🛗
🖥 **nuraghearrubiu.it**

The Arrubiu Nuraghe, one of several archaeological sites near Orroli

⓳ Perdasdefogu

Road map D4 & D5. 🗺 2,500. 🚌
ℹ 0782 94 614. 🎟 12 Sep: San Salvatore. 🖥 **comune.perdasde fogu.nu.it**

An isolated mountain village in the lower Ogliastra area, Perdasdefogu lies at the foot of the striking *tacchi*, vertical limestone walls that tower over the maquis *(see p93)*. The road that meanders northeast towards Jerzu is one of the most scenic in Sardinia. It runs along a plateau at the base of these dolomitic walls, offering a spectacular view of the sea and Perda Liana peaks in the distance. Along the way is the rural church of **Sant'Antonio**, set in a meadow at the foot of Punta Coróngiu, one of the most impressive of the limestone *tacchi*.

㉑ A Trip on the Trenino Verde

It takes just over five hours to travel 160 km (99 miles) on the narrow-gauge *trenino verde* (little green train), but the reward is a trip backwards in time through some of the wildest landscapes in Sardinia. The line passes through the softly rolling hills of Trexenta, carpeted with almond and olive trees, to the rugged mountains of Barbagia di Seui, where the train runs along the foot of a magnificent *tònnero*, with a broad view of its vertical limestone walls. This particular route – one of several across Sardinia – follows the craggy contours of the mountain and there are so many bends that it is easy to lose your sense of direction. The train makes two hairpin turns through the town of Lanusei in order to get over a steep slope. At peak service times it is possible to make the entire return journey in one day, but perhaps inadvisable: the hard seating makes such a long trip uncomfortable.

Lake Alto Flumendosa, on the southern side of Gennargentu

⑥ **Villanovatulo** This isolated shepherds' village has a view of the Flumendosa river basin. The walls of the houses have murals by Pinuccio Sciola.

The Trenino Verde
This picturesque train skirts the hillsides, well away from the road amid unspoilt scenery. As well as the timeless landscape, you can appreciate the atmosphere of a forgotten age.

VISITORS' CHECKLIST

Practical Information
🛈 Cagliari (070 57 93 03 46). Trenino Verde:
Tel 070 265 71.
🅦 treninoverde.com

Train timetable: Check the website for latest times and updated routes as the train schedule is revised at the beginning of each year. The train is also available for private hire all year round.

⑧ **Mandas** 69 km (43 miles) from Cagliari, Mandas is the leading agricultural town in the area. The church of San Giacomo, with statues of San Gioacchino and Sant' Anna, is worth a visit.

⑦ **Orroli** Surrounded by oak forests, the town of Orroli lies on a basalt tableland crossed by the Flumendosa river. Look out for the Arrubiu nuraghe (*see p95*).

Flumendosa

Lago di Flumendosa

SS198

③ **Montarbu Forest** This is one of the best preserved forests in Sardinia, where moufflons live among ash, holm oak and yew trees. A striking feature here are the *tònneri*, massive vertical limestone walls.

② **Lanusei** This village lies on the slope of a hill commanding a fine view of the sea *(see p92)*.

① **Tortolí** The capital of the Ogliastra region is 3 km (2 miles) from the sea, on the edge of a large marsh which attracts thousands of migratory birds in winter. Watch out for the ruins of Castello di Medusa.

The train usually consists of one or two carriages

⑤ **Sadali** Lying in the middle of a karstic plateau, Sadali boasts a 7-m (23-ft) waterfall fed by springs that flow into an underground chasm. There are numerous caves, such as Is Janas, 205 m (672 ft) long with an underground lake and impressive stalagmites and stalactites.

④ **Seui** The village of Seui, on the side of a steep valley, retains some traditional stone houses. The 17th-century Spanish prison is now occupied by the Civic Museum of Rural Culture with displays of traditional farm utensils and reconstructions of an 18th-century kitchen and bedroom.

0 kilometres 4
0 miles 4

Winding routes following the sheer slopes

Key

🚊 Train route
▬ Major road
═ Minor road
— River

Tips for Travellers

Refreshments are not served on the train and the few stations en route are not equipped to offer restaurant facilities, so it is advisable to take along something to eat and drink. Going towards Mandas, the best views can be appreciated from the left-hand side of the train (and vice versa). The "normal" train, called TL, is superior to the AT (single-unit rail diesel car), which is noisier and less comfortable.

CENTRAL SARDINIA AND BARBAGIA

The central region of Sardinia is the area that most vividly reflects the ancient character of the island. Rugged mountains are marked by shepherds' trails and villages perch over steep valleys. The inhabitants of this isolated region are known as hardy and proud and have retained many aspects of their traditional way of life.

The name Barbagia derives from the Latin word *barbària*, used by the Romans to designate the inaccessible regions of the interior inhabited by "barbarians" (any culture that did not share the values and beliefs of the Roman civilization). Inhabited since prehistoric times and rich in archaeological sites, such as the nuraghic village of Tiscali *(see pp108–9)*, the heart of Sardinia resisted Roman invasions for many centuries and preserved its nuraghic religious rites up to the advent of Christianity.

Getting to know this rugged land requires some effort, since the roads are slow and winding, road signs are sometimes missing and many sights can be reached only via rough dirt tracks. The people, however, are often hospitable and tradition is still an essential part of local life. The churches and villages come to life during the colourful folk festivals, the patron saints' feast days and at religious festivities. At Mamoiada the *Mamuthones* lead the Mardi Gras processions wearing forbidding masks, cow bells and sheepskins *(see p106)*.

The mountainous landscape dominates central Sardinia. Trekkers can enjoy walks from the rocks of Supramonte di Oliena to the dense forests of holm oak on the slopes of Monte Novo San Giovanni *(see p111)* and the chestnut woods along the old railway near Belvì *(see p113)*.

The local cuisine is flavoured with herbs from the maquis, such as rosemary and thyme, while the handicrafts draw inspiration from pastoral life. Woven carpets, baskets and pottery with traditional motifs can be seen in Nuoro's Museo Etnografico *(see p103)*.

The giants' grave, an archaeological site in Fonni

◀ The Gocéano mountain range near Burgos

Exploring Central Sardinia and Barbagia

Nuoro is the capital of Sardinia's interior region: to the east lies the Supramonte mountain range, with Oliena, Orgòsolo, Urzulei, Baunei and Dorgali at its feet, while to the west the valleys descend towards Lake Omodeo and Macomer. In this landscape of hills and steep limestone walls (the *tònneri* formations) are some of the most important towns in the region: Mamoiada, Bitti and Sarule. To the south is the Gennargentu massif, carpeted with dense forests, on the slopes of which are typical mountain villages such as Gavoi and Fonni. Heading northeast and skirting the slopes of Monte Ortobene, which towers above the city of Nuoro, the road descends among almond trees and vineyards towards the Baronia region.

Barren slopes on the Gennargentu mountain range

Sights at a Glance

1. Nuoro pp102–3
2. Bitti
3. Bono
4. Burgos
5. Ottana
6. Ollolai
7. Sarule
8. Mamoiada
9. Oliena
10. Tiscali pp108–9
11. Orgòsolo
12. Gavoi
13. Fonni
14. Teti
15. Sòrgono
16. Làconi
18. Aritzo
19. Belví
20. Dèsulo
21. Tonara

Tours

A mural painted on rocks near Orgòsolo

The steeple of the church in Aritzo

Getting Around

Public transport in the interior of Sardinia is slow and unreliable if it exists at all, and is not the best way to visit the area. If you have a car, the main roads are the SS131 from Siniscola to Nuoro up to Lake Omodeo; the SS125, the Orientale Sarda road, which skirts Supramonte and links Orosei to Arbatax, and the SS389, which also goes to Arbatax from Nuoro, passing Gennargentu on the east. For sights such as Tiscali and Punta La Marmora, you have to hike up fairly steep footpaths.

A pleasant alternative mode of transport is to travel on the little narrow-gauge train that runs between Mandas and Sòrgono on the Cagliari-Sòrgono line (see p113).

Key

- ▬▬ Major road
- ▬▬ Secondary road
- ▦▦ Minor road
- ▬▬ Scenic route
- ─── Minor railway
- △ Summit

0 kilometres 10
0 miles 10

1 Nuoro

Nùgoro, as the locals still call their city, is one of Sardinia's most important centres. The city began to expand in the 14th century, but by the 18th century there was social unrest and riots erupted. In 1746 the Piedmontese prefect, De Viry, described the city as "a hotbed of bandits and murderers". A decree in 1868 that put an end to the common use of farmland culminated in a popular rebellion known as *Su Connottu*. At the beginning of the 20th century Nuoro became the heart of the island's cultural life, producing political and social writers such as Grazia Deledda. The city became the provincial capital in 1926, and today it is the commercial heart of Barbagia.

Santa Maria della Neve, Nuoro's imposing Neo-Classical cathedral

The huge granite blocks in Piazza Sebastiano Satta

Exploring Nuoro

The city is set in spectacular surroundings on a granite plateau beneath Monte Ortobene. Its isolated position and limited exposure to tourism have helped to preserve local culture, traditions and costumes.

The modern city retains many picturesque streets and buildings in the old centre. Corso Garibaldi, once known as Bia Maiore, leads up to the quarter of San Pietro and the city's Neo-Classical cathedral, **Basilica di Santa Maria della Neve** (1836). Near Corso Garibaldi is the whitewashed Piazza Sebastiano Satta, paved in 1976 with large granite blocks.

Nuoro is the birthplace of some of Sardinia's most notable men and women of letters, who at the end of the 19th century injected new life into the island's culture. Apart from Grazia Deledda, other native literary figures are politician and essayist Attilio Deffenu (1893–1918) and poet Sebastiano Satta (1867–1914).

𝄪 Museo Nazionale Archeologico

Via Mannu 1. **Tel** 0784 316 88. **Open** 9am–1pm Tue–Sat (also 3–5pm Tue & Thu). logiconuoro.beniculturali.it

This museum combines the collections of fossils and fossil plants of the *Gruppo Speleologico Nuorese*, with archaeological finds excavated over many years in the area. Exhibits range from Neolithic to medieval objects, including the skeletons of an ancient hare, *Prolagus sardus*, and a collection of cave finds. Also of interest are nuraghic bronze statuettes. Finds from the Roman era include belt buckles and other everyday household objects.

𝄪 Museo Deleddiano

Via Grazia Deledda 28. **Tel** 0784 25 80 88. **Open** 10am–1pm, 3–8pm Tue–Sun (till 7pm in winter).

Grazia Deledda's birthplace retains the atmosphere of a mid-19th-century Sardinian home. The house has been arranged according to her own description, set out in her novel *Cosima*, with objects marking the stages of her career. The courtyard leads to what was the kitchen garden (now the venue for cultural events), while the upper floors are given over to displays of the

Grazia Deledda (1871–1936)

Grazia Deledda won the Nobel Prize for Literature in 1926 in recognition of her perceptive portrayal of the power and passions in the primitive communities around her. Born in Nuoro in 1871, she has become a symbol of Sardinian culture and an example of the island's prolific artistic production. The eventful and difficult years of her early career are described in the autobiographical novel *Cosima* (1937). Her world of fiction revolves around Barbagia, with its mysteries and strong sense of identity. Among her best-known novels are *Elias Portolu* (1900), *Cenere* (1903), and *Canne al Vento* (1913). She died in Rome in 1936.

The author Grazia Deledda

For hotels and restaurants in this region see pp177–8 and pp187–8

The whitewashed Museo Etnografico in Nuoro

Traditional costume from Dèsulo,
Museo delle Tradizioni Sarde

covers of her books, programmes for her plays, and a copy of the diploma for the Nobel Prize for Literature.

🏛 Museo Etnografico
Via Antonio Mereu 56. **Tel** 0784 25 70 35. **Open** mid-Mar–Sep: 9am–1pm, 3–7pm Tue–Sun; Oct–mid-Mar: 10am–1pm, 3–8pm Tue–Sun. 🎫 🚫
W **isresardegna.it**

The Museum of Sardinian life and popular traditions was designed in the 1960s by architect Antonio Simon Mossa. The aim of the project was to recreate a typical Sardinian village, with courtyards, alleys and stairways, as a setting for artifacts, objects and costumes representing Sardinian daily life.

On display in this popular ethnographic museum are traditional pieces of furniture, such as a 19th-century chest and cover and silver jewellery used to adorn aprons or hand-kerchiefs. Characteristic costumes worn daily or on special occasions by women are also on show, as are different types of traditional bread moulds, looms and hand-woven carpets. One room is dedicated to carnival masks and costumes. A collection of musical instruments is also on display alongside a multimedia system that enables visitors to hear the sounds of these instruments, which are used to perform traditional Sardinian folk music.

The museum also has a library specializing in anthropological literature, an auditorium and an exhibition centre. Every other October, the museum features a festival of ethnographic and anthropological films.

Environs
🏔 Monte Ortobene
East of Nuoro.
Nuoro was founded on the granite slopes of this mountain and the inhabitants have always held it in high regard. To reach its wooded areas, take the SS129 Orosei road east out of the city. The road passes the church of **Nostra Signora della Solitudine**, where Grazia Deledda is buried. At the summit is a statue of the Redentore (Christ the Redeemer) that overlooks the city below and next to it is the church of **Nostra Signora di Montenero**. On the last Sunday in August this church is the focus of the solemn procession known as the *Processione del Redentore*, in which representatives from almost every town in Sardinia take part (see p32).

🪨 Necropoli di Sas Concas
SS128. **Tel** 0784 23 88 78. **Open** daily. 🎫
To visit this necropolis, take the SS131 15 km (9 miles) west out of Nuoro and then the SS128 south for 3 km (2 miles) towards Oniferi. The complex consists of a series of *domus de janas*, some decorated with bas reliefs, such as the *Tomba dell'Emiciclos* (Tomb of the Hemicycle). The area is unattended, so a torch for the tombs may be useful.

The Sagra del Redentore procession on Monte Ortobene

Su Tempiesu well-temple near Bitti, a relic of Sardinia's nuraghic civilization

❷ Bitti

Road map D3. 🖽 3,800. 🅸 Town Hall, Piazza G Asproni (0784 41 51 24). 🖼 23 Apr: San Giorgio. 🆆 **comune. bitti.nu.it**

This picturesque pastoral village has become known thanks to the *Tenores de Bitti* musical group, whose interpretations of traditional Sardinian close-harmony songs have won them acclaim throughout Europe (*see pp20–21*). Experts say the local dialect is the one that most resembles Latin.

The 19th-century church of **San Giorgio Martire** stands in the central Piazza Giorgio Asproni. In the nearby parish home is a fine small collection of local archaeological finds.

Environs

Not far from Bitti on the road to Orune (watch out for the signs, which can be difficult to follow) is the **Su Tempiesu** well-temple. This consists of several

chambers made of large square basalt stones, and houses the sacred well. The well water was used in nuraghic rituals. A little way east of Bitti are five churches, Santo Stefano, Santa Maria, Santa Lucia, San Giorgio and *Babbu Mannu* (Holy Ghost). These become lively during religious festivities.

❸ Bono

Road map C3. 🖽 4,100. 🅸 Town Hall, Corso Angioj 2 (079 79 169). 🖼 31 Aug: San Raimondo Nonnato. 🆆 **comunebono.gov.it**

Set at the foot of the Gocèano mountain range, Bono is an ideal starting point for trips to the wooded Monte Rasu and the Foresta di Burgos. In the centre of town is the parish church of **San Michele Arcangelo**, which has been rebuilt several times over the years. Inside is a curious clock driven by the weight of four cannonballs, shot at the town during the 1796 siege, when the government troops were driven out by the city's inhabitants. This episode is re-enacted every year during the traditional festival held on 31 August. On this day the largest pumpkin from the local kitchen gardens is awarded to the person who comes in last in the festival horse race as a facetious sign of recognition of the "valour" of the routed army. Until recently, this pumpkin was rolled down the mountain to the valley to symbolize the government

troops escaping from the local inhabitants.

In early September Bono plays host to the colourful *Fiera dei Prodotti Tipici Artigiani del Gocèano*, a fair featuring typical handicrafts from the Gocèano region.

Environs

From the Uccaidu pass, northwest of Bono, you can hike up the ridge to the summit of Monte Rasu at an altitude of 1,258 m (4,125 ft). From here there are magnificent sweeping views of the Foresta di Burgos and surrounding mountain range as well as most of Sardinia.

The countryside between Bono and Burgos

❹ Burgos

Road map C3. 🖽 1,100. 🅸 079 79 31 34. 🆆 **comuneburgos.gov.it**

The hamlet of Burgos lies below a cone-shaped peak in the Gocèano mountains. The town was founded in

The village of Burgos, dominated by the 12th-century castle

Small Giara horses in the Foresta di Burgos

1353 by Mariano d'Arborea and is dominated by the ruins of **Burgos Castle**, built in 1127. The castle was the scene of many battles between the Sardinian principalities and mainland colonists during the Middle Ages. It was from here that in 1478 Artaldo di Alagon's troops marched from the castle to the battle of Macomer, marking the start of Aragonese dominion. Inside the outer defensive walls, further fortifications surround a restored tower. The entrance to the tower was once through a wooden stairway that could be raised in case of a siege.

Environs
The **Foresta di Burgos**, 5 km (3 miles) northwest of Burgos, is a well-kept forested area with holm oak and cork oak trees, cedars, conifers and some chestnut trees. The area is also known for the small Sardinian Giara horses that graze in fenced-off pastures.

❺ Ottana
Road map C3. 🏔 2,700. 🚹 Town Hall (0784 75 623). 🎭 Carnevale. 🌐 **comune.ottana.nu.it**

Ottana lies in the valley of the river Tirso, not far from the slopes of the Barbagia di Ollolai region. In the Middle Ages the town was an important religious centre. On the southern outskirts of town is the church of

San Nicola, once the cathedral of the regional diocese. It was built in 1150 in austere Romanesque style, with black and purple trachyte ashlars showing strong Pisan influence. Inside is a 14th-century polyptych showing the Madonna flanked by the bishop of Ottana and Mariano d'Arborea, count of Gocèano. In the apse is a 16th-century wooden crucifix.

Almost abandoned in the 16th century due to an outbreak of malaria, Ottana was chosen in the 1970s as an industrial development site, promoted by ENI, the National Hydrocarbon Corporation. The industries have not produced the expected profits, however, and the ecological problems

are so serious that the entire project is to be abandoned.

Carnival is a popular festival in Ottana, when locals dress in sheepskin and bells and wear bull-like masks (see p33).

❻ Ollolai
Road map C3. 🏔 1,800. 🚹 Town Hall (0784 51 051). 🎭 24 Aug: San Bartolomeo. 🌐 **comune.ollolai.nu.it**

Ollolai was once the medieval administrative centre of the Barbagia di Ollolai region, an area that included the northern part of Barbagia and still retains the name today. The town's decline began in 1490 after a terrible fire destroyed most of it and today it is a small hamlet.

Some original houses decorated with dark stone doorways are visible in the old centre and there are still a few craftsmen who weave the traditional asphodel baskets in their courtyards.

Asphodel used in basket-weaving

Environs
A short distance west of Ollolai is the church of **San Basilio**. A traditional rural religious festival is held here on 1 September. A rough road climbs up to S'Asisorgiu peak to an altitude of 1,127 m (3,700 ft). From here there are fabulous views of the surrounding mountain range and the summit is popularly known as "Sardinia's window".

Typical masked figures dressed for the Carnival at Ottana

The village of Sarule as seen from the nearby hills

❼ Sarule

Road map C3. 🏔 1,840. ℹ Town Hall (0784 760 17). 🎭 8 Sep: Madonna di Gonare. 🅦 **comune sarule.gov.it**

Sarule is a village of medieval origin which has preserved its tradition of carpet-weaving. Along the main street you can still see the workshops where these vividly coloured carpets with stylized figures are woven on antique vertical looms and then sold on the premises.

Perched on a spur overlooking the village is the sanctuary of **Nostra Signora di Gonare**, one of the most sacred shrines in Sardinia. The church was built in the 13th century for the ruler of the principality, Gonario II di Torres, and by the 16th century it had already become a famous pilgrimage site. The sanctuary was enlarged in the 17th century with a dark stone exterior and austere buttresses.

To reach the sanctuary, a rough road heads east from Sarule and climbs up Monte Gonare for 4 km (2.5 miles). This granite rock mountain is interspersed with layers of limestone and outcrops of schist covered in vegetation. The mountain slopes are populated by many species of birds, including partridges, turtle doves, woodpeckers, shrikes and various birds of prey. The forest has holm oaks and maples, while in the spring the undergrowth is enlivened by brightly coloured cyclamen, peonies and morning glory. The road ends at an open space with pilgrims' houses (cumbessias), and a winding footpath up the bluff through the holm oak forest leads to the sanctuary. From here there are marvellous views of Monte Ortobene towering over Nuoro, Monte Corrasi near Oliena, and the Gennargentu mountains in the distance.

From 5–8 September a lively festival takes place at the sanctuary for the Madonna di Gonare, to which pilgrims travel on foot from all of the neighbouring villages. As well as religious festivities, a horse race is held, and the square resounds with poetry readings and sacred songs sung in traditional dialect.

The sanctuary of Nostra Signora di Gonare at Sarule

❽ Mamoiada

Road map D3. 🏔 2,700. ℹ Town Hall (0784 560 23). 🎭 17 Jan, Carnival Sun & Shrove Tue: Mamuthones procession. 🅦 **comune.mamoiada.nu.it**

Some old buildings, possibly of Aragonese origin, are still visible among the modern houses that line the main street of Mamoiada. In 1770 the town was mentioned by the Savoyard viceroy, Des Hayes, as a place of some interest with numerous vineyards and an exceptional number of sheep. Flocks are still taken every summer to the slopes of Barbagia di Ollolai to graze. Mamoiada is best known for the dark, forbidding masks of the *Mamuthones*,

---

Traditional Festivals in the Barbagia

S'Incontru, the procession held in the streets of Oliena on Easter Day, commemorates the resurrection of Christ and his subsequent encounter with the Virgin Mary. The statues of Virgin Mary and Christ are carried to the main square. The statue of Virgin Mary is covered in

The carnival *Mamuthones* at Mamoiada

a mourning veil, which is removed at the end of the procession to reveal a blue dress to symbolise the joy of resurrection. On this occasion, and during the festivities in honour of San Lussorio on 21 August, you can admire the colourful traditional costumes and watch the impressive procession of horsemen through the streets of the town.

At Mamoiada the lively celebrations on the night of Sant'Antonio Abate (17 January), Shrove Tuesday and the last night of Carnival, all revolve around the figures of the *Mamuthones* and *Issohadores*. The former wear tragic masks and shepherds' garb, with a set of cow bells tied on their backs. The bells jangle in time with their rhythmical steps as they go through the village to the main square, where there is music and dancing all evening. The *Issohadores*, with their red waistcoats, are more colourful: they "capture" spectators and drag them inside the circles of the traditional round dance.

Woman in traditional costume on Easter Day in Oliena

The underground cave of Grotta Sa Oche in Oliena

who appear in the village streets on the feast days of Sant'Antonio Abate (17 January), the Sunday of Carnival and in particular on Shrove Tuesday, during the Barbagia's most famous Carnival celebrations *(see p33)*.

Environs
About 5 km (3 miles) southwest of Mamoiada, along a secondary road towards Gavoi, is the **Santuario di San Cosimo**. This typical rural church has a central structure surrounded by *cumbessias,* lodgings for pilgrims to the sanctuary. The present-day church dates from the 17th century and its main feature is the single nave. At the end of the nave, restoration has brought to light an Aragonese niche with columns and an architrave made of volcanic rock.

A further 6 km (4 miles) to the south is the **Santuario della Madonna d'Itria**, an imposing church with *cumbessias.* Here, on the last Sunday of July, there is a horse race around the church, known as *Sa Carrela.*

❾ Oliena

Road map D3. 🏔 8,000. 🛈 Town Hall (0784 28 02 00). 🎭 Easter am: S'Incontru; 21 Aug: San Lussorio.
🌐 **comune.oliena.nu.it**

The approach to Oliena towards evening, along the northern road from Nuoro, is an unforget-table sight. The lights of the town shine at the foot of the steep white mass of Supramonte, which rises eastwards towards the Golfo di Orosei. The country-side is covered in vineyards, which yield the famous

Sardinian wine Cannonau. Some original houses, built around courtyards with external stairways and pergolas and brightly coloured rooms, are still visible along the narrow streets and alleyways. There are also several religious buildings, such as the church of **Santa Croce**, said to be the oldest in the town. Rebuilt in the 17th century, it has a bell tower decorated with an unusual trident motif.

The **Jesuit College** on Corso Vittorio Emanuele II is a reminder of the arrival of this religious order in Oliena. From the beginning of the 17th century onwards, the Jesuits encouraged the town's economy by promoting wine-making and the breeding of silkworms. Next door to the Jesuit college, the church of **Sant'Ignazio di Loyola** has wooden statues of Sant'Ignazio and San Francesco Saverio, as well as an altarpiece depicting San Cristoforo.

Oliena, known for its good wine, is also famous for its jewellery, cakes and the traditional costumes worn by the women: a black shawl, interwoven with silk and gold, and a light blue blouse. There are two important festivals at Oliena that end with impressive processions: *San Lussorio* in August and *S'Incontru* on Easter morning.

Environs
South of Oliena, it is possible to take various hiking tours on the rugged and spectacular rocks of the **Supramonte di Oliena**. Starting from the Monte Maccione refuge, you can cross the chain and descend into the Lanaittu valley floor.

The **Su Gologone** natural springs are 8 km (5 miles) east of Oliena. The waters, which have cut channels through the mountain rock, are refreshingly cool in summer and turn into an extremely cold, rushing torrent in winter. Su Gologone is the largest spring in Sardinia, with an average production of 300 litres (66 gallons) per second. It lies in a pleasant wooded area ideal for picnics in the shade.

For many years speleologists have been exploring the depths of the underground cave of **Grotta Sa Oche**, in the Supramonte mountains. Every year divers penetrate further underground into the Supramonte mountains to study the various aspects of this natural phenomenon.

The Su Gologone natural spring at the foot of Supramonte

⑩ Tiscali

A little over a century ago some woodcutters, travelling over the mountain range that dominates the Lanaittu valley, discovered a nuraghic settlement hidden in the depths of an enormous chasm in Monte Tiscali. The village of Tiscali, which had been inhabited up to the time of the Roman invasion, consists of a number of round dwellings with juniper wood architraves around the doors and roofs. Years of neglect have led to the partial deterioration of the site, but it is still one of the most exciting nuraghic finds in Sardinia, in particular because of its unique position. The climb to Tiscali can be hazardous and tiring, and is over rocky ground.

The Path to the Village
Red arrows on the rocks indicate the way to the village.

Dwellings
Round nuraghic dwellings are still visible among the crumbling rocks and ruins.

KEY

① **The chasm** had no natural springs, so the inhabitants collected water that dripped down the walls of the rock.

② **The roofs** were made of juniper wood.

③ **The walls** of the dwellings were made of limestone blocks.

Bronze Model
Cagliari's Museo Archeologico *(see p62)* has a model of the dwellings.

Monte di Tiscali
Hidden inside this 518-m (1,700-ft) high mountain, the nuraghic village of Tiscali was discovered in the 19th century. Archaeological excavations did not begin until many years later.

VISITORS' CHECKLIST

Practical Information
Road map D3.
Open 9am–7pm
(Oct–May: 5pm). 🚗 🅿️
ℹ️ Town Hall, Dorgali (0784 927 200) or Pro Loco, Dorgali (0784 962 43). The following organize tours and hikes: Gennargentu Escursioni: **Tel** 0784 943 85. 🆆 **gennar gentu.com**; Cooperativa Ghivine: **Tel** 338 834 1618. 🆆 **ghivine.com**

Entrance to the Chasm
The difficult terrain and steep walls were the best defence for the inhabitants of Tiscali.

Tips for Drivers

From Oliena take the road east towards Dorgali. After about 5 km (3 miles), take the right-hand turn for Su Gologone. Just after the hotel of the same name *(see p177)*, take the dirt road to the right that goes to the Lanaittu plain. Proceed along the floor of the valley (keeping to the left) until the road becomes too difficult for vehicles. Clear red arrows on the rocks and trees indicate the footpath to the chasm of Tiscali. The walk will take you about 3–4 hours and can be extremely difficult. It is highly advisable to go with a tour guide.

It is possible to make other trips in this area, and again it is recommended you go with a guide. Places to head for include the Gole di Su Gorroppu ravines, parts of the caves of Su Bentu, Sa Oche or S'Elicas Artas, or the climb down to the Codula di Luna valley *(see p89)*.

The Nuraghic Village of Tiscali

This reconstruction of the nuraghic village shows how the settlement would have looked. A crater opening allows natural light in and steps from the entrance made the descent easy.

Murals in Sardinia

Sardinian murals began to appear on walls at Orgòsolo in the 1960s and soon became a feature of many of the island's villages and towns. The most famous of these is San Sperate (*see p66*), the home town of the artist Pinuccio Sciola. The themes of this particular artistic genre are satirical, political or social. The styles vary greatly but are always characterized by bright colours. Even in the open country you may come across faces, shapes, hands and penetrating stares painted onto the boulders, rocks or cliffs. The *Associazione Italiana Paesi Dipinti* (Italian Association of Painted Towns) was founded to preserve and publicize the towns with these murals and also to encourage creativity and cultural exchange between different regions.

Mural at Orgòsolo

Mural on a wall at San Sperate

A mural painted on rock near Orgòsolo

⑪ Orgòsolo

Road map D3. 🏠 4,800.
ⓘ Town Hall (0784 40 09 01).
🎪 first Sun of Jun: Sant'Anania;
15 Aug: Festa dell'Assunta.
ⓦ comune.orgosolo.nu.it

This characteristic village in the interior of the island has been compared to an eagle's nest and a fortress, perched precariously on the mountainside. The villagers are known as rugged and hardy shepherds, proud of their lifestyle and traditions. Rampant banditry in the 1900s was documented in Vittorio De Seta's film *Bandits at Orgòsolo*, in which the hard life of the shepherds and their mistrust of the government is narrated with cool detachment. The passion of the locals for social and political issues is also visible in the hundreds of murals painted on the walls of houses and on the rocks around Orgòsolo. The images describe the harsh life of the shepherds, their struggles to keep their land and Sardinian traditions, as well as injustices committed in other parts of the world.

Simple low stone houses line the steep and narrow streets of the town and some original features are still visible on a few isolated houses. On Corso Repubblica, the church of **San**

Pietro retains its 15th-century bell tower. Traditional dress, a brightly coloured apron embroidered with geometric patterns and a saffron-yellow headscarf, is still worn by some local women.

In summer two popular local festivals draw large crowds: the Assumption Day Festival on 15 August and Sant'Anania's feast day on the first Sunday of June.

Environs

Just outside Orgòsolo is the 17th-century church of **Sant'Anania**. The church was built where the saint's relics are said to have been found. Orgòsolo is an ideal starting point for excursions up to the surrounding Supramonte mountains, where open pastures are interspersed with dense forests of oak. A road leads to the **Funtana Bona**, 18 km (11 miles) south of Orgòsolo. These natural springs emerge at an altitude of 1,082 m (3,550 ft), at the foot of the limestone peak of **Monte Novo San Giovanni**, 1,316 m (4,316 ft) high. From here it is also possible to reach the shady **Foresta di Montes**, a forest of holm oak that stretches out to the south.

⑫ Gavoi

Road map C3. 🏠 3,100. ⓘ Town Hall (0784 531 97). 🎪 last Sun of Jul: rural festival at Sanctuary of the Madonna d'Itria; second Sun after Easter: Sant'Antioco's feast day.
ⓦ comune.gavoi.nu.it

For many centuries this village was famous in Sardinia for the production of harnesses and bridles. Today its most characteristic product is cheese, including *fiore sardo* pecorino, made from sheep's milk (*see p183*). The centre of town is dominated by the pink façade of the 14th-century church of **San Gavino**, which overlooks the square of the same name. Some of Gavoi's oldest and most characteristic streets begin here. A stroll down these narrow alleys will reveal historic buildings with dark stone façades and balconies overflowing with flowers, such as the two-storey building on Via San Gavino.

In the little church of **Sant' Antioco**, in the upper part of town, dozens of ex votos in gold and silver filigree are pinned to the wall. There is also a fine statue of the saint, whose feast day is celebrated the second Sunday after Easter.

Sculpted detail on San Gavino, Gavoi

The Lago di Gusana as seen from Gavoi

⑬ Fonni

Road map D3. 🏔 4,600. 🛈 Town Hall (0784 591 31). 🎭 first Sun & Mon in Jun: Madonna dei Martiri. 🌐 comunefonni.gov.it

Fonni is one of the highest towns in Sardinia, lying at an altitude of 1,000 m (3,280 ft). Its economy relies on tradition and tourism, offering locally made produce, such as traditional sweets, as well as fabrics and rugs known for their fine workmanship. Although the modern building has slightly diminished its charm, at first sight the town gives the impression of sprouting from the mountainside.

On the edge of town is the Franciscan **Madonna dei Martiri** complex, which dates from the 17th century. Inside is a curious statue of the Virgin Mary made from pieces of ancient Roman sculptures.

The town's major festival is held in mid-June to celebrate the return of the shepherds and their flocks from the winter pastures.

On the road towards Gavoi, 4 km (2 miles) west of Fonni, is the **Lago di Gusana**, a large artificial lake. Its tranquil shores, surrounded by holm oaks, make it a popular spot.

⑭ Teti

Road map C4. 🏔 900. 🛈 Town Hall (0784 680 23). 🎭 third Sun in Sep: San Sebastiano. 🌐 comune.teti.nu.it

Perched on the rocky mountains that dominate Lago di Cucchinadorza, the village of Teti distinguishes itself by its small museum, the **Museo Archeologico Comprensoriale**. Run by a team of enterprising young local people, the museum illustrates with clarity and detail the history of the area's ancient nuraghic settlements (in particular the village of S'Urbale and the sacred precinct of Abini). The display cases contain pieces found during excavations, including everyday objects used by the nuraghic people. One hall features a reconstruction of a round dwelling dating from about 1000 BC. Inside are spinning tools, pots, small axes and granite mills. In the middle of the house is the area used as a fireplace.

The halls of the lower floor are used for temporary exhibitions on local culture and traditions, such as traditional costumes and handicrafts.

Bronze statuettes found at Teti, Cagliari Museo Archeologico

Environs

About 1 km (half a mile) southwest of Teti is the entrance to the nuraghic archaeological site of **S'Urbale**. The village was inhabited from 1200 to 900 BC, and the ruins of many prehistoric dwellings are still visible. The ancient nuraghic village of **Abini** is found 10 km (6 miles) to the north of Teti.

🏛 **Museo Archeologico Comprensoriale**
Via Roma. **Tel** 0784 681 20. **Open** 9am–12:30pm, 3–6pm (to 5:30pm Oct–May) Tue–Sun. 🎨 🍴 ♿

Foresta di Montes

At the foot of the rocky bluffs of Monte Novo San Giovanni and Monte Fumai is the largest holm oak forest in Europe. Although many trees were destroyed in the past by fires – often started by shepherds in order to acquire more grazing land – the vast forest is once again increasing in size thanks to replanting, and today it attracts visitors from all over the island. Even in the heat of the summer, a walk through this area and the plateau around the River Olai is very enjoyable, as the dense forest offers shade from the sun and there is a chance to see sheep and pigs, as well as asphodels in bloom. The many footpaths around the Funtana Bona forest headquarters offer opportunities for hiking and mountain-biking.

Monte Novo San Giovanni

The rural Sanctuary of San Mauro, near Sòrgono

⓯ Sòrgono

Road map C4. 🏔 2,100. 🛈 Town Hall (0784 62 25 20). 🎭 26 May: San Mauro feast day. 🔲 **comune. sorgono.nu.it**

Situated in a densely cultivated area of orchards and vineyards, famous for producing Cannonau wine (see p184), Sòrgono has been an important town since Roman times. Today it is the administrative centre of the Mandrolisai area.

Two rather dilapidated sites in the town are worth a visit; the 17th-century **Casa Carta**, featuring a typical Aragonese window, and a medieval fountain of Pisan origin.

Just west of town is one of the most interesting and oldest rural sanctuaries in Sardinia, the **Santuario di San Mauro**. This imposing church is surrounded by the traditional *cumbessias*, the houses used by the pilgrims during their stay at the sanctuary. The building is a mixture of local architectural features and the characteristic Gothic-Aragonese style. A fine stairway flanked by two stone lions leads to the grey trachyte façade, which boasts a beautiful carved Gothic rose window. Numerous inscriptions are recorded on the stones of the church, some many centuries old and others more recent, carved by pilgrims to commemorate their visits to the sanctuary.

The interior of San Mauro has a single vault and is interrupted only by an arch that leads into the presbytery. Here there are a Baroque altar and some statues. Various buildings were added to the original church to accommodate pilgrims and offer them adequate dining facilities, in particular during the San Mauro feast day. One of Sardinia's most important livestock and horse fairs used to be held on this day in the grounds of the sanctuary.

Not far from the church are two further sites worth visiting: the **Tomba di Giganti di Funtana Morta** (Tomb of the Giants) and, on a hilltop overlooking the church, the **Talei Nuraghe**, built with large granite stones and partly into the surrounding rock.

The Pisan fountain at Sòrgono, a relic from the Middle Ages

⓰ Làconi

Road map C4. 🏔 2,500. 🛈 Town Hall (0782 86 62 00). 🔲 **comune. laconi.or.it**

The town of Làconi is built around a rocky spur of the Sarcidano mountain range and boasts beautiful panoramic views. Làconi also features the ruins of **Castello Aymerich** in the park above the town. Only a single tower from the original fortress, built in 1053, remains. The rest of the castle includes later additions such as the 15th-century hall and the 17th-century portico. The magnificent park around the castle includes a botanical garden and waterfall, and today it is a popular destination for walks and picnics.

Once the seat of the local noble overlords, Làconi has preserved the Neo-Classical **Palazzo Aymerich**, built in the first half of the 1800s by architect Gaetano Cima from Cagliari. Within the palace is the **Menhir Museum**, a collection of 40 pre-nuraghic megalithic monuments.

Near the 16th-century parish church is the birthplace and small museum of **Sant' Ignazio da Làconi**, a miracle worker who lived here in the second half of the 18th century. There is also a monument in his honour in the square.

Environs

The area around Làconi has many prehistoric remains. Among these are several anthropomorphic menhirs, single stones on which ancient sculptors carved human features. These can be seen at Perda Iddocca and Genna 'e Aidu, but it is advisable to be accompanied by a local guide.

The ruins of Castello Aymerich at Làconi

⑰ The Cagliari–Sòrgono Railway

Compared to travelling by car, the train line between Cagliari and Sòrgono offers a slow but picturesque approach to the foothills of the Gennargentu mountain range. In the first stretch, up to Mandas, the train goes over the rolling hills of Trexenta. It then climbs up to the road house at Ortuabis, an area of thick vegetation with a backdrop of mountain peaks, and on beyond Belvì through a wood of dense tree heathers. At Mandas, you will need to break your journey to pick up the little *trenino verde* service *(see also pp100–1)* up to Sògorno. This part of the rail route offers both spectacular scenery and an insight into travel from another age. DH Lawrence described the trip in his book *Sea and Sardinia* (1921).

Lush scenery and waterfalls characterize the stretch between Làconi and Meana.

Several touristic routes are covered by Sardinia's *trenino verde* (little green train) services. The timetabling of these services is very variable, but although journeys need some planning, they offer a delightful way to see the countryside.

Chestnut and hazelnut woods cover the foothills of the Gennargentu. Near the station at Belvì you can visit the *Museo di Scienze Naturali* (Natural Science Museum) *(see p114).*

Làconi is a popular tourist destination in the Sarcidano region.

0 km ———— 10
0 miles ———— 10

San Pantaleo Cathedral, at Dolianova, is a Romanesque building built by the Pisans. Inside is a 5th–6th-century christening font, vestige of the original early Christian basilica that stood on this site.

Tips for Travellers

ℹ️ Stazione di Cagliari, Piazza Repubblica (070 49 13 04); Trenino Verde (070 265 71).
🌐 **treninoverde.com**
The Mandas–Sògorno *trenino verde* operates on a restricted summer-only timetable; on days without a service the train can be chartered for groups of 30 people or more.

Key

🚂 Train route
▬ Major road
═ Minor road
— River

**Map labels:**
Sorgono
128
Belvì
295 • Aritzo
Meana Sardo
Laconi
Nurallao
128
Isili •
198
Màndas •
128
547
Senorbì •
547   387
131
466
Dolianova
387
130
Cagliari

Houses in the town of Aritzo

⓲ Aritzo

Road map C4. 🏔 1,700. 🛈 Town Hall (0784 62 72 23). 🎭 second Sun in Aug: Sant'Isidoro; first weekend Nov: chestnut festival. **W** comune. aritzo.nu.it

The small town of Aritzo was once famous for selling snow, at a very high price, packed in straw-lined boxes and transported throughout the island during the hot summer months. Under Aragonese rule, the town had the privilege of being governed by its own inhabitants, locally elected.

There are still many traces of the old town. Some houses retain typical stone façades and long, wooden balconies. Among the most important buildings are the **Casa degli Arangino** (in Neo-Gothic style) and the impressive 17th-century stone **Aritzo prison** on Via Maggiore.

The market for snow no longer exists, but the town has continued its tradition of making wooden furniture, such as hand-carved wedding chests. These are sold from the craftsmen's workshops.

The good climate, the high altitude and panoramic views make Aritzo a pleasant tourist destination in the summer. Rodeos are a popular attraction outside town and interesting walking tours and horseback rides take place towards the Gennargentu massif and the upper Flumendosa river valley. Here canoeing on the river is a popular activity.

Environs
Just north of Aritzo is the **Tacco di Texile**, a vertical limestone pinnacle, 975 m (3,200 ft) high, in the shape of a mushroom. From here there are spectacular views of the mountains of the Barbagia region.

During the Middle Ages, the humble saint Efisio lived in this area. For many years he preached to the local inhabitants and eventually converted them to Christianity.

Wedding chest made by Aritzo craftsmen

⓳ Belvì

Road map C4. 🏔 810. 🛈 Town Hall (0784 62 92 16). 🎭 28 Aug: Sant'Agostino feast day. **W** comune.belvi.nu.it

The village of Belvì lies in a dominating position overlooking the Iscra river valley, which is full of fields of hazelnut trees and orchards.

In the past it must have been an important economic and trading centre, as the surrounding mountain region, Barbagia di Belvì, has also adopted the name.

The railway which connects Mandas and Sòrgono runs along the stretch of road near the village. The route goes through magnificent scenery as well as tackling a thousand tortuous bends and high viaducts *(see p113)*.

In the village, several old houses are still visible. One of these, on the main street, Via Roma, houses the private **Museo di Scienze Naturali** (Natural Science Museum). Founded in 1980 by a group of enthusiasts (including a German naturalist who lived in Belvì for almost ten years), the museum has palaeontology and mineralogy departments, as well as occasional exhibitions of its collection of typical Sardinian fauna and insects.

🏛 **Museo di Scienze Naturali**
Via San Sebastiano. **Tel** 339 753 1025.
Open by appt only. 🅿 🅲

The rodeo held near Aritzo

Overlooking Dèsulo

⓴ Dèsulo

Road map C4. 🏔 3,200. ℹ️ Town Hall (0784 61 92 11). 🎭 second Sun of Pentecost, Corpus Domini.
Ⓦ **comune.desulo.nu.it**

Perched at an altitude of 895 m (2,900 ft) on the slopes of Gennargentu, the village of Dèsulo was not converted to Christianity or ruled by outsiders until the 7th century. Unfortunately, unregulated building development has had a devastating impact on the village and has almost eliminated the traditional schist houses. It is still quite common, however, to see villagers in traditional dress.

The local economy is based on sheep-raising and the ancient tradition of cultivating the chestnut groves and mountain pastures. In the past the inhabitants, skilled in wood-carving, used to travel to the various markets and fairs throughout Sardinia to sell their hand-made spoons, cutting boards and other wooden objects, as well as locally grown chestnuts.

The parish church of **Sant' Antonio Abate**, and other churches such as the **Madonna del Carmelo** and **San Sebastiano**, are worth a visit for a series of colourful wooden statues sculpted in the mid-1600s. But the main reason to visit this village is its natural scenery and the splendid views of the highest peak on the island. There are plans to give the area National Park status, incorporating it into the Gennargentu National Park. Dèsulo is a favourite destination for hikers keen to climb up Gennargentu and Punta La Marmora *(see p86)*. As groups of walkers become more common, a number of hotels and hostels catering for this form of tourism have been built.

㉑ Tonara

Road map C4. 🏔 2,600. ℹ️ Town Hall (0784 63 823). 🎭 second Sun in Aug: Sagra del Torrone.
Ⓦ **comunetonara.gov.it**

In the past the economy of Tonara was based largely on the chestnut and hazelnut groves that surround the town, and on other products typical of a mountain environment. Since tourism discovered this side of the mountain, the local production of cow bells, *torrone* (nougat) and hand-woven rugs has become famous. During the local festivals in the town square, blacksmiths forge the celebrated Tonara bells by hammering the metal

Chestnuts

on specially shaped stone moulds. The inhabitants will be more than willing to tell you how to arrange to see craftsmen at work and purchase traditional rugs. The atmosphere of a typical mountain village can still be seen in the shepherds' houses, which have not changed in over a century.

Tonara is another popular starting point for excursions to the Gennargentu massif. One of the most interesting is the tour to **Punta Mungianeddu** (1,467 m, 4,800 ft). A road climbs through holm oak and chestnut woods to reach the summit, from which there are magnificent views.

Stone used as a mould for making cow bells at Tonara

Sardinian Nougat

Nougat *(torrone* in Italian) is one of the most common sweets in the culture and tradition of central Sardinia. Every local fair or festival will have stalls selling the delicious, hard nougat made in Tonara, Dèsulo or one of the other mountain villages. The main ingredients are almonds, walnuts, hazelnuts, various qualities of honey and egg whites (in some cases the yolk is also used). Cooking – during which the mixture has to be stirred continuously – takes more than 5 hours. The different styles of nougat are created by variations in the type of honey, the flavour of the nuts or number of eggs used. There are many nougat confectioners and, no matter how big or small the premises, visitors are always welcome to watch the preparation and choose a favourite flavour. Blocks of nougat are cut for you while you wait. One excellent outlet is Torronificio Marotto in Tonara, at No. 6 Via Roma; they make particularly delicious and fragrant nougat.

The Nougat Festival at Tonara

THE WESTERN COAST

Each year thousands of flamingoes choose the marshes and wetlands of western Sardinia as their favoured place for over-wintering, creating clouds of pink against the vegetation of the maquis. The coastline is vulnerable to the cool mistral, and years of strong winds have sculpted massive dunes along the shore.

The natural harbours and fertile land in this part of Sardinia have attracted foreign ships for centuries. The Phoenicians discovered the safe harbours of Sulki and Tharros as well as the great commercial potential of the obsidian from the slopes of Monte Arci. The Romans and Spaniards also left their mark at Bosa, the latter transforming Alghero into a Catalonian town.

The area around Oristano is one of the largest wetland areas in Europe. As well as freshwater pools and marshy lakes, there are saltwater lagoons, sandbanks and sand dunes. A combination of the waters of the Tirso river and the mistral is responsible for this particular ecosystem. Over the course of centuries massive dunes have formed at the river mouth, whipped up by the violent winds from the west, effectively blocking the flow of water out to sea.

At the beginning of the 20th century, this marshland was infested with malaria-transmitting mosquitoes but, thanks to land reclamation in the 1930s and the Rockefeller-funded anti-malaria campaign, the soil can now be cultivated without risk. Today this is one of the most fertile areas in Sardinia, producing spring vegetables for sale to mainland Italy, as well as olives and citrus fruits. Vineyards cover the land around Oristano and near the beaches in the Sinis region, yielding quantities of white Vernaccia wine. The coastline is lovely – small beaches and seaside resorts nestle against sand dunes shaded by thick pine forests. Some beaches are made of grains of translucent quartz, which suits wild lilies. Some stretches of cliff, wild and rocky, can only be reached by boat or after a lengthy trek.

The historic town of Bosa seen from the Temo river

◀ Flamingoes flocking in the shallow lagoons around Oristano

Exploring the Western Coast

The western coast of Sardinia offers a wide variety of activities –
whether you prefer to explore the towns and countryside, or relax
on a beach at places like Is Arutas near San Salvatore or Bosa Marina.
There are extensive nature reserves teeming with wildlife, and
fortified cities with Romanesque cathedrals. One of Sardinia's best-
known wines, Vernaccia, is made in this region, from the vineyards
north of Oristano. At Tharros you can explore the ruins of a Phoenician
coastal town, founded in the 8th century BC. The relatively short
distances between sights and the flattish terrain, especially in the Sinis
and Campidano di Oristano regions, make this area ideal for cycling
tours. Walkers may prefer the hiking trails and riders can choose from
the bridle paths that converge on the coast near Arborea. At the
headland of Capo Caccia you can explore caves and grottoes, some
of which extend for kilometres under the cliff.

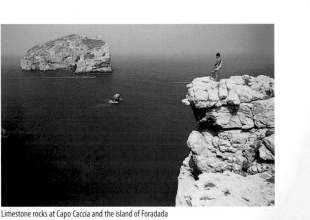

Limestone rocks at Capo Caccia and the island of Foradada

Archaeological excavations at Tharros

For keys to map symbols *see back flap*

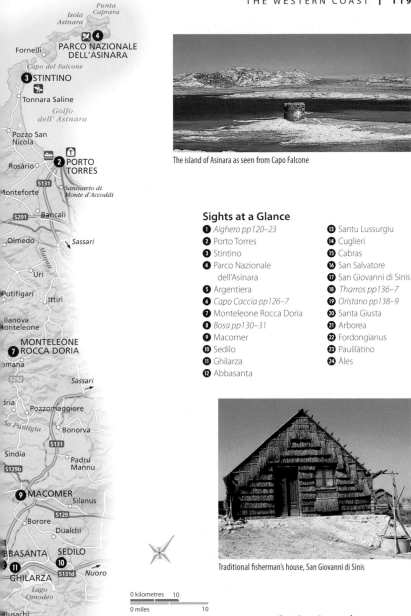

Punta
Caprara

Isola
Asinara

Fornelli

**PARCO NAZIONALE
DELL'ASINARA**

Capo del Falcone

3 STINTINO

Tonnara Saline

*Golfo
dell' Asinara*

Pozzo San
Nicola

Rosário

**2 PORTO
TORRES**

S131

Monteforte

*Santuario di
Monte d'Accoddi*

S291 Bancali

Olmedo

Sassari

Mannu

Uri

Putifigari Ittiri

Villanova
Monteleone

**MONTELEONE
7 ROCCA DORIA**

omana

S292 *Sassari*

dria

Pozzomaggiore

Sa Puntigia Bonorva

S131

Sindia

Padru
Mannu

S129b

9 MACOMER Silanus

S129

Borore

Dualchi

ABBASANTA **SEDILO**

11 **10**

GHILARZA **S131d** *Nuoro*

*Lago
Omodeo*

Busachi

S388

Ortueri

Sughèo

Atzara

S128

The island of Asinara as seen from Capo Falcone

Sights at a Glance

1. *Alghero pp120–23*
2. Porto Torres
3. Stintino
4. Parco Nazionale
   dell'Asinara
5. Argentiera
6. *Capo Caccia pp126–7*
7. Monteleone Rocca Doria
8. *Bosa pp130–31*
9. Macomer
10. Sedilo
11. Ghilarza
12. Abbasanta
13. Santu Lussurgiu
14. Cuglieri
15. Cabras
16. San Salvatore
17. San Giovanni di Sinis
18. *Tharros pp136–7*
19. *Oristano pp138–9*
20. Santa Giusta
21. Arborea
22. Fordongianus
23. Paulilàtino
24. Àles

Traditional fisherman's house, San Giovanni di Sinis

0 kilometres   10

0 miles   10

Key

═══ Major road

─── Secondary road

═══ Minor road

─── Scenic route

─·─ Main railway

─── Minor railway

△ Summit

Getting Around

The coastal road is quite good but not especially fast; the same is true of the roads connecting the villages and those used for mountain tours. The SS131, known as the Carlo Felice road, goes from Oristano to Sassari. There are good railway connections from Oristano to Cagliari, Olbia and Porto Torres, the main ports for ferry connections.

● Street-by-Street: Alghero

In the early 12th century, the aristocratic Doria family from Genoa decided to establish two strongholds in Sardinia, which became Castelgenovese (now Castelsardo) and Alghero. Because of the abundant quantities of algae off the coast, the latter city was named Alquerium – *s'Alighera* in Sardinian dialect and *l'Alquer* in Catalan. After a very short period of Pisan rule, Alghero was conquered by the Aragonese in 1353, and has always been the most Spanish city on the island. The old centre lies within the ancient fortified quarter and the local economy is based on tourism and handicrafts – particularly jewellery and other items made of coral.

★ San Francesco
Parts of this jewel of Catalan architecture date back to the first half of the 14th century. The lovely cloister becomes an open-air concert venue in summer.

Porta Terra tower

Sign in Catalan
The street signs in Alghero are still written in Catalan.

The Maddalena tower and ramparts

PIAZZA CIVICA

MAGELLANO

VIA ROMA

BASTIONI

Alghero Marina
Via Garibaldi starts at the marina and runs alongside Alghero's long, sandy beach towards the lido and Fertilia.

BASTIONI

M A

Torre di Sant'Erasmo

Torre della Polveriera

★ Duomo Doors
Built in the mid-1500s, the carved doorway, together with the bell tower, is the oldest part of Alghero's cathedral.

Key

━ Suggested route

For hotels and restaurants in this region see p178 and p188

San Michele
This Baroque church contains two stucco altars dating from the second half of the 17th century.

Torre di San Giovanni

VISITORS' CHECKLIST

Practical Information
Road map B2. 🏛 41,148.
ℹ Piazza Porta Terra, 079 97 90 54. 🆆 **alghero-turismo.it**

Transport
✈ Alghero Fertilia, 12 km (7 miles) N.

Torre dello Sperone
This is one of the towers in the walls surrounding Alghero. It overlooks Piazza Sulis, the heart of city life.

Chiesa della Misericordia

Torre di San Giacomo

Chiesa del Carmelo

The Al Tuguri Restaurant
This small restaurant in the historic centre of Alghero offers some of the best food in Sardinia. Al Tuguri specializes in fresh fish cooked according to old Catalan recipes.

Via Carlo Alberto is the central shopping street in the city. In the summer months craftsmen set out their coral jewellery to tempt visitors to buy.

| 0 metres | 50 |
| 0 yards | 50 |

★ Ramparts
Positioned between the old city and the sea, the ramparts are now popular places for strolling, especially on warm evenings.

Exploring Alghero

Despite the considerable damage wrought by Allied bombardments in World War II, the heart of the old city is, for the most part, intact and can easily be explored on foot. The main roads from Bosa (to the south) and Sassari (to the northwest) lead to the city walls, and the best way to explore is to leave your car outside and walk around the narrow, high-sided streets of the old city. Strongly influenced by Spanish culture, Alghero remains the most Spanish city in Sardinia. The Alghero dialect is closely related to that of Catalonia, so much so that since 1970, street signs have been printed in Italian and Catalan, and you are likely to hear as much Catalan spoken on the streets as Italian.

The old town, Alghero

🏛 Porta a Terra
Piazza Porta a Terra.
This 14th-century city gate now has a rather stranded air, as most of the associated fortifications were demolished to make room for present-day Via Sassari. The gate was once known as Torre degli Ebrei (dels Hebreus in Catalan), or Tower of the Jews, because of the contribution made by the Jewish community to Catalan king Pietro III's conquest of the city. The tower was originally one of two gates. A drawbridge linked Porta a Terra and the large Gothic arch which is now a war memorial. The ground floor, covered by a stone vault, is now used as a small exhibition centre.

🏛 Torre di San Giacomo
Situated in front of the 17th-century church of Carmen, on the waterfront, is the restored Torre di San Giacomo. It differs from the other towers

in Alghero with its unique octagonal form. It is also known as the Torre dei Cani (the Dogs' Tower) reflecting its earlier use as an enclosure for the stray dogs of the town.

🏛 Bastione and Forte de la Magdalena
Around sunset locals and tourists alike enjoy the pleasant stroll along the seafront. Starting from the south, Lungomare Dante is followed by Lungomare Cristoforo Colombo and Lungomare Marco Polo, which has a series of ramparts with towers (the Torre di San Giacomo, the Mirador rampart, the Torre de la Polvorera, the Torre de Castilla), leading to the port. Not far from the steps which run from the seafront to the old Porta a Mare city gate, is Forte de la Magdalena, the city's most important Spanish fortification. On its walls a plaque commemorates Giuseppe Garibaldi's landing here on 14 August 1855.

A window at Palazzo d'Albis

🏛 Palazzo d'Albis
Piazza Civica (Plaça de la Dressana).
This 16th-century palace with twin lancet windows is also known as Palazzo de Ferrera. It is a rare example of Catalan civic architecture, and is famous for having hosted Charles V in October 1541. The emperor stopped at Alghero with his fleet on the way to Algiers, and was very flattering in his reactions to the city. According to tradition, the emperor spoke to the populace from the balcony of Palazzo d'Albis, and had the following to say about the city: "Bonita, por mi fé, y bien assentada". ("Beautiful, by my faith, and quite solid") and told the inhabitants "Estade todos caballeros" ("You are all gentlemen"). The monarch's sojourn ended with a massive requisition of cattle, which he needed for the Spanish troops. The animals were then slaughtered after an impromptu bullfight, held by the palazzo in Piazza Civica.

⛪ Cattedrale di Santa Maria
Piazza Duomo. **Tel** 079 97 92 22.
Open Jul–Aug: 10am–1pm, 7–9:30pm Mon, Tue & Thu–Sat; Apr–May & Sep–Oct: 10:30am–1pm, 4–6:30pm Mon, Tue & Thu–Sat.

The doorway of Alghero's Neoclassical Cathedral opens out onto the small Piazzetta Duomo. The cathedral, dedicated to Santa Maria, was first built in the 14th century. In the mid-1500s the building was restructured in the Catalan-inspired late Gothic style. The unusual octagonal bell tower dates from the same period.

The 15th-century Torre di San Giacomo

For hotels and restaurants in this region see p178 and p188

The harbour and broad seafront in Alghero

In the interior there is a striking difference between the layout of the central part, which is late Renaissance, and that of the 16th-century Gothic presbytery. Items of Catalan jewellery are on display in the sacristy.

Displays of coral jewellery

Via Principe Umberto

This narrow street, which begins at the Cathedral, was one of the main arteries in the old walled city. Of interest are the Casa Doria (16th century), Palazzo della Curia and, in Piazza Vittorio Emanuele II, the 19th-century Savoyard Teatro Civico.

San Francesco and Cloister

Via Carlo Alberto. **Tel** 079 97 92 58. **Open** 9:45am–12:30pm, 5–6:30pm daily (Sun evenings only).

San Francesco may very well be the most important Catalan monument in the whole of Sardinia. Built at the end of the 1300s and then partially rebuilt when some of the structure collapsed, the church displays different stylistic influences.

The bell tower is Gothic, with a hexagonal body set on a square base. The cupola, dressed with multicoloured tiles, has become the symbol of Alghero.

The two-aisle, white sandstone interior still has Baroque altars made of carved wood and, under the star-spangled Gothic vault of the presbytery, there is an 18th-century altar. The sculptures include a *Dead Christ* and *Christ at the Column*.

The cloister, accessible from the sacristy, is well worth a visit. It is an eclectic sandstone construction, built in different periods. The lower part dates from the 14th century, while the upper part was added in the 1700s. The 22 columns are in two sections, with round or polygonal bases and sculpted capitals. During the summer music season, the Estate Musicale Internazionale di Alghero, concerts and other cultural events are held in these lovely surroundings. In other seasons of the year events and art exhibitions are held in the old refectory.

The Beaches

The port of Alghero has never been an important trading place, partly because of its position and the low-lying coast. There is no heavy industry here and, as a result, the sea is not polluted. A series of resorts can be found just outside the old town. The best-known beach is the Bombarde, a strip of pure white sand bordered by crystal-clear sea, 8 km (5 miles) northwest of the city. Another good beach nearby is the Lazzaretto, which

owes its name to the hospital for the poor which was there during the period of the black plague. When the weather is clear, the impressive vertical profile of Capo Caccia stands out on the horizon.

Environs

To the north is the coastal town of **Fertilia**, a small yacht harbour built during the Fascist era as the centre of the land reclamation programme. Nearby you can still see the 13 arches of the Roman bridge at the ancient city of Carbia. At one time the bridge connected Carbia to Portus Nympharum, now Porto Conte bay. A few minutes away stands the site of **Palmavera Nuraghe**. This prehistoric complex contains two towers and a courtyard surrounded by a barbican.

East of Alghero are the **Necropolis Anghelu Ruju**, the largest pre-nuraghic burial place of its kind in Sardinia, and the Sella & Mosca vineyard and museum *(see p191)*.

Entranceway to the prehistoric site of Palmavera Nuraghe

❷ Porto Torres

Road map B2. 🏛 22,000. 🔢 079 50 08 000. ⓦ comune.porto-torres.ss.it

The chief port in northern Sardinia lies in the Golfo dell'Asinara. Porto Torres was known to the Romans as Turris Libisonis, and was once a prosperous colony. Trade with the city of Kàralis (today's Cagliari) was carried out along the main road on the island. Relations with Rome were very close, as can be seen from the ancient mosaics at the Foro delle Corporazioni in Ostia Antica.

After a lengthy period of decline that began in the Middle Ages, Porto Torres began to recover in the 19th century, when it became the port for Sassari, and again in the 20th century with the development of local industries.

The basilica of **San Gavino** is one of the most important Romanesque churches in Sardinia, built in the Pisan style in 1111. Noteworthy elements are the portal in the northern façade, with its 15th-century bas relief, and the other Gothic doorway, which shows Catalan influences.

Inside there is a crypt, with access to an area of late Roman-early Christian ruins, as well as the 18th-century statues of the martyrs Gavino, Proto and Gianuario, and a medieval inscription celebrating emperor Constantine.

The **Terme Centrali** archaeological area presents a reasonably faithful picture of an ancient Roman quarter, and the **Antiquarium Turritano** contains finds from the excavations here. Not far away, the 135-m (440-ft), seven-arched **Ponte Romano** (Roman bridge) crosses the Mannu river.

Environs

A short distance from here lies one of the most interesting sites in ancient Sardinia, the pre-

The Romanesque basilica of San Gavino, in Porto Torres

nuraghic **Santuario di Monte d'Accoddi**. From Porto Torres, head towards Sassari along the SS131; a short distance after the Sorso junction (at kilometre marker 222.3) a signposted road leads to the archaeological site. The sanctuary dates from the Copper Age (2450–1850 BC) and provides the only example of a megalithic altar in the entire western Mediterranean. The shape is that of a truncated pyramid with a trapezoid base, supported by walls of stone blocks. On the southern side, a ramp leads to the top, about 10 m (33 ft) high, while the base is about 30 m by 38 m (98 ft by 124 ft).

Gold bracelet from the Porto Torres excavations

Around the altar you can see foundations for houses, some sacrificial stone slabs and fallen menhirs. A group of *domus de janas* (rock-cut tombs) was once part of this complex. The material found at this site, including ceramics, is on display at the Museo Nazionale in Sassari *(see p167)*.

🏛 **Antiquarium Turritano**
Via Ponte Romano 99. **Tel** 079 51 44 33. **Open** 9am–8pm Tue–Sun. 🔲 📷 ♿

🏛 **Santuario di Monte d'Accoddi**
Open Apr–Oct: 9am–6pm Tue–Sat (to 7pm Jul & Aug), 9am–2pm Sun; Nov–Mar: 9am–2pm Tue–Sun. **Tel** 334 807 44 49. 🔲 📷 🏛

❸ Stintino

Road map B2. 🏛 1,200. 🔢 Town Hall (079 52 30 53). 🎏 end Aug: Vela Latina; 8 Sep: Santissima Maria Immacolata. ⓦ comune.stintino.ss.it

The road to Capo Falcone, the northwestern tip of Sardinia, passes by the large wind turbines at the Alta Nurra ecological energy plant. Beyond this is the pleasant fishing village of Stintino (named from the Sardinian word *s'isthintinu*, or narrow passageway, the traditional name for the inlet where the village lies). Now a holiday town, Stintino was once important for its tuna fishing grounds, off the island of Asinara. In the summer the two ports, Portu Mannu and Portu Minori, have facilities for aquatic sports of all kinds. The long, sandy beach is the most accessible in the area and very popular.

North of Stintino, the road skirts the coastline as far as **Capo Falcone**. The place is still "defended" by a tower on its highest point and by the two Spanish fortifications at Pelosa and Isola Piana, in the inlet of Fornelli, opposite the island of Asinara.

Portu Mannu, one of the two harbours in Stintino

The barren cliffs on the island of Asinara

❹ Parco Nazionale dell'Asinara

Road map B1. **i** 079 50 33 88.
📷 🎥 compulsory.
w parcoasinara.org

This rugged island, once home to the Fornelli maximum-security prison, became a National Park in 1997. Asinara is less than 18 km (11 miles) long and 7 km (4 miles) wide and ends at the headland of Scomunica. The island's ecosystem is unique in the entire western Mediterranean and includes rare or endangered animal species.

In fact, the pristine coastline and lack of traffic on its 51 sq km (19 sq miles) make Asinara an ideal refuge for raptors, various species of sea birds, moufflons and wild boar. There is also a rare species of small endemic albino donkey, after which the island must have been named (*asino* meaning donkey). The rocky, volcanic terrain supports a holm oak forest, and the typical low-level maquis brush shields numbers of rare plants.

As a protected area, the island cannot be visited unaccompanied. Day boat trips start at Stintino and Porto Torres. Tours are by bus, on foot or, for the most comprehensive, by offroad vehicle.

Albino donkey from Asinara

❺ Argentiera

Road map B2. 🚌 70.

Many places in Sardinia still carry reminders of the island's former mining industries. At Argentiera, not far from the modern town of Palmadula, the ancient Romans, and the Pisans in the Middle Ages, dedicated themselves to mining the precious metal that gave its name to the area (*argento* means silver).

In the 19th century, mining complexes, with wooden and masonry buildings, were constructed along the coast, so that the mined silver could then be transported by sea to other destinations, where it could be processed and eventually sold. A number of ambitious restoration and restructuring projects, many of which are yet to be completed, have changed the face of the town, but it still remains one of the most fascinating examples of industrial archaeology in Sardinia.

In the summer, the tranquil bay at Argentiera, with its crystal-clear water, is a great favourite with visitors.

The old mine buildings at Argentiera

❻ Capo Caccia

Towering above the sea, the Capo Caccia promontory, with a lighthouse perched on the outermost point, offers wonderful views of Alghero. Wild pigeons, swifts, peregrine falcons and herring gulls nest in the crevices and gullies of the precipitous cliffs. On the western side of the headland – opposite the barren profile of the island of Foradada – 656 steep steps (known as the Escala del Cabirol, or Roe-deer's Staircase) take you down the cliff to the fascinating caves of the Grotta di Nettuno (Neptune's Grotto). The cave can also be reached in about three hours by boat from Alghero.

Griffon vulture
Only a few of these rare creatures survive in Sardinia.

Herring gulls
These birds nest in cliff crevices and ravines.

Peregrine falcons
These raptors prefer calm, open spaces with rocky cliffs – Capo Caccia is a favoured ground.

KEY

① Torre Pegna
② Torre del Tramariglo
③ Cala d'Inferno
④ Isola Foradada
⑤ Lago La Marmora
⑥ Punta del Bollo
⑦ Punta del Quadro

Capo Caccia
In the past this promontory was frequented by travellers and prominent naturalists such as Alberto La Marmora. The name Capo Caccia derives from the *caccia*, or wild pigeon hunting, that was once popular here.

Grotta Verde
The name of this large cave, Green Grotto, derives from the colour of the moss and other plants that cover the stalagmites and stalactites. On the shores of a small lake at the far end of the gallery, ancient graffiti have been discovered.

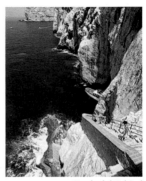

Escala del Cabirol
From the ridge of land separating the headland from the lighthouse point, the Escala del Cabirol steps wind down to the entrance of the Grotta di Nettuno.

Grotta di Nettuno
Neptune's Grotto, one of the most picturesque caves in Sardinia, was first explored in the 1700s. The grotto extends for 2,500 m (8,200 ft), while the guided tour covers 200 m (650 ft).

Romanesque Santo Stefano, at Monteleone Rocca Doria

❼ Monteleone Rocca Doria

Road map B3. 🗺 140.
ℹ 079 92 51 17. 🌐 **comune. monteleoneroccadoria.ss.it**

Situated on the top of the Su Monte cliff (420 m, 1,380 ft), the little village of Monteleone Rocca Doria has a sweeping view of Lake Temo and the Nurra plain. Today it is tranquil, although inhabitants look back proudly on a noble, warlike past. In the 13th century the Doria family from Genoa built a fortress here which was totally destroyed in 1436 after a three-year siege by troops from Aragon, Sassari, Bosa and Alghero.

Many inhabitants departed to found the town of Villanova Monteleone, but a few people remained behind. Monteleone was not included in development programmes and, at one point, locals tried to improve their lot by putting the village up for sale. In the centre of Monteleone is the 13th-century Romanesque parish church, **Santo Stefano**.

❽ Bosa

See pp130–31.

❾ Macomer

Road map C3. 🗺 12,000. ℹ Town Hall (0785 79 08 51). 🌐 17 Jan: Sant'Antonio Abate. 🌐 **comune. macomer.nu.it**

Built on a platform of volcanic rock, Macomer is one of the most important commercial

centres in the interior of Sardinia. Macomer developed around key communication routes – the Carlo Felice road (the N131 that runs through most of the island) and the railway – and owes its prosperity to agriculture, livestock raising, dairy products and light industry, while retaining traces of its past. The parish church of **San Pantaleo** is an example of 17th-century Spanish Gothic. On the evening of 17 January the traditional *Sa Tuva* celebration is held in honour of Sant'Antonio Abate. The event takes place in the large square in front of Santa Croce, and a huge bonfire lights up the entire quarter.

San Pantaleo, in Macomer

Environs
Not far from the town centre, near the Carlo Felice road, a short walk will take you to the impressive **Santa Barbara Nuraghe**. Its sheer size means that it dominates a series of smaller towers and ramparts.

❿ Sedilo

Road map C3. 🗺 2,700.
ℹ 0785 560 01. 🌐 5–8 Jul: S'Ardia at Santu Antine sanctuary.
🌐 **comunesedilo.gov.it**

The rocky terrain in the Abbasanta plateau gave the people of Sedilo the raw material to build their houses. There are still a few originals remaining, representing a style that has virtually disappeared. The main sight of interest is the church of **San Giovanni Battista** in the centre of town. However, Sedilo's most notable claim to fame is the **Sanctuary of Santu Antine**, otherwise known as San Costantino, or Constantine, after the early champion of Christianity who is much revered in Sardinia. The church, with the typical *cumbessias* houses for pilgrims, stands on a cliff overlooking Lake Omodeo. Within the precinct there are numerous nuraghic sculptures on display, including the so-called *Perda Fitta*, a monolith which, according to legend, is actually the body of a woman who was turned into stone because she was disrespectful towards the patron saint.

The open space opposite the sanctuary is the setting for the annual *S'Ardia* competition. This horse race ends the July festivities commemorating Constantine the Great's victory over Maxentius in the battle of the Milvian Bridge in AD 312. The inside walls of Santu Antine are covered with quantities of ex votos.

The S'Ardia horse race run around the Santu Antine sanctuary, Sedilo

The Losa nuraghe near Abbasanta

⑪ Ghilarza

Road map C3. 🏛 4,700.
ℹ️ Town Hall (0785 56 10).
Ⓦ comune.ghilarza.or.it

An unfinished Aragonese tower stands in the centre of Ghilarza, but the place is known principally as the town in which the famous Italian political thinker and writer Antonio Gramsci spent his childhood years. A small door on Corso Umberto leads to the **Casa di Gramsci**, now occupied by a research and study centre. There is also an exhibition of historical material relating to the Communist leader, who died in prison during the Fascist era. On the second floor is the small bedroom that was Gramsci's from 1898 to 1908.

Environs
A short distance from Ghilarza, on the road to Nuoro, is the beautiful church of **San Pietro di Zuri**, which was relocated, along with the village of the same name, after the artificial lake Omodeo was created in 1923.

The original church dates from 1291. The building was commissioned by Mariano d'Arborea, and carried out by architect Anselmo da Como. The architecture is prevalently Romanesque, with some interesting details which anticipate the transition towards the Gothic style.

🏛 **Casa di Gramsci**
Corso Umberto 36. **Tel** 0785 541 64.
Open May–Sep: 10am–1pm, 4–7pm Mon, Wed–Sun (daily in Aug); Oct–Apr: 10am–1pm, 3:30–6:30pm Fri–Sun.
Ⓦ casagramscighilarza.org

⑫ Abbasanta

Road map C3. 🏛 2,700.
ℹ️ Town Hall (0785 56 16).
Ⓦ comune.abbasanta.or.it

This village, the centre of which still has some old traditional houses made of dark local basalt stone, revolves around the parish church of Santa Cristina, with its impressive Renaissance-inspired architecture. Situated in the middle of a highly developed agricultural region, Abbasanta owes its importance to its strategic position near main artery routes, both ancient and modern.

In the vicinity are two of the most important archaeological sites in the whole of Sardinia: the **Losa Nuraghe** and the **Santa Cristina** nuraghic complex near Paulilàtino (*see p141*). In order to reach the Losa Nuraghe, take the Carlo Felice road towards Cagliari until you reach kilometre marker 123 (indicated on a road sign).

Here, a turning to the right leads to the entrance to the archaeological site, which is fenced off. Together with the monuments at Barùmini (*see pp68–9*) and Torralba (*see pp28–9*), this nuraghic complex is one of the most important remaining from the immediate pre-Punic period.

In the middle of this vast structure is a keep thousands of years old, dating from the second millennium BC, while the ramparts were built some centuries later. The outer defensive walls were the last to be built, and date from the 7th century BC.

Inside the nuraghe there are three roofed chambers with a great many niches, which were probably used for storage. A spiral staircase leads to the upper floor, which features a terrace above.

All around the main structure are the foundations of a series of later buildings, dating from the Bronze Age to the Middle Ages.

A small **Antiquarium** stands about 100 m (328 ft) from the nuraghi themselves. It houses an interesting exhibition of plans and illustrations of a number of nuraghic monuments in this part of Sardinia.

🏛 **Losa Nuraghe**
SS Carlo Felice 123.5 km.
Tel 0785 52 302. **Open** 9am–1 hour before sunset daily. ♿ 📷 💻 🏛

Antonio Gramsci

Antonio Gramsci was born at Àles in 1891 to a humble family. After completing his studies at Turin, he entered politics full-time. He was one of the co-founders of the radical weekly *L'Ordine Nuovo* and in 1921 helped to found the Italian Communist Party, later becoming its Secretary-General. He was elected to parliament but was arrested by the Fascists in 1926 and given a 20-year prison sentence. He did not see freedom again, dying in prison in 1937. The complete edition of his writings, *Quaderni del Carcere* (Prison Notebooks) was not published until 1976. *Lettere dal Carcere* (Letters from Prison) are a moving statement of his sufferings as a prisoner.

The young Gramsci

❽ Bosa

Dominated by the Castello dei Malaspina, the pastel-coloured houses of Bosa lie on the right bank of the Temo river, the only navigable river in Sardinia. The town was originally founded by the Phoenicians on the opposite bank of the river. In the Middle Ages, under threat from constant pirate raids, the townspeople sought the protection of the Malaspina family on the slopes of the hill of Serravalle. Bosa was granted the status of royal city under Spanish rule and always maintained a close relationship with the Iberian peninsula. This fascinating town is famous for its artisan traditions of gold-filigree jewellery and lace-making. In the Sa Costa medieval quarter, a labyrinth of cobblestone alleys and steps, you can still see women sitting outside their homes making lace. Environmentalists say the nearby seaside is the cleanest in Italy.

Interior of the Cathedral in Bosa, with Baroque ornamentation

🏛 Cathedral
Piazza Duomo. **Tel** 0785 37 32 86.
Open 9–11:30am, 3–5pm daily (3:30–6:30pm in summer).

Dedicated to the Virgin Mary, the Cathedral was rebuilt in the 19th century in the majestic late Baroque Piedmontese style. In the interior is a statue of the *Madonna and Child*, of the Catalan school, sculpted in the 16th century. On either side of the main altar are two marble lions killing dragons. The side altars are made of multi-coloured marble.

🏚 Corso Vittorio Emanuele II
The main street in Bosa, paved with stone, runs parallel to the river. It is lined with aristocratic buildings and goldsmiths' workshops where filigree and coral jewellery are made.

🏛 Casa Deriu
Corso Vittorio Emanuele II 59.
Tel 0785 37 70 43.
Open summer: 10am–1pm, 4–8pm Tue–Sun; winter: by appointment. 📷

Casa Deriu is a typical 19th-century Bosa building which has been transformed into an exhibition centre. The first floor features traditional local products such as cakes, wine and bread, as well as a display

Detail of the architrave of San Pietro

of old black-and-white photographs. On the second floor is a fine reconstruction of the elegant Deriu apartment, with its olive wood parquet, frescoed vaulted ceiling, majolica tiles from Ravenna and locally made lace curtains.

The top floor houses the Pinacoteca Civica (municipal art gallery), featuring the collection of Melkiorre Melis, a local artist and one of the leading promoters of 20th-century applied arts in Sardinia.

The works on display span a 70-year period of graphic art, oil painting, ceramics and posters. There are also Arab-influenced works of Melis, executed while he headed the Muslim School of Arts and Crafts in Tripoli.

🏰 Castello Malaspina
Via Ultima Costa 14. **Tel** 340 395 50 48.
Open 15–31 Mar & 1–15 Nov: 10am–1pm daily; Apr–Jun: 10am–7pm daily; Jul–Aug: 10am–7:30pm daily; Sep: 10am–6pm daily; Oct: 10am–5pm daily; 16 Nov–14 Mar: by appt only. 🅿 📷 🌐 **castellodibosa.it**

Built in 1112 by the Malaspina dello Spino Secco family, this castle is still impressive, even though only its towers and outer walls have survived. It was enlarged in the 1300s, when the main tower, built of light ochre trachyte, was added. Inside the walls the only building standing is the church of **Nostra Signora**

Bosa as seen from the Temo river, with fishing boats

For hotels and restaurants in this region see p178 and p188

The Aragonese tower at Bosa Marina

di Regnos Altos, built in the 14th century. Restoration carried out in 1974–5 brought to light a cycle of Catalan school frescoes, one of the few left in Sardinia. From the ramparts there are splendid views of the church of San Pietro, the lower Temo river valley and the red roofs of the Sa Costa quarter. You can walk down to the centre of town by following the steps skirting the walls that once defended Bosa to the east.

🚏 Sas Conzas

The buildings on the left bank of the Temo river were once used as tanneries. Abandoned years ago after a crisis in the leather goods market, the buildings are currently being restored. Two of the buildings now house a tannery museum and a small restaurant. The Sas Conzas quarter can best be admired from the palm-lined

street on the other side of the river, Lungotemo De Gasperi, where the fishermen of Bosa moor their boats.

🛈 San Pietro

Tel 340 395 50 48. **Open** Apr–Sep: 9:30am–12:30pm, 3:30–6pm (4–7pm in Aug) Tue–Fri, 9:30am–12:30pm Sat, 3:30–6pm Sun; Oct–Mar: by appt.
🖼 ✓

About 1 km (half a mile) east of the left bank of the Temo stands the church of San Pietro, built in red trachyte stone, one of the most interesting of Sardinia's Roman-esque churches. It was built in different periods, beginning in the second half of the 11th century, while the bell tower, apse and side walls were added the following century. The façade combines elements of Romanesque with touches

of French Gothic, imported by the Cistercian monks. On the architrave of the doorway is a singular *Madonna and Child with Saints Peter, Paul and Constantine*.

Bosa coat of arms

Environs

Bosa Marina, just over 2 km (1 mile) from the centre of town, has a lovely secluded beach with dark sand. Isola Rossa is linked to the mainland by a long jetty. The Aragonese tower is open in July and August and hosts temporary exhibitions.

The coastline between Bosa and Alghero is spectacular. Part of the Trenino Verde route (see pp96–7) goes from Bosa Marina to Macomer, skirting the Pedras Nieddas (black stones) beach before going up the Rio Abba Mala valley to Modolo, Tres-nuraghes and Sindia.

The Castello Malaspina in Bosa

The paired horse race held during Carnevale at Santu Lussurgiu

⑬ Santu Lussurgiu

Road map B3. ⚲ 2,900. ⚍
ⓘ Town Hall (0783 55 19).
⚑ Carnevale: horse race in town centre; 2 Jun: Horse Fair;
21 Aug: San Lussorio.
Ⓦ comunesantulussurgiu.it

The village of Santu Lussurgiu lies at 500 m (1,640 ft) above sea level on the eastern slope of the extinct volcanic mountain, Mount Montiferru, laid out like an amphitheatre on the edge of a volcanic crater, and surrounded by olive groves.

The historic centre is fascinating, with its steep, narrow streets and tiny squares surrounded by beautiful tall stone houses painted in bright colours. Some have decorated architraves and wrought-iron balconies. On Via Roma, an elegant 11-room 18th-century building houses the **Museo della Tecnologia Contadina**, (Museum of Rural Culture), founded by the local Centro di Cultura Popolare. The "Su Mastru Salis" collection is the work of Maestro Salis, the museum curator, who in over 20 years has collected more than 2,000 objects related to the culture and traditions of Santu Lussurgiu.

A guided visit to this interesting museum is like making a trip backwards in time. Room after room contains fascinating displays of everyday objects used by the farmers, shepherds and coal merchants who worked at the foot of Mount Montiferru. Some of the most interesting exhibits are in the sections given over to spinning and weaving, cooking and crafts. The room devoted to winemaking is also interesting. Equipment includes a fulling-mill, the implement used to soften and felt fabric. Over 40 of them were once in use in the Santu Lussurgiu area.

In the upper part of town is the 15th-century church of **Santa Maria degli Angeli**, which has a fine 18th-century carved wooden altar.

There are still several craftsmen in Santu Lussurgiu who specialize in making knives and fittings for horse-riding (bridles, bits, saddles and leather riding boots).

At Carnevale the street in front of the museum is turned into a track for a breakneck horse race between pairs of riders dressed as knights.

Environs
A few kilometres from Santu Lussurgiu there is a forest of

Church of Santa Maria degli Angeli in Santu Lussurgiu

Flamingoes in the Sale Porcus Reserve

The Sale Porcus marsh is one of the largest reserves on the Sinis peninsula, its many white sand dunes covered with maquis vegetation. In winter and spring over 10,000 flamingoes and thousands of cranes, wild geese, cormorants and mallards make their home here. In summer, drought reduces the water level, transforming the lake into a white area with a thick, hard salty crust that you can walk across. One of the least intrusive ways to explore this natural oasis is by horse. For more details on environmentally friendly visits to the reserve, contact Engea Sardegna, the regional chapter of an association of horseback guides.

🦩 **Oasi Sale Porcus**
Open daily. **Tel** 0783 52 20 (bird-watching), 0783 52 81 00 (horse rides).
Ⓦ sitogea.net

Flamingoes in the Sale Porcus reserve

One of the seven springs at San Leonardo de Siete Fuentes

pine, holm oak and oak near the village of **San Leonardo de Siete Fuentes**, which is famous for its seven springs of radio-active, diuretic water that flow out of seven fountains at a constant temperature of 11°C (52°F). The streams meander through a wood popular for family outings. In the centre of town is the small church of San Leonardo, which once belonged to the Knights of Malta. It was constructed with dark trachyte stone in the 12th century, and acquired its present Romanesque-Gothic appearance the following century. The single-nave interior bears the insignias of the Knights of Malta. Opposite the church stands a small public library.

In early June, San Leonardo plays host to an important saddle-horse fair packed with horse races and other events.

Ⅲ Museo della Tecnologia Contadina
Via D Meloni 1. **Tel** 0783 55 06 17 or 340 770 66 73. **Open** by appt only.

⑭ Cuglieri

Road map B3. 🏛 3,400.
🅸 Via Carlo Alberto 33 (0785 36 82 00). 🎪 Good Friday: procession and 'Iscravamento; 5 Aug: Madonna della Neve. 🆆 **comune.cuglieri.or.it**

The agricultural town of Cuglieri lies 500 m (1,640 ft) above sea level on the western slopes of Mount Montiferru, with a panoramic view of the sea. It is dominated by the striking silver-domed **Basilica di Santa Maria della Neve**, which has an 18th-century façade and twin bell towers. The barrel-vaulted interior of the church is adorned with stucco and features eight chapels, four on each side of the nave, and there is also an impressive Baroque-style altar made from marble and stone. The walk up to the church is lovely, winding through alleyways and stepped streets lined with tall stone houses.

The square in front of Santa Maria offers a fine view of the town and the coast between Santa Caterina di Pittinuri and Porto Alabe.

Environs
The coast is 15 km (9 miles) away on main road 292. **Santa Caterina di Pittinuri** is a seaside town set around a white-stone inlet enclosed by a limestone cliff, where the Spanish Torre del Pozzo tower stands. This stretch of coast is scenic, with rocky headlands and white sand and pebble beaches, as well as caves and beautiful ravines. The most famous sight is **S'Archittu**, a large natural bridge created by coastal erosion. A dirt road off main road 292, between Santa Caterina di Pittinuri and S'Archittu, goes to the ruins of the Punic-Roman city of **Cornus**, the setting for the last battle between the Romans and Sardinian Carthaginians headed by Amsicora (215 BC).

In the 9th century the city was abandoned because of repeated Saracen raids and the inhabitants founded a new city, Curulis Nova, present-day Cuglieri, on the nearby mountainside. The dirt road peters out just before the Early Christian town of Columbaris, while the acropolis of Cornus is visible on the hill to the southwest. Although the archaeological site may seem abandoned, it still has some sarcophagi and the remains of a three-nave basilica. It seems likely that all of these date back to the 6th century.

S'Archittu, the famous natural bridge at Santa Caterina di Pittinuri, near Cuglieri

An archaeological site in Tharros

⓯ Cabras

Road map B4. 🗺 10,000. 🚌
ℹ Town Hall (0783 3971). 🎉 first
Sun in Sep: Festa di San Salvatore.
🌐 **comunedicabras.it**

The town of Cabras, not far
from Oristano, is characterized
by its old, one-storey houses.
It stands on the edge of the
largest freshwater lake and
marsh in Sardinia (21 sq km,
8 sq miles), and is connected to
the sea via a series of canals.
    The presence of both fresh
and salt water attracts coots,
marsh harriers, peregrine
falcons and purple gallinules.
    In the past, local fishermen
used long, pointed boats, called
is fassonis, made of dried rushes
and other marsh plants using
a technique similar to that
known to the Phoenicians.
Another Phoenician technique
is the marinading process
called *sa merca*, in which fresh
fish is wrapped in plant leaves
from the lake and left to soak
in salt water.

Environs
At the northern end of the
Golfo di Oristano is the **Laguna
di Mistras**. Separated from the
sea by sandbars, in wetlands
of international scientific
importance, this lagoon makes
an ideal habitat for flamingoes,

cormorants, grey herons and
ospreys. In a modern complex
by the lagoon, the **Museo Civico
di Cabras** displays finds from
Tharros *(see pp136–7)* and other
local archaeological sites, and
explores the ethnographic and
ecological makeup of the area.

🏛 Museo Civico di Cabras
Via Tharros. **Tel** 0783 29 06 36. **Open**
9am–1pm, 4–8pm (winter 3–7pm)
daily. 🎫 (ticket also valid for Tharros).

⓰ San Salvatore

Road map B4. ℹ Cabras. 🎉 end of
Aug–first Sun in Sep: Corsa degli Scalzi
di San Salvatore.

Typical white houses for
pilgrims, or *cumbessias*,
surround the country church

of San Salvatore. They are
occupied for nine days each
year in late August and early
September, for the novena
of the saint's feast day. In the
1960s the church's central
square was used as a location
for "spaghetti westerns".
    San Salvatore was built in the
17th century on the site of a
nuraghic sanctuary for the
worship of sacred waters. In the
6th century the site was transformed into an underground
church. In the left-hand nave
stairs lead to the hypogeum,
which has six chambers: two
rectangular ones flanking a
corridor leading to a circular
atrium with a well, around
which three further chambers
lie. The hypogeum was partly
hewn out of the rock;

The annual Corsa degli Scalzi (barefoot race) at San Salvatore

Marsh samphire, a typical plant growing in the Cabras marshes

depictions of ships, which experts believe are ex votos.

The Latin letters RVF, interlaced as in a monogram and repeated several times, seem to derive from the Phoenician language and are said to stand for "cure, save, give health".

On the first Saturday in September, the feast day of San Salvatore is celebrated. The event is marked with a barefoot (*scalzi*) race in memory of local youths, who, in the Middle Ages, left the village to escape from the Saracens but returned to save the statue of the saint.

Just east of the sanctuary are the ruins of the Domu 'e Cubas Roman baths.

the vaulted ceilings are made of sandstone and brick. On the walls are graffiti of animals (elephants, panthers and peacocks) and heroes and gods (Hercules fighting the Nemean lion, Mars and Venus with a small winged cupid). There are even Arabic writings about Allah and Mohammed, and numerous

⑰ San Giovanni di Sinis

Road map B4. 🚗 40. 🚹 Cabras.

At the edge of the Sinis peninsula is a bathing resort once famous for its fishermen's

huts made of wood and reeds (*see p119*). Today only a few survive; the largest group lies east of the motorway, not far from the archaeological site of Tharros (*see pp136–7*).

As visitors enter the small village of San Giovanni di Sinis they will see the early Christian church of **San Giovanni** which, together with San Saturnino in Cagliari, is the oldest in Sardinia. It was built in the 5th century, though much of the present-day church was the result of 9th- and 10th-century rebuilding. The three-nave interior is barrel-vaulted.

Environs

Near San Giovanni di Sinis is the WWF **Torre 'e Seu** reserve, where some of the last dwarf palms in the area survive. A dirt road at the northern end of San Giovanni di Sinis leads to the reserve. At the gate there is a path to the sea and the Torre 'e Seu Spanish tower.

The Vernaccia Wine of Sardinia

Vernaccia grapes

The countryside north of Oristano is one of the most fertile areas in Sardinia, carpeted with olive trees and grapevines. The Vernaccia made in Oristano is perhaps Sardinia's most famous white wine and is produced in the towns of San Vero Milis, Cabras, Zeddiani, Narbolia, Riola and Baratili. The wine is full-bodied and strong, with 15 degrees of alcohol, and is aged for at least three years in large oak barrels. You can take a tour of the wine-producing area, and pause for wine-tasting at the Vino Vernaccia.

🏛 **Vino Vernaccia**
Via Oristano 6A. **Tel** 0783 33 383. **Open** 8am–1pm, 3:30–6:30pm Mon–Fri, 8am–1pm Sat. 🅿 🚫 book in advance.
🌐 **vinovernaccia.com**

The 18th-century gate at the entrance to Cantina Sociale winery, Oristano

Wine barrels in the Vino Vernaccia

Rows of Vernaccia vines

⑱ Tharros

The city of Tharros was founded by the Phoenicians around the end of the 8th century BC, on a spit of land called Capo San Marco, which offered safe anchorage for cargo-laden ships. By the 6th and 5th centuries BC, Tharros had become a flourishing port and this prosperity continued under the Romans, from 238 BC on. With sea on two sides, this is one of the most intriguing ancient sites in the Mediterranean. Only a third of the area has been unearthed so far. Most of the visible remains date back to the Punic-Roman era, but there is also evidence of previous civilizations: the nuraghic village (late Bronze Age) and the Tophet (Phoenician) located on the hill, Su Murru Mannu.

7th–6th century BC necklace
Made of gold and cornelian, this necklace was found in the southern necropolis.

Capo San Marco
At the southern tip of the Sinis peninsula, Capo San Marco still has the remains of nuraghe Baboe Cabitza, dating back to the late Bronze Age. During this time, the whole peninsula was likely subject to intense settlement.

Remains of the Fortifications
At the foot of San Giovanni is a quadrangular base of squared sandstone blocks thought to date back to the 3rd century BC.

KEY

① **San Giovanni Spanish tower**

② **Deep tombs** were installed by the fortifications north of the city during Roman times.

③ **Tophet**

④ **Sanctuary of Demeter**

⑤ **The Castellum Acquae** is an imposing rectangular building, the function of which is still in doubt. The archaeologist G Pesce thought that this was the cistern feeding the city's water system.

⑥ and ⑦ **Baths**

Distinctive Residence
The presence of a courtyard of basalt millstones in this house has led archaeologists to believe that this was an area dedicated to working wheat, or possibly even a bakery.

Drainage System
A drain ran along the middle of the paved road. The system was linked to the rows of houses on either side of the street.

VISITORS' CHECKLIST

Practical Information
Road map B4.
San Giovanni di Sinis.
🛈 Cooperativa Penisola Sinis (0783 37 00 19). **Open** 9am–7pm summer, 9am–5pm winter.
🚗 📷 🌐 penisoladelsinis.it

Head of Goddess
Found in the Punic necropolis, this 5th-century BC head is now in Cagliari's archaeological museum (see p62).

★ **Corinthian Columns**
These reconstructed columns are part of the process of re-erecting monuments that occupied Tharros between the 1st and 3rd centuries AD. One of the columns has an original Corinthian capital.

★ **Cistern**
This quadrangular cistern (3rd–4th centuries AD) on the southern side of the temple is made of large blocks of sandstone and adorned with Doric half-columns.

⑲ Oristano

Placed at the northern border of the Campidano region, between the mouth of the Tirso river and the Santa Giusta marshlands, Oristano is the largest town in western Sardinia. It was founded in 1070, after the powerful and prosperous city of Tharros was abandoned, the inhabitants defeated by constant pirate raids. The period between 1100 and 1400 saw the rise of the city under enlightened rulers such as Mariano IV and his daughter Eleonora, who controlled most of Sardinia. Oristano became the provincial capital only in 1974. The town stands in the middle of a fertile plain with a network of pools, well-stocked with fish. The historic centre, once protected by the city walls, is small and mostly a pedestrian-only zone.

The Cathedral of Oristano with its octagonal campanile

🏛 Cattedrale

Piazza Mannu. **Tel** 0783 786 84. **Open** 7am–noon, 4–6:30pm daily. 🚹

Dedicated to the Blessed Virgin Mary, the Cathedral was built in 1220 by Lombard architects and masons for Mariano di Torres. It was totally rebuilt in the 17th century in the Baroque style and now displays a mixture of influences. The remaining original elements are the octagonal bell tower with its onion dome and brightly coloured majolica tiles, the bronze doors and the Cappella del Rimedio, which has a fine marble balustrade decorated with Pisan bas relief sculpture depicting Daniel in the lions' den. The Renaissance choir behind the main altar is another important work. The rich and varied Tesoro del Duomo, the cathedral treasury, is housed in the chapterhouse, and silverwork, vestments and illuminated manuscripts can be seen upon request. On Piazza del Duomo are the Palazzo Arcivescovile (arch-bishop's palace) and the Seminario Tridentino.

🏰 Torre di Mariano II

Piazza Roma.

Also called Torre di San Cristoforo or Porta Manna, this sandstone tower at the northern end of the former city walls was built in 1291 by the ruler of the Arborea principality, Mariano II. This and the Portixedda tower, just opposite, are the sole surviving remains of the old city walls. At the top of the tower is a large bell made in 1430. The Torre di Mariano is open on its inner façades and looks over Piazza Roma, the heart of city life, with its fashionable shops and outdoor cafés.

🏰 Corso Umberto

This pedestrian street, also known as Via Dritta, is the most elegant in Oristano with impressive buildings such as Palazzo Siviera, once the residence of the Marquise d'Acrisia, which has a dome on top, and Palazzo

The Knights of the Star

The Sa Sartiglia procession and tournament is centuries-old and is held on the last Sunday of Carnival and on Shrove Tuesday. It was probably introduced in 1350 by Mariano II to celebrate his wedding. On 2 February the procession leader, *su Componidori*, is chosen. On the day of the event he is dressed by a group of girls. A white shirt is sewn on him, his face is wrapped in fasciae and covered with a woman's mask, and a bride's veil and black hat are placed on his head. He then leads a procession of knights, trumpeters and drummers through the city to the tournament grounds by the Arcivescovado and the Cathedral. At a given signal the tournament begins. The leader has to run his sword into the hole in the middle of a star hanging from a string, and pick it up. If he succeeds, this signals a prosperous year.

The Sa Sartiglia tournament at Oristano

Falchi, built in the 1920s. Oristano's smartest shops are found here and it is the most popular street for the traditional evening stroll.

⚏ Piazza Eleonora D'Arborea

This long, irregular, tree-lined square is named after the ruler who established the famous Carta de Logu body of laws in 1392. A 19th-century statue of Eleonora stands in the middle of the square. This piazza also boasts noble buildings such as Palazzo Corrias and the Palazzo Comunale, the town hall, once the Scolopi monastery. The octagonal church of San Vincenzo was part of the monastery.

Eleonora d'Arborea

⌂ San Francesco

Piazza Mannu. **Tel** 0783 782 75. **Open** 9:30–11:30am, 5–6:30pm. This Neo-Classical church was built over the remains of a Gothic church which was completely destroyed in the early 19th century. The façade has six columns with Ionic capitals. In the interior is one of the most interesting statues in Sardinia: a crucifix executed by

an unknown late 14th-century Catalan artist. Another important work, by Pietro Cavaro, depicts *The Stigmata of San Francesco*.

⌂ Santa Chiara

Via Garibaldi. **Tel** 0783 780 93. **Open** for Mass only (6pm daily). The Gothic church of Santa Chiara was built in the 14th century. The façade displays sandstone ashlars, a severe rose window and small bell gable. The interior has wooden Gothic corbels with carved animal figures.

ⓜ Antiquarium Arborense

Palazzo Parpaglia, Via Parpaglia 37. **Tel** 0783 79 12 62. **Open** mid-Jun–mid-Sep: 9am–2:30pm, 3:30–9pm daily; mid-Sep–mid-Jun 9am–8pm daily. ⧠⧠⧠⧠ⓦ antiquarium arborense.it

Housed in the Neo-Classical Palazzo Parpaglia, this interesting museum features archaeological finds from Tharros, an art gallery and a section given over to medieval Oristano. The gallery has interesting altarpieces in Catalan style: the San Martino *retablo* (15th century) attributed

to the workshop of the Catalan artist Ramon de Mur; the *Retablo di Cristo* (1533), by followers of Pietro Cavaro, of which only nine panels remain; and the *Retablo della Madonna dei Consiglieri* (1565) by the Cagliari artist Antioco Mainas, representing the councillors of Oristano kneeling before the Virgin Mary.

The archaeological collection contains over 2,000 Neolithic obsidian scrapers, bone hair slides, small amphoras from Greece and Etruria, and Roman glass objects and oil lamps. These all belong to the Collezione Archeologica Efisio Pischedda. Among the most notable objects in the collection are a terracotta mask used to ward off evil spirits, scarabs made out of green jasper, and carved gemstones from the Roman period.

Oristano

① Cattedrale
② Torre di Mariano II
③ Corso Umberto
④ Piazza Eleonora
⑤ San Francesco
⑥ Santa Chiara
⑦ Antiquarium Arborense

0 metres 300
0 yards 300

Fishermen using *fassonis*, traditional sedge boats, on the Santa Giusta lake

⑳ Santa Giusta

Road map B4. 🚗 4,700.
ℹ️ Via Amsicora 17 (0783 35 45 00).
🎉 14 May: Sagra di Santa Giusta.

This agricultural town, built on the banks of the Santa Giusta lake and marsh, was built over the ruins of the Roman city of Ottona. The cathedral of **Santa Giusta**, a jewel of Pisan Romanesque architecture blended with Arab and Lombard elements, stands on the rise as you enter the town. The cathedral was built in the first half of the 12th century and has a narrow façade, with a triplelancet window. The columns in the interior are in various styles, and originally came from the nearby Roman cities of Neapolis, Tharros and Othoca. From the sacristy there is a lovely view of the lake, one of the best fishing areas in Sardinia, where you can still see the long *is fassonis* sedge boats of Phoenician derivation. On the feast day of Santa Giusta in May, a lively regatta is held here. The local gastronomic speciality is *bottarga* (salted mullet roe).

Soapstone scarab found in Santa Giusta digs

🏛 **Santa Giusta**
Via Manzoni. **Tel** 0783 35 92 05.
Open 8am–5:30pm. 🎫 call 346 963 0329 or 340 403 0572.

㉑ Arborea

Road map B4. 🚗 3,900. ℹ️ Town Hall (0783 80 331). 🎉 Good Friday: living representation of the Passion of Christ. 🌐 comune.arborea.or.it

Arborea was founded in 1930 during the Fascist period and was initially named Mussolinia. The town was built on a regular grid plan typical of modern cities. All the civic buildings (school, parish church, hotel and town hall) are found in Piazza Maria Ausiliatrice, from which the main streets radiate. The avenues are lined with trees and the two-storey Neo-Gothic houses are surrounded by gardens. The **Museo della Bonifica** is dedicated to the land reclamation scheme of the 1920s and 1930s, and also contains finds from excavations in the area, including the Roman necropolis of S'Ungroni, north of Arborea, discovered during the land reclamation. About 9 km (6 miles) to the southwest is the pretty fishing village of Marceddi, on the edge of the marsh of the same name, dominated by the 16th-century Torrevecchia.

🏛 **Museo della Bonifica**
Corso Italia 44. **Tel** 0783 803 3217 (by appt only). **Open** 9:30am–noon, 4:30–7pm Tue–Fri, 5–7:30pm Sat & Sun. 🎫 🌐 museoarborea.it

㉒ Fordongianus

Road map C4. 🚗 1,200. ℹ️ Via Traiano 7 (0783 601 23). 🎉 21 Apr & 21 Aug: Festa di San Lussorio.

Ancient Forum Traiani was once the largest Roman city in the interior. Located in the Tirso river valley, it was fortified against the local Barbagia people. Today the

Cathedral of Santa Giusta, a masterpiece of Romanesque architecture centre consists of houses in red and grey stone. One of the best preserved is Casa Madeddu, a typical old "Aragonese house" of the early 1600s with Catalan-style doorways and windows. On the same street is the 16th century parish church of San Pietro Apostolo, in red trachyte, which has been almost entirely rebuilt. The **Roman Baths** lie on the banks of the river, with a fine portico and several rooms with mosaic pavements. The rectangular pool still contains warm water from the hot springs.

A short distance south of Fordongianus stands the rural church of San Lussorio, built by Victorine monks around AD 1100, over an early Christian crypt.

🛈 Roman Baths
Via Terme. **Tel** 0783 60 157. **Open** 9:30am–1pm, 3–6:30pm daily. 🖼

㉓ Paulilàtino

Road map C4. 🏛 2,500. 🛈 Viale della Libertà 33 (0785 556 23). 🎪 second Sun in May: Sagra di Santa Cristina.

This rural village at the edge of the Abbasanta basalt plateau is surrounded by olive groves and cork oak woods. The houses are built of dark stone and have Aragonese doorways and small wrought-iron balconies. The same stone was used to build the church of San Teodoro in the 17th century. This Aragonese Gothic church has a stained-glass rose window and a bell tower with an onion dome. **Palazzo Atzori** houses a museum of folk culture with domestic tools and objects on display.

🏛 Palazzo Atzori
Via Nazionale 127. **Tel** 0785 554 38. **Open** summer: 9:30am–1pm, 4–7pm; winter: 9:30am–1pm, 3–5:30pm. **Closed** Mon. 🖼 🟢 ♿

Environs
About 4 km (3 miles) from town, a turning off state road 131 takes you to the nuraghic village of **Santa Cristina**. A stone wall

Village of Àles at the foot of Monte Arci

encloses the archaeological area, where there is a well temple dedicated to the local mother-goddess dating from the 1st millennium BC. The well is in a good state of preservation, and a broad stone stairway leads to its vaulted underground chamber. Nearby is an enclosure that was probably used for general assemblies. The sacred nature of this site has been maintained over the centuries with the construction of a church dedicated to Santa Cristina. Worshippers continue to flock to the church, which is surrounded by *muristenes*, houses intended for those who come here for novena on the saint's feast day.

To the right of the church, among the olive trees, another archaeological zone includes a well-preserved nuraghe and two rectangular nuraghic-age stone dwellings. The best preserved of these is 14 m (46 ft) long and 2 m (6 ft) high.

Earrings found at the Forum Traiani

🛈 Santa Cristina
Km 114,300, SS131 Cagliari-Sassari. 🛈 Cooperativa Archeotour (0785 554 38). **Open** 8:30am–dusk.

Steps leading to the temple of Santa Cristina at Paulilàtino

㉔ Àles

Road map C4. 🏛 1,700. 🛈 Town Hall (0783 91 131). 🎪 first Sun in Aug: Santa Madonna della Neve.
🌐 comune.ales.or.it

Àles, the main village in the Marmilla area, lies on the eastern slope of Monte Arci. In the upper part stands the cathedral of San Pietro, built in 1686 by Genoan architect Domenico Spotorno, who used the ruins of the 12th-century church on this site as material for his construction.

Twin bell towers with ceramic domes rise above the elegant façade, while in the Baroque interior, the sacristy has lovely carved furniture and a rare 14th-century crucifix. The Archivio Capitolare contains elegant gold jewellery.

In the same square stand the Palazzo Vescovile and the seminary and oratory of the Madonna del Rosario.

Àles is also the birthplace of Antonio Gramsci (1891–1937) *(see p129)*. The house is marked with a plaque.

Environs
Àles is a good starting point for a hike to the top of Trebina Longa and Trebina Lada, the highest peaks on **Monte Arci**, the remnants of an ancient crater. Along the way you are likely to spot pieces of obsidian, the hard black volcanic glass which was cut into thin slices and used to make arrowheads, spears and scrapers. The obsidian of Monte Arci was in great demand, and not only supplied the whole of Sardinia, but was also sold throughout the Mediterranean in the 4th–3rd millennia BC.

THE NORTH AND THE COSTA SMERALDA

Northeastern Sardinia's beauty is familiar from the classic images of a rugged coastline, beautiful inlets, sparkling turquoise sea and beaches of brilliant white sand. To the north, the islands crowded in the Straits of Bonifacio, a stone's throw from Corsica, have great appeal for those in search of unspoilt calm.

The most well-known development in the northeast is the famous Costa Smeralda, founded by a consortium of financiers including the Aga Khan in 1962. Since then, few areas in Sardinia have undergone such profound changes as the northeastern coastline. Villas and residential hotels have sprung up almost everywhere, and small harbours have been equipped as marinas. The surroundings are undeniably beautiful, with spectacular scenery at headlands such as Capo d'Orso and Capo Testa. The perfume of the Mediterranean maquis still manages to reach the beaches of pure white sand, and there are still unspoilt areas that have resisted the encroachment of holiday homes. Tourism brings its own problems however, and there is increasing recognition of the need for stricter controls on building, if the growing influx of visitors is not to damage the island's unique environment.

In the interior, the Gallura region displays quite a different character, with extensive forests of cork oak trees and rough, rocky terrain. Granite outcrops create enchanting landscapes like the Valle della Luna near Aggius *(see p156)*. This part of Sardinia is characterized by its wholesome cooking, the continuing practice of traditional handicrafts and frequent reminders of its long history. As well as prehistoric nuraghe, an exceptional series of Romanesque churches survives in the Logudoro area *(see pp160–61)*, culminating in the black and white striped stone church of Santissima Trinità di Saccargia *(see pp162–3)*.

The shore of San Teodoro, ideal for bathing and sunbathing

◄ Crystal clear waters at a pristine beach at Porto Cervo

Exploring the North and the Costa Smeralda

The port and airport in Olbia handle most of the visitors headed not only for the Costa Smeralda holiday villages, but the rest of Sardinia as well. The appeal of the northern part of Sardinia is the beautiful long coastline, with magnificent beaches and wind-eroded cliffs. From Olbia the road winds northwards to Santa Teresa di Gallura, then turns westwards, beyond the Castelsardo headland, until it reaches Porto Torres. In the interior, Tempio Pausania, capital of the Gallura region, makes an excellent starting point for local tours.

The bear-like cliff at Capo d'Orso

Sights at a Glance

The Romanesque abbey church of Tergu

For keys to symbols *see back flap*

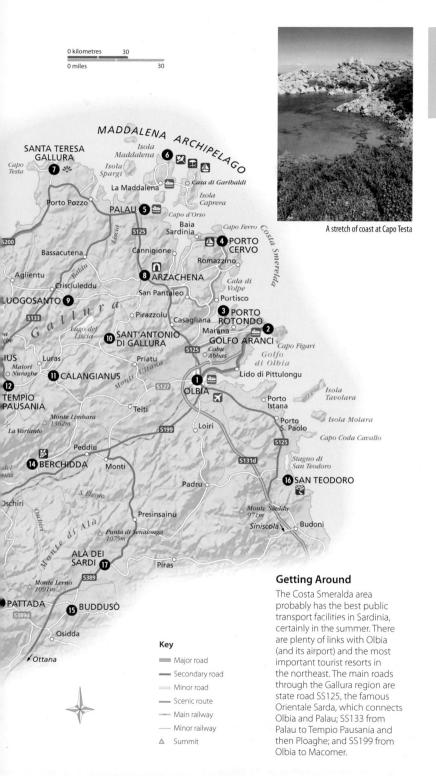

0 kilometres 30

0 miles 30

A stretch of coast at Capo Testa

MADDALENA ARCHIPELAGO

SANTA TERESA GALLURA **7**

Isola Maddalena

Capo Testa

Isola Spargi

6

La Maddalena

Casa di Garibaldi

Isola Caprera

Porto Pozzo

PALAU **5**

Capo d'Orso

S125

Baia Sardinia

Capo Ferro

Bassacutena

Cannigione

4 PORTO CERVO

Liscia

Aglientu

Crisciuleddu

San Pantaleo

Romazzino

8 ARZACHENA

Portisco

Cala di Volpe

LUOGOSANTO **9**

Pirazzolu

Casagliana

3 PORTO ROTONDO

S133

Gallura

Lago del Liscia

10 SANT'ANTONIO DI GALLURA

Marana

GOLFO ARANCI **2**

IUS

Luras

Priatu

Cabu Abbas

Capo Figari

Maiori Nuraghe

Monti Ottana

S125

Golfo di Olbia

12

11 CALANGIANUS

S127

Lido di Pittulongu

TEMPIO PAUSANIA

Telti

1 OLBIA

Porto Istana

Isola Tavolara

Monte Limbara 1362m

S199

Loiri

Porto S. Paolo

Isola Molara

La Variante

Peddiu

Capo Coda Cavallo

S125

14 BERCHIDDA

Monti

S131d

Stagno di San Teodoro

Oschiri

S. Elene

Padru

16 SAN TEODORO

del nas

Monte di Alà

Presinsainu

Monte Nieddu 971m

Siniscola

Budoni

Punta di Senalonga 1075m

17 ALÀ DEI SARDI

Piras

Monte Lerno 1091m

S389

PATTADA

S389d

15 BUDDUSÒ

Osidda

Ottana

Key

▬ Major road

▬ Secondary road

▬ Minor road

▬ Scenic route

▬ Main railway

▬ Minor railway

△ Summit

Getting Around

The Costa Smeralda area probably has the best public transport facilities in Sardinia, certainly in the summer. There are plenty of links with Olbia (and its airport) and the most important tourist resorts in the northeast. The main roads through the Gallura region are state road SS125, the famous Orientale Sarda, which connects Olbia and Palau; SS133 from Palau to Tempio Pausania and then Ploaghe; and SS199 from Olbia to Macomer.

The ruins at Cabu Abbas, a nuraghic site just outside Olbia

❶ Olbia

Road map D2. 🏔 43,000. ✈
🚋 🚌 🚢 ⓘ 0789 52 206.
📅 15–20 May: San Simplicio.
🌐 **olbiaturismo.it**

Olbia is only 200 km (125 miles) from the port of Civitavecchia on the mainland of Italy, and has always been the main arrival point on the island, rather than the capital Cagliari. The building of the airport just outside Olbia, to serve the Costa Smeralda, has confirmed this role.

Olbia is a modern city and usually considered as a stopoff on the way to the coast. Of interest in the town are a Roman cistern in Piazza Margherita, proof of ancient Roman occupation, and the Romanesque **San Simplicio.** This church was built from the 11th century onwards and enlarged in the 13th century.

Environs

There are two interesting prehistoric sites near Olbia: the **Cabu Abbas** nuraghic complex (4 km, 2 miles to the northeast) and the **Sa Testa** holy well.

To reach Cabu Abbas from the old port of Olbia, go along Corso Umberto and then Via d'Annunzio. Once past the railway you will see the country church of Santa Maria Cabu Abbas. From here a dirt path winds up towards the top of the mountain, another 15 minutes on foot. The site offers a great view of the island of Tavolara. There is a central well with a tower where remains of sacrifices – burnt bones and pieces of pottery – were found in 1937. This large megalithic zone extends for about 200 m (656 ft).

To reach the Sa Testa holy well, take road SP82 to Golfo Aranci as far as the Pozzo Sacro hotel. This site consists of a wide paved courtyard, from which 17 covered steps lead down to a well chamber.

❷ Golfo Aranci

Road map D1. 🏔 2,100. 🚋 🚌 🚢
15 Aug: Assunta. 🌐 **golfoaranci.com**

The name "Aranci" means oranges, but you will not see orange groves here. Golfo Aranci owes its name to a mistaken interpretation of the local place-name *di li ranci,* meaning

"some crabs". Formerly a part of Olbia, the village of Golfo Aranci became an independent town in 1979. Since 1882 increasing numbers of ferries from the mainland have used Golfo Aranci as a stopping place. Corsica Sardinia Ferries *(see p207)* has a direct service from here to Livorno.

Luxury sailing craft moored at the Porto Rotondo Yacht Club

❸ Porto Rotondo

Road map D1. ⓘ 0789 34 105.

Porto Rotondo is not so much a town as a large, well-planned tourist village which grew from nothing during the Costa Smeralda boom. The buildings, placed around the inevitable yacht marina, were designed to fit in as much as possible with the natural surroundings. The result is certainly pleasant, and Porto Rotondo has been a great success as a tourist resort, despite its perhaps slightly artificial air.

Mussel beds at sunset in the Bay of Olbia

For hotels and restaurants in this region see pp178–9 and p189

The Porto Rotondo quay and Piazzetta San Marco are lined with famous designer shops, and throughout the summer the cafés and restaurants are crowded with visitors, lunching, dining, meeting friends, or just watching the world go by. Out of season Porto Rotondo is quiet and even deserted.

The church of San Lorenzo, designed by Andrea Cascella, holds pretty wooden statues by Mario Ceroli depicting Biblical figures.

Just outside Porto Rotondo is the attractive headland called Punta della Volpe, which separates the Golfo di Marinella from the Golfo di Cugnana.

Boats moored in the scenic town of Porto Rotondo

Architecture on the Costa Smeralda

In the early 1960s, a stretch of coastline in northeastern Sardinia was transformed into the most exclusive tourist resort in the Mediterranean, the Costa Smeralda, or Emerald Coast. Back in 1962 the beaches were the preserve of grazing cattle, then taken to overwinter on the islands of Mortorio, Soffi and Li Milani. The Consorzio Costa Smeralda was formed to transform the area. The group initially consisted of the landowners, but expanded to include property owners. Building regulations were established and an architectural committee was founded to supervise any new building in the area. The prominent architects Luigi Vietti, Jacques Couelle, Giancarlo and Michele Busiri Vici, Antonio Simon, Raimond Martin and Leopoldo Mastrella were appointed to design the resorts. The area has since changed beyond recognition. Luxury hotels, sumptuous villas and huge holiday villages have gone up, together with sporting facilities: the famous Yacht Club and one of the most attractive golf courses in the Mediterranean, as well as small villages such as Porto Cervo.

The Neo-Mediterranean style is a combination of the various elements frequently seen in Mediterranean architecture.

In planning Porto Rotondo, the architects decided that only native plants should be used, so trees such as pine, poplar and eucalyptus are banned because they would not blend in with the local strawberry trees, myrtle, lentiscus, oleanders and mimosa.

The materials used must be traditional – local stone, pebbles, curved tiles and brick.

Pastel-coloured traditional buildings in Porto Cervo

❹ Porto Cervo

Road map D1. 📞 0789 89 20 19.
🌐 portocervoonline.com

The heart of the Costa Smeralda and a paradise for European VIPs, Porto Cervo is centred around two yacht harbours with some of the most spectacular private craft in the world. In summer there is a series of top sporting events, including regattas and golf tournaments (see p194 and p197). The traditional evening stroll along the quay is almost obligatory, with fashionable designer shops on one side, and luxury yachts on the other. The church of Stella Maris has a canvas attributed to the painter El Greco.

Environs
There are plenty of good beaches around Porto Cervo, such as Liscia Ruja to the south, framed by the sheltered Cala di Volpe.

❺ Palau

Road map D1. 📞 3,300. 📞 0789 70 70 25. 🌐 palauturismo.com

The logical departure point for a trip to the Maddalena archipelago, Palau also owes its success to the appeal of the narrow-gauge Sassari-Tempio-Palau railway, part of the Trenino Verde (see pp96–7). Life here is rather frenetic in the summer and revolves around the ferry boat wharf and the yacht harbour. From Palau you can travel to some of the most fascinating and famous places on the coast, such as the jagged Capo d'Orso (Bear Cape)

promontory, which ends in a large, bear-shaped rock, sculpted by the wind.

To get to Punta Sardegna, take the road that goes up to Monte Altura and then go on foot to the beach of Cala Trana, on the tip of the headland. There is an extraordinary view of the coast and the islands, which is particularly lovely in the early morning and at sunset, despite the fact that 21st-century

construction work is slowly but surely spoiling the unique beauty of this part of Sardinia.

❻ The Maddalena Archipelago

See pp150–51.

❼ Santa Teresa Gallura

Road map C1. 📞 4,200.
ℹ️ Piazza Vittorio Emanuele 24, 0789 75 41 27. 📅 15–18 Oct: Festival.
🌐 santateresagalluraturismo.com

The area around Santa Teresa was inhabited in Roman times and was also important to the Pisans, who used the local granite for building. The present-day town was built from scratch during the Savoyard period. It has a regular grid plan with streets intersecting at right angles, in

Sunset at Palau, departure point for the Maddalena Archipelago

The Aga Khan and the Costa Smeralda

The Consorzio Costa Smeralda group of foreign investors was founded in 1962 with Prince Karim Aga Khan IV at its head. The Harvard-educated prince, rich and charismatic, was then in his mid-twenties. He is reputed to have spent more than 1,000 million dollars in creating an opulent jet-set playground, complete with yachting marinas, luxury hotels, villas and elegant restaurants along the Gallura coastline, all designed to harmonize with the rugged Sardinian landscape. The project has proved very successful: Porto Cervo and the nearby villages quickly became popular holiday spots, especially for the wealthy and famous of the international jet set, who can be seen on the quays of Porto Cervo in the summer.

Aga Khan IV

Overlooking Santa Teresa Gallura

the middle of which is a small square and the church of San Vittorio. The local economy is based on fishing (including coral fishing) and tourism.

On the rocky headland stands the Torre Longosardo, a tower built in the 16th century during the Aragonese period; it affords a magnificent view of Porto Longone bay and, in the distance, the white cliffs circling the city of Bonifacio in Corsica, which is located only 12 km (7.5 miles) away.

To the left the coast falls away to the beach of Rena Bianca, which ends not far from the Isola Monica, a tiny island which has the remains of an abandoned quarry.

The Capo Testa lighthouse

Environs
About 5 km (3 miles) away is **Capo Testa**, a rocky promontory connected to the mainland by a thin sandbar. The headland can be reached via a very pretty route around the bays of Colba and Santa Reparata. A walk through the ancient and modern quarries – which supplied the Romans with the granite for the columns in the Pantheon – accompanied by the sweet fragrance of the maquis will take you to the Capo Testa lighthouse.

❽ Arzachena

Road map: D1. 🚗 12,000.
ℹ Piazza Risorgimento, 0789 84 40 55. 🆆 **turismoarzachena costasmeralda.it**

As recently as the 1960s, this was a peaceful shepherds' village. Today it is the centre of one of the most famous tourist resorts in the world, the Costa Smeralda, and has undergone considerable change. Towering above the houses is a curious rock formed by wind erosion, called the Fungo (mushroom), and there are many traces of prehistoric settlements in the vicinity. Prehistoric sites to be noted include the **Albucciu Nuraghe**, the **Tomba di Giganti Coddu Vecchju** and the **Li Muri Necropolis**.

🏠 Albucciu Nuraghe
🎫 Tours by Anemos, call for reservation. **Tel** 333 738 99 73. 📷 📸 🆆 **anemos-arzachena.com/ museo-eta-nuragica**

From Arzachena, take the road to Olbia and after about 600 m (650 yds), at the end of town, follow the turn-off and then take the footpath on the right.

Once at the nuraghe, go up the ladder to the upper level, to visit the side section.

The stone brackets that once supported the original wooden structure are still intact.

🏠 Tomba di Giganti Coddu Vecchju
For contact details & opening hours see Albucciu Nuraghe. 🎫 📷 📸
To get to the Giants' Tomb, take state road SS427 towards Calangianus and, after about 3 km (2 miles), take the turning to the right signposted Luogo-santo. After about 1,800 m (1 mile) you join the Capichera road; another 500 m (550 yds) on there is a path leading to the tomb, which lies to the right. In the middle of the funerary monument there is a stele 4 m (13 ft) high, surrounded by a semicircular wall of stone slabs set into the earth.

🏠 Li Muri Necropolis
For contact details & opening hours see Albucciu Nuraghe. 🎫 (book ahead for a trek combining archaeology and nature).

Once outside Arzachena, follow signs for Calangianus (SS427) and then the right-hand turning for Luogosanto. Continue for 4.5 km (3 miles) and take another turning to the right (a dirt road), which goes to the necropolis of Li Muri.

This site includes a number of ancient tombs: burial chambers surrounded by concentric circles of stones. These funerary circles constitute the most important monumental complex left from the era archaeologists now refer to as the Arzachena Culture.

The mistral whipping up the surf off Capo Testa

⓺ The Maddalena Archipelago

Seven islands (Maddalena, Caprera and Santo Stefano to the southeast, Spargi, Budelli, Razzoli and Santa Maria to the northwest) make up the Arcipelago della Maddalena. Beyond lie the Straits of Bonifacio, which became a marine reserve of international status at the beginning of 1997. Rugged, jagged coasts, rocks hewn by wind and water erosion, and tenacious maquis vegetation characterize this group of islands, known during the Roman period as *Cuniculariae*, or "rabbit islands". In the 18th century Maddalena was used as a military base – a convenient landing place, it lay in a strategically important position. A tour of the island would be incomplete without a visit to Caprera, to see the places where the Italian hero Giuseppe Garibaldi lived and is buried.

Razzoli Sar
Ma

Budelli

Budelli
Cactus grows on the shores of this island, popular with divers.

Spargi

La Madd

Spargi
Uninhabited, like Budelli, Razzoli and Santa Maria, this island has marvellously clear water and secluded beaches, making it an ideal site for swimmers, snorkellers and scuba divers.

KEY

① **A scenic route** of just over 20 km (12 miles) runs around the island, providing magnificent views of the archipelago, Corsica and the four Corsican islands of Lavezzi.

② **Guardia Vecchia** is the highest mountain on the island. The Savoy rulers chose it as the site for the fort of San Vittorio, which is now occupied by a lighthouse.

③ **The bridge over Passo della Moneta** was constructed in 1891 to link the islands of Maddalena and Caprera.

④ **Monte Teialone** is the highest point on Caprera.

Regattas
The west wind, an almost constant presence in the Maddalena archipelago, makes this a popular place for yachting competitions.

★ **La Maddalena**
This is the most important town in the archipelago. Town life centres around Piazza Umberto I and Piazza Garibaldi. There is a wide choice of boat trips to the nearby islands from the harbour.

VISITORS' CHECKLIST

Practical Information
Road map D1. 🛈 0789 79 02 11. Caprera: can be reached from Maddalena via a 600-m (2,000-ft) bridge over the Passo della Moneta. 🆆 **comune lamaddalena.gov.it**

Transport
🚤 from Palau, departures every 20 mins in the summer (once an hour after midnight) and winter.

★ **Tomb of Garibaldi**
The "hero of two worlds" was buried here on 2 June 1882.

Santo Stefano

Caprera

Caprera
The island of Caprera extends over nearly 15 sq km (6 sq miles).

Bird Life
The many rock formations in this archipelago are frequently visited by sea birds such as cormorants, to the delight of bird-watchers.

Exploring the Maddalena Archipelago

The small Maddalena Archipelago is a favourite with sailing fanatics, fans of underwater fishing and with people who appreciate tranquillity and unspoilt surroundings. Except for the two largest islands, the archipelago is uninhabited and, together with the many other small islands, make perfect summer destinations for boat trips, sunbathing and swimming in solitude.

The Sardinia Regional Naval headquarters at La Maddalena

La Maddalena

Road map D1. 🏔 12,000. 🛈 0789 79 02 11. ⛴ from Palau. 🎉 20–22 Jul: Santa Maria Maddalena.

The town that is now the capital of the island was founded in 1770 and replaced a small village built on the shores of the Cala Gavetta bay. After the unsuccessful invasion on the part of the French in 1793, British admiral Horatio Nelson stopped at La Maddalena in 1804 and in 1887 the entire Maddalena Archipelago was turned into a naval base by the Savoy rulers. On Via Amendola, which runs along the seafront, a series of 19th-century buildings bears witness to the rapid development of the town in this period. In Piazza Garibaldi, the Municipio (town hall) has on display a French bomb dating from France's attempt to conquer Sardinia in 1793.

In the evening, particularly in summer, the residents of the island can be found taking a leisurely stroll around Via Garibaldi. Not far away is the church of Santa Maria Maddalena, which has two candelabra and a silver cross given by Admiral Nelson to the island's

inhabitants. La Maddalena is still the headquarters of the Sardinia Regional Navy.

🚩 The Scenic Route

The road around the island is about 20 km (12 miles) long and goes through the Cala Spalmatore, Stagno Torto and Baia Trínita bays.

On your way from La Maddalena, you will see the church of the Trinità, then the turn-off for Monte Guardia Vecchia, on the summit of which is the Savoyard fort of San Vittorio, and lastly the island of Giardinelli, which is connected to La Maddalena by a narrow

strip of land. Further north are Porto Massimo, the inlets of Abbatoggia and Cala d'Inferno, and the other large fortification on the island, Forte dei Colmi. In the first stretch of this tour is the **Museo Archeologico Navale "Nino Lamboglia"**, the maritime museum with finds from the "ship of Spargi", an ancient Roman cargo vessel discovered in the 1950s.

🏛 Museo Archeologico Navale "Nino Lamboglia"

Località Mongiardino.
Open 10am–1pm Mon–Sat.
Tel 0789 79 06 60/33. 🅿

Caprera

Road map D1. 🛈 0789 73 63 21.
This small island has 34 km (21 miles) of coastline, and is connected to the island of Maddalena by the 600 m (1,968 ft) Passo della Moneta bridge. Walkers will enjoy the climb up the steps to the top of Monte Teialone (212 m, 695 ft).

The island of Caprera became the property of Giuseppe Garibaldi in 1856 (see pp44–5). His estate is now part of the **Compendio Garibaldino** museum area. A visit here includes a fascinating tour of the stables, moorings and the Casa Bianca (white house) where Garibaldi lived. The stable still has a period steam engine used for threshing, while the Casa Bianca contains mementos of Garibaldi's adventurous life, including weapons, flags, portraits, the hero's clothes (including his famous red shirt) and a model of the Battle of Solferino.

Garibaldi and Caprera

The legendary Italian revolutionary and hero Giuseppe Garibaldi escaped to the island of Caprera in 1849, after the fall of the Roman Republic. He returned in 1855 after the death of his wife Anita and decided to buy most of the island. The rest of the land was then given to him by some English friends. Garibaldi, who went on to play a key role in the unification of Italy, settled on Caprera permanently in 1857, and died here in 1882.

Giuseppe Garibaldi wearing the famous red shirt

The famous pink sand beach at Budelli

Garibaldi's favourite room was the salon, and he asked to be taken there before he died. The calendar and clocks in the room have not been changed since that day, and still show the exact time of his death: 6:20pm on 2 June 1882.

Caprera also has a famous sailing school, the Centro Velico Caprera (see p195).

🏛 Compendio Garibaldino

Tel 0789 72 71 62. **Open** 9am–8pm Tue–Sun (in summer); winter hours vary, call ahead. **Closed** 1 Jan, 25 Dec. 🖂 🗺 🗓 W compendio garibaldino.it

Santo Stefano

Road map D1. 🚹 0789 73 63 21. The small island of Santo Stefano lies about halfway between Palau and the island of Maddalena and can be reached via the boats that depart at regular intervals from La Maddalena harbour. Dominating the scene is the Santo Stefano (or San Giorgio) fortress, also known as Napoleon's fort, built at the end of the 18th century.

There is a tourist village on the beach of Pesce, on the western coast.

Spargi

Road map D1. 🚢 from La Maddalena. 🚹 0789 73 63 21. Spargi is little more than 2 km (1 mile) in diameter and is completely uninhabited. The terrain is fairly barren and the coast steep and inaccessible, but there is a lovely beach for bathing, although keep in mind that it has no facilities. An ancient Roman ship was found opposite the Cala Corsara cove on the southern coast; its cargo is now in the Museo Archeologico Navale "Nino Lamboglia" at La Maddalena. Tourist boats make regular stops at Cala Corsara.

Budelli

Road map D1. 🚹 0789 73 63 21. This beautiful uninhabited island is remarkable for its unique beach of rose-coloured sand. Even though there are no facilities, Budelli is popular with visitors because of its beautifully unspoiled natural setting. It was also used in a film by the director Michelangelo Antonioni.

The clear, unpolluted water is also ideal for scuba diving, either to observe marine life or for underwater fishing.

Sailing in Northern Sardinia

The Straits of Bonifacio are dotted with small islands and rocks with lighthouses which create natural buoys, making the area ideal for yacht and dinghy racing. The wind is pretty constant, and in summer the west wind blows steadily at 40 km per hour (24 mph).

The Yacht Club Costa Smeralda in Porto Cervo, founded by H.H the Aga Khan, is the main sailing facility in this area. This world-famous club organizes several major sailing races and other competitions. Among the most well-known are the Sardinia Cup, an international offshore championship held in even-numbered years, and the Settimana delle Bocche, a summer race for yachts from all over the world.

In June and September the new marina at Porto Cervo plays host to fleets of sailing superyachts and the largest gathering of Maxi class yachts takes place at the Club each year. Other important races, such as the European and world championships of various yacht categories, also take place here. The Yacht Club Costa Smeralda represented Italy in the 1983 America's Cup with the yacht *Azzurra* and in 1987 the Club organized regattas to select the Italian representative in the America's Cup in Perth, Australia.

Yachts racing in the Straits of Bonifacio

San Trano, a 12th-century hermitage near Luogosanto

❾ Luogosanto

Road map C1. 🏘 1,900. 🛈 Town Hall (079 65 790). 🎭 first Sun in Aug: San Quirico's feast day. 🆆 **comune luogosanto.gov.it**

The small village of Luogosanto is surrounded by maquis, and is well known for the production of bitter honey, often served with *sebadas (see p183)*. The village is typical of the Gallura region, backed by greenery and wind-eroded pinkish-grey rocks. Every seven years a colourful and solemn ceremony celebrates the opening of the Porta Santa (holy door) of the church of Nostra Signora di Luogosanto.

San Quirico's feast day ends with a dinner for all of the villagers. The traditional dish *carr'e cogghju*, made with pork and cabbage, is served.

About 1 km (half a mile) to the east of Luogosanto is the **San Trano hermitage**, perched at 410 m (1,345 ft), dominating the landscape towards the north of the town. This small church was built in the 12th century in memory of the hermit saints San Nicola and San Trano, who, according to the legend, lived in the small cave to the rear of the altar.

Nearby is the Filetta spring, the waters of which are famous throughout the island. Squares, steps and street lamps have been set around the spring.

❿ Sant'Antonio di Gallura

Road map D1. 🏘 1,700. 🚌 🛈 Town Hall (079 66 90 13). 🎭 last weekend in Sep: Sant'Antonio. 🆆 **comunesantantoniodi gallura.ot.it**

This village has always been an important farming and sheep-raising centre. In the heart of the town, situated on a rocky spur, is a small, archaeological park, known for its intricate landscape of windsculpted rocks. This same site was inhabited in prehistoric times. During the first week of September, the feast days of Sant'Antonio, San Michele and Sant'Isidoro are celebrated with a procession. Decorated oxen and tractors follow the statues of the saints through the streets.

Environs
Two kilometres (1 mile) away is the artificial lake of Liscia, capable of holding 150,000,000 cubic m (5 billion cubic ft) of water.

⓫ Calangianus

Road map C2. 🏘 4,800. 🚌 🛈 Town Hall (079 66 02 00). 🎭 third Sun in Sep: Sant'Isidoro's feast day. 🆆 **comune.calangianus.ot.it**

In the forests around the town of Calangianus you can see evidence of cork harvesting everywhere: the barked cork oaks have that characteristic reddish colour that will remain until the bark grows again, while the cork strips themselves are heaped up in large piles to dry.

Calangianus is the cork production centre of the Gallura region and there are numbers of workshops and factories for processing the material. There is also an important trade school whose curriculum focuses on the cultivation of cork oaks and

The artificial lake of Liscia near Calangianus

For hotels and restaurants in this region see pp178–9 and p189

making the maximum use of cork bark. In September every year Calangianus hosts an exhibition and trade fair of cork oaks and their many by-products, both on an industrial and domestic scale.

In the centre of the old town, in a small, isolated square, is the small parish church of Santa Giusta, which was built in the 17th century.

Cork items produced in the Gallura region

Environs
Near the village of **Luras** (northwest of Calangianus), a series of prehistoric dolmens is open to visitors. To reach the site, go through the village in the direction of Luogosanto and then turn right just before the end of town. At the point where the paved road ends, take the dirt road on the right, which takes you to the **Ladas Dolmen**, the most impressive of them all. It has a rectangular plan, is roofed with two granite slabs, and is 6 m (19 ft) long and 2.20 m (7 ft) wide.

⑫ Tempio Pausania

Road map C2. ⚉ 14,000. ▦
ℹ Pro Loco (079 631 273).
⚑ Shrove Tuesday: Carnival.
Ⓦ comune.tempiopausania.ot.it

The capital of Gallura, Tempio Pausania consists of a large number of modern buildings which tend to obscure the charming old town. Investigate further and discover two- and three-storey buildings with dark granite stone walls and characteristic balconies. A short walk from the central Piazza Gallura, site of the town hall and other public buildings, is the **Cathedral** – founded in the 15th century but rebuilt in the 1800s. Also nearby are the Oratorio del Rosario and the small **Santa Croce** church.

Detail of Santa Croce

Not far from town are the **Rinaggiu springs**, whose mineral water is famous for its beneficial qualities. As well as the traditional festivals, an international folklore festival is held here in July (see p31).

Environs
A short distance away, on state road SS133, is the turning for the **Maiori Nuraghe**, one of the best preserved megalithic structures in the area. By heading south from the town on state road 392 for 17 km (10 miles) you will pass close to the summit of **Monte Limbara** (1,359 m, 4,459 ft), which can be reached in a few minutes on foot from the paved road. Along the way you will see the Curadoreddu road house (about 6 km, 4 miles, from Tempio Pausania); here, a turning to the left will take you to an abandoned fish farm, from which you can admire an impressive view of mountain rock pools and waterfalls. Water flows from one great mass of rocks to the other, creating cascades and hollows. The spectacle is at its most striking during the winter months.

The bed of the mountain stream near Curadoreddu

Cork and the Handicrafts of Gallura

Strips of cork bark ready for processing

Cork is obtained from the stripped bark of cork oak trees (*Quercus suber*) and has always been a fundamental part of the Gallura regional economy. The material is used for everyday purposes as well as local handicrafts. Among kitchen utensils in use are cork spoons and ladles (such as the *s'uppu*, a small ladle used to collect water), buckets and different containers for water and wine, and large serving dishes – called *agiones* in dialect – for roasts and other dishes. Today the Tempio Pausania region produces 90 per cent of the bottle stoppers used in Italy, although the cork is also used as a building and insulating material.

Cork is very versatile, thanks to its lightness, resistance to air and water, its insulating properties and long life. Cork cannot be stripped from the tree before it is at least 25–30 years old. The first layer stripped is porous and elastic and of scant commercial use. Only nine to ten years after this first barking process is the true – and profitable – new layer of cork obtained. The trees are then stripped every nine to ten years, and the layers thoroughly seasoned before use.

A barked cork oak tree

The Valle della Luna (Valley of the Moon) near Aggius

⑬ Aggius

Road map C2. ⚄ 1,200. **ℹ** Town Hall (079 62 10 60). 🎭 first Sun in Oct: feast days of Santa Vittoria and Madonna del Rosario. **w comune aggius.gov.it**

Natural features have shaped this village and its surroundings. A granite outcrop dominates the landscape of Aggius, both in the high ground of the Parco Capitza, which towers over the town, and in the amazing labyrinth of rock formations in the nearby Valle della Luna.

Once the dominion of the Doria family from Genoa, and then ruled by the Aragonese, Aggius owes its present prosperity to the quarrying and processing of granite. Local handicrafts are also important to the economy – especially rug-making, every stage of which is carried out using traditional techniques.

The centre of Aggius is a pleasant place to walk; the old stone houses have been lovingly preserved and they are among the most attractive in the Gallura region. On

the first Sunday in October traditional festivities are held, including the *di li 'agghiani*, for unmarried men, at which the Gallura *suppa cuata* (bread and cheese soup) is served.

The road to Isola Rossa will quickly bring you to the **Valle dolla Luna**, with its weird rock formations, which are the legacy of glaciation. On a left-hand curve a dirt road veers right. Follow this almost up to the bridge, then continue along the small road on the right, which leads to the **Izzana Nuraghe** in the middle of the valley.

Rock formations above Aggius

⑭ Berchidda

Road map C2. ⚄ 3,400. 🚌
ℹ Town Hall (079 70 39 01).
w comune.berchidda.ot.it

Built on the southern slopes of Monte Limbara, in a hilly landscape which stretches as far as Monte Azzarina, Berchidda is a large village whose economy is based on sheep raising, dairy products, cork processing and viticulture. The leading local wine is Vermentino (one of the best known of Sardinian white wines), and the local pecorino cheese is also of excellent quality.

About 4 km (2 miles) from the centre of Berchidda, a steep climb will take you to the ruins of the **Castello di Montacuto**, which was the fortress of Adelasia di Torres and her husband Ubaldo Visconti before becoming the domain of the Doria and Malaspina families from the mainland. Monte Limbara, the geographical heart of the Gallura region, towers in the background.

Cheese and white Vermentino wine, locally made produce from Sardinia

⑮ Buddusò

Road map C2 & D2. ⚄ 6,500.
ℹ Town Hall (079 715 90 00).

The town of Buddusò is fairly prosperous thanks to sheep farming, granite quarrying and the processing and sale of cork.

The stone-paved streets in the old part of town wind around buildings made of dark stone. In the Roman era the main road from Kàralis (Cagliari) to Olbia crossed the town, then known as Caput Thirsi. The church of **Santa Anastasia** and the paintings in the sacristy are worth a visit. A tour through the **Monti di Alà** is another worthwhile excursion.

Environs

Nearby are **Iselle Nuraghe** (on the road to Pattada) and **Loelle Nuraghe**, towards Mamone.

A *cuile*, or seasonal shepherd's hut, still a common sight in this region

⓰ San Teodoro

Road map D2. 🚹 2,900. 🛈 0784 86 57 67. 🌐 santeodoroturismo.it

To the south of the Capo Coda Cavallo headland, just opposite the rocky island of Tavolara, the village of San Teodoro has grown rapidly in recent years due to increasing numbers of tourists.

The village also makes an excellent starting point for excursions to the Cinta beach, a long strip of sandy terrain that separates the **Stagno di San Teodoro** from the sea. Fairly close to the Orientale Sarda road, this lake and marsh

The Island of Tavolara

This island is a mountain of limestone rising from the sea to a height of 500 m (1,640 ft). The eastern side is an inaccessible military zone, but the low sandy area called Spalmatore di Terra has beaches, a small harbour, a couple of restaurants and a few houses. Together with the neighbouring islands of Molara and Molarotto, home to over 150 moufflons, Tavolara is a marine reserve. The granite cliffs are pierced by caves and crevices. Sea lilies grow in the Spalmatore di Terra area and the rock is covered with juniper, helichrysum, rosemary and lentiscus. According to tradition, Carlo Alberto, the king of Piedmont and Sardinia, landed on the island to find the legendary "goats with golden teeth" (a phenomenon caused by a grass they eat), and was so fascinated by the island that he officially dubbed its only inhabitant, Paolo Bertolini, "king of Tavolara". In the summer there is a regular boat service to the island from Olbia (*see p146*) and Porto San Paolo.

The unmistakable profile of the island of Tavolara

is one of the few remaining coastal marshes that once lay south of the Bay of Olbia. Mallards and coots are easily sighted on the water. When the birds glimpse a bird of prey or other danger, they gather in large groups

and make a loud noise to defend themselves. Grey and red heron as well as Kentish plovers can be seen in search of food. Another common sight is the hovering kestrel, one of Italy's smallest raptors.

Granite outcrops are used as a resting place by ducks.

Kestrel

The clear, still water is rich in food for birds.

Grey heron

The shores are ideal for mud-dwelling creatures.

Lapwing

The Stagno di San Teodoro

The Ruju nuraghe outside the village of Alà del Sardi

⑰ Alà dei Sardi

Road map D2. 🏛 2,000. 🚹 Buddusò
Town Hall (079 723 90 10). 🎭 4 Oct:
countryside feast day of San Francesco.
W comune.aladeisardi.ot.it

Rocks and maquis, and forests
of enormous cork oaks with the
characteristic marks of recent
stripping, make up the landscape
of Alà dei Sardi and its plateau,
the last tract of the rocky interior
overlooking the Bay of Olbia.

The main street of the village
is lined with the small granite
stone houses characteristic
of this region.

Environs
Not far from Alà dei Sardi,
off the road which leads to
Buddusò, is the **Ruju nuraghe**,
with the remains of a prehistoric
village almost buried in the
scrub. Following signs to the
town of Monti, the route crosses
a sizeable plateau studded
with astonishingly varied
rock formations. At a
fork, the road deviates
for the sanctuary of
San Pietro l'Eremita,
and passes through
some stunning
scenery, with gaps
allowing occasional
views of the sea and
the unmistakable
profile of the island of
Tavolara *(see p157)* in
the distance. Every year
in August at Ferragosto
(Assumption Day), the
restored Romanesque
church of San Pietro
l'Eremita is crowded
with pilgrims from the
surrounding villages.

⑱ Pattada

Road map C2. 🏛 3,800. 🚹 Town
Hall (079 75 51 14). 🎭 29 Aug: Santa
Sabina. **W** comune.pattada.ss.it

Situated in the middle of a
territory rich in prehistoric
nuraghi and other vestiges
of the past, Pattada is world-
famous for the production
of steel knives, which began
here because of a rich vein
of iron ore which has been
worked for centuries. The
village blacksmiths still carry
on the tradition of making steel
blades, and handles from
animal horn, and dozens of

The Sa Fraigada forest near Pattada

The Knives of Pattada

The best-known style of shepherd's knife made
in Pattada is the *resolza* (the word derives from
the Latin *rasoria*, or razor). The *resolza* is a jack-knife
with a steel blade that may be as much as 14 cm
(5 inches) long. The blacksmiths of Pattada only
use traditional materials. Steel is hammered into
shape in a forge and on an anvil; the handle is
made from wood, or from moufflon, sheep or deer horn. The
production of Pattada knives dates from the mid-19th century, and
the best knives are
still hand-made by
skilled craftsmen.
Among the masters
at work today
some, like Salvatore
Giagu and Maria Rosaria Deroma, draw inspiration
from the oldest types of Pattada knives, such as the
fixed-blade *corrina*, which dates back to the 18th
century. It is not easy to find real Pattada knives on
sale, and you should avoid imitations. Production is a
slow and complicated affair, but it is possible to order
a Pattada knife to be made for you, although this
procedure will take about a year.

Sheath

The handles are
made of wood
or horn.

The blade is
made of hand-
wrought steel.

An assortment of Pattada knives

The artificial lake created by the Rio Mannu at Pattada

imitations of these Sardinian knives can now be found on the Italian mainland.

Environs

In the vicinity of Pattada is the **Fiorentini** – an area of greenery resulting from reforestation – and the ruins of the medieval castle of Olomene.

Earthenware found in the Grotta di San Michele

⑲ Ozieri

Road map C2. ⚐ 12,000. ☒
ℹ Town Hall (079 78 12 00); Pro Loco (079 78 30 13); Comunità Montana del Monte Acuto (079 781 06 00).
🎉 second Sun in May: Sant'Antioco di Bisarcio. 🆆 comune.ozieri.ss.it

Ozieri lies in a natural hollow and its situation is one of the most attractive sights in northeast Sardinia. Both the traditions and architecture here are interesting, and the town has a fascinating history that goes back millennia and has added to the knowledge of the remote pre-nuraghic cultures which developed here.

The fabric and layout of the town are quite varied and blend in well with the slopes of the hills. Among the tall houses the occasional covered roof terrace filled with flowers can be glimpsed. The major sights in the old town are **Piazza Carlo Alberto** and **Piazza Fonte Grixoni**, centred around an ancient fountain. On the edge of the historic quarter is the Neo-Classical **Cathedral**, which contains a splendid 16th-century Sardinian polyptych by the artist

known as the Maestro di Ozieri. The painting depicts the famous miracle of the Sanctuary of the Madonna of Loreto, and reveals Spanish influences as well as traces of Flemish mannerism. The 17th-century San Francesco monastery houses the **Museo Archeologico**, with finds from the archaeological digs in the area. Most of this material belongs to the era of the Ozieri civilization, the predominant culture here from 3500 to 2700 BC. It is also known as San Michele, from the name of the cave in which major finds were discovered.

The territory surrounding Ozieri is also rich in historic and archaeological sites and ruins, such as the *domus de janas* at Butule, the San Pantaleo necropolis and the dolmen at Montiju Coronas.

The **Grotta di San Michele** is a cave that lies behind the Ozieri hospital, near the track and field stadium (in fact, during the construction of the latter, part of the cave was destroyed). Large quantities of decorated ceramics were found here, as well as human bones, a mother-goddess statuette and pieces of obsidian from Monte Arci. All these finds support the theory that there was some continuity from the earlier Bonu Ighinu culture to the time of the Ozieri.

🏛 **Museo Archeologico di Ozieri**
Piazza Pietro Micca. **Tel** 079 785 10 52.
Open 9am–1pm, 3–7pm Tue–Sun (until 6pm Sun. ♿ 🅿 🆆 **museo. comune.ozieri.ss.it**

🏛 **Grotta di San Michele**
Ozieri Hospital. **Tel** 079 78 76 38.
Open 10am–1pm, 3–5pm (4–6pm in summer) Tue–Sun.
🎫 combined ticket for both sites.

The cathedral surrounded by houses in the town of Ozieri

⑳ Tour of the Logudoro

After the fall of the Roman Empire, Sardinia did not return to a central role in the Mediterranean until after the year 1000, when Pisan and Genoese merchants, soldiers and preachers came into contact with the different regional cultures of the island. The Romanesque churches in the north of Sardinia are the result of these encounters. It is difficult to assess how much of each single monument was created by local artists and artisans and how much by those from Pisa and Genoa. Whatever the facts, east of Sassari there is a series of Romanesque churches that has few equals in the rest of mainland Italy.

⑦ Nostra Signora di Tergu
This church was built over the remains of a monastery founded by monks from Montecassino in Tuscany.

① Santissima Trinità di Saccargia
The Santissima Trinità, built in striped layers of black and white stone, is the most significant example of Romanesque architecture in northern Sardinia. The apse is decorated with frescoes of Christ and the saints. The church was restored in the early 1900s *(see pp162–3)*.

② San Michele di Salvènero (Ploaghe)
In the 12th century the monks of Vallombrosa built this church near the village of Salvènero, which has since disappeared. The church now stands abandoned in the middle of a series of road interchanges. Restored in the 13th century and again in 1912, this splendid monument needs to attract greater care and respect to safeguard its future.

③ Santa Maria del Regno (Ardara)
Consecrated in 1107, this Pisan-Romanesque church is famous for the *Retablo Maggiore di Ardara*, one of the best on the island. The paintings on the altar-step are by the Sardinian Giovanni Muru (1515).

Castelsardo

Valledoria

200

134

127

⑦

132

Sassari

Nuraghe di Camarzu

127

①

Ploaghe

②

597

⑥ San Pietro di Simbranos (or delle Immagini)

The traditional name of this church derives from the bas-relief on the façade depicting an abbot and two monks (the *immagini* or "images"). San Pietro, in the Bulzi area, was first built in 1113 and rebuilt in its present form a century later. This isolated and tranquil monument has a particular fascination because of its desert setting among canyons and rocks.

⑤ Nostra Signora di Castro (Oschiri)

Dominating Lake Coghínas, this church blends Lombard and local architectural elements. It was built in the second half of the 12th century and is surrounded by the *cumbessias* enclosure of pilgrims' houses, built at a later date.

④ Sant'Antioco di Bisarcio (Ozieri)

Sant'Antioco is a combination of Pisan Romanesque and French influences. Sant'Antioco was built from the second half of the 11th century to the late 12th century and was initially the cathedral of the Bisarcio diocese. It differs from the other churches on this tour in its architectural complexity, shown in the unusual two-storey porch, small windows and the decorative detail on the façade.

Key

━━ Major road
══ Other roads
─── River

0 kilometres 5
0 miles 5

㉑ Santissima Trinità di Saccargia

Both simple and impressive, Sardinia's most famous Romanesque church stands in the middle of a windswept valley. Its name probably derives from *sa acca argia*, "the dappled cow". According to legend, this animal used to kneel in prayer on the site, which is why there are carvings of the cow on four sides of one of the capitals in the portico. Another account relates how, around the year 1112, the ruler of the region, Constantine, donated the small church to the Camaldolesi monks, who then decided to enlarge it with the help of Tuscan architects, craftsmen and labourers. Initially they added the apse and the bell tower with its alternating layers of black trachyte and white limestone. At a later stage they built the porch, the only one of its kind on a Sardinian church. The austere interior, with a tall, narrow nave lit by small openings or slots in the side walls, is very atmospheric.

Animal Frieze
The severity of the exterior of the church is lightened with sculptures of animals.

Portico Capitals
The portico is supported by columns with carved capitals. They carry the classic Romanesque motifs of plants and animals.

★ Façade
Two rows of blind arches adorn the façade, each level decorated with rose windows and multicoloured diamonds. The central arch has an opening in the form of a cross.

★ Carved Cows
It may be that the church was named after the carved cows on this capital, even though the portico was built after the main church.

KEY

① **The campanile** is 41 m (134 ft) tall and each side is 8 m (26 ft) wide.

② **The black and white stripes** reveal Pisan influence.

③ **The aisleless nave** was built after the apse, which dates from 1116.

Double-lancet Windows
These date from the late 12th century.

Fresco of Christ
Christ is depicted holding a book in the act of benediction.

Monastery Ruins
Only a few black and white stone archways are left of the first and most important Camaldolese monastery in Sardinia.

★ The Apse Frescoes
Romanesque frescoes are rare in Sardinia – these are attributed to Pisan artists.

㉒ Sassari

Sardinia's second most important city commercially, politically and culturally, Sassari lies on a tableland that slopes down to the sea among olive groves and well cultivated valleys. The city has a long history of invasions, conquests and raids, but also boasts a tradition of stubborn rebellion and uprisings. Pisans, Genoese and Aragonese have all attempted to subdue the city, but the indomitable spirit of the Sassari citizens has always succeeded in asserting independence. The city's hero is a rebel named Carlo Maria Angioj, who headed a revolt in 1796 against the Savoyard government, which had sought to impose a feudal system. Two presidents of the Italian Republic, Antonio Segni and Francesco Cossiga, were born in Sassari, as was the prominent Italian Communist Party leader Enrico Berlinguer *(see pp48–9)*.

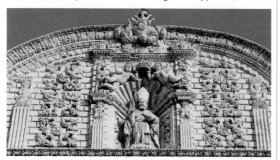

Detail of the façade of Sassari Cathedral

Exploring Sassari

The old town, with its winding alleyways branching off from the main streets, was once surrounded by walls. Only a few parts of the city walls (such as the section at the beginning of Corso Trinità) have survived the effects of time, but the old centre has preserved its original layout, even though it is now somewhat dilapidated.

A morning should be enough time for a walk around the old town. The main sights are the Duomo (cathedral), the Fontana del Rosello fountain, the churches of Sant'Antonio, Santa Maria di Betlem and San Pietro in Silki, and the Sanna museum.

🏛 Duomo

Piazza Duomo. **Tel** 079 23 20 67. **Open** 8:30am–noon, 4–5:30pm daily. ♿
Sassari cathedral is dedicated to San Nicola (St Nicholas). Its impressive Baroque façade is in rather striking contrast to its size and to the small, simple and elegant 18th-century Piazza Duomo with its characteristic

semicircular shape. The end result of successive enlargements and changes carried out over the centuries, the Duomo was originally built on the site of a Romanesque church. The base of the façade and bell tower are still intact.

At the end of the 15th century the original structure underwent radical transformation that not only changed its shape but created today's unusual proportions. The side walls were propped up by buttresses decorated with gargoyles of

mythical and monstrous animals, while the interior was rebuilt in the Gothic style.

In the late 18th century grand decorations were added to the façade: volutes, flowers, cherubs and fantastic figures. In the middle, the statue of San Nicola is surmounted by the figures of the three martyr saints, Gavino, Proto and Gianuario, set in three niches. At a later stage, an octagonal section decorated with multi-coloured majolica tiles was superimposed on the original Lombard-style lower part of the campanile. The interior, which has been totally restored, has retained its simple Gothic lines despite the presence of lavishly decorated Baroque altars. The choir, the work of 18th-century Sardinian artists, is particularly striking.

The Museo del Duomo, reached through the Cappella Aragonese (Aragonese chapel) on the right, houses the processional standard, a 15th-century panel painting. There is also a silver statue of San Gavino, embossed using a Mexican technique that was in fashion in the late 17th century.

🏛 Santa Maria di Betlem

Piazza Santa Maria. **Tel** 079 23 57 40. **Open** 7am–noon, 5–8pm daily (winter: to 7pm daily).
The church of Santa Maria di Betlem is situated in the square of the same name, at the northwestern entrance to the city. Built by Benedictine monks in 1106, it was later donated to the Franciscans. Unfortunately, the elegant original structure was the subject of frequent rebuilding in the 18th and 19th centuries, and the church has lost its early

The *Li Candareri* festival in Sassari

qualities of lightness and purity of form. The only intact part of the earlier church is the 13th-century façade, decorated with small columns and capitals and pierced by a lovely 15th-century rose window. The Gothic interior, once austere, has been spoiled by the heavy-handed Baroque decoration and altars; yet the original side chapels are intact, each dedicated to a craftsmen's guild as a reminder of the social role the church played in the community. To this day, on 14 August, the date of the *De li Candareri* festivities, the votive candles donated by the various guilds are carried here in procession from the Chiesa del Rosario.

The cloister is partly walled in but can still be visited. It contains the 14th-century granite stone Brigliadore

The church of Santa Maria di Betlem in Sassari

fountain, once the source of most of Sassari's water supply.

🚇 Corso Vittorio Emanuele

The city's main street crosses the heart of the old town and connects Piazza Sant'Antonio and Piazza Cavallino. The Corso is lined with 19th-century houses and 16th-century Aragonese buildings, and you can often catch a glimpse of courtyards and interiors that testify to their former splendour. This is Sassari's main shopping street, with shops of all kinds, from clothing to ironmongery.

🏛 Sant'Antonio Abate

Piazza Sant'Antonio. **Open** 7–10am daily, 4:30–7:30pm Sat.

Dating from the early 1700s, the stately Baroque façade of this church, with its simple elegance, dominates the tree-lined square at the end of Corso Trinità. The upper part of the portal still bears the emblem of

the brotherhood responsible for building the church. The Latin cross interior boasts one of the most elegant high altars in Sassari, which bears a carved and gilded wooden altarpiece. The panels were executed in the late 1700s by the Genoese painter Bartolomeo Augusto.

The church stands in Piazza Sant'Antonio, once the site of the old northern gate of the same name, and formerly the hub of the city's commercial and political life. The only vestiges of the past are a part of the medieval city walls, and a battlemented tower to the left of the church.

Sassari

1. Duomo
2. Santa Maria di Betlem
3. Corso Vittorio Emanuele
4. Sant'Antonio Abate
5. Fontana del Rosello
6. Palazzo di Città
7. Chiesa di Santa Caterina
8. Piazza d'Italia
9. Museo Archeologico Nazionale

0 metres 300
0 yards 300

The Fontana del Rosello, dating from the Renaissance

📷 Fontana del Rosello
Via Col di Lana.

On the right-hand side of the church of Santissima Trinità, in Piazza Mercato, a small stone stairway known as the Col di Lana will take you to the Fontana del Rosello, the fountain at the lower end of the Valverde gorge.

Unfortunately, very little remains of the steep valley and woods that were once the natural backdrop for this little jewel of late Renaissance art. However, this has not diminished the locals' love for their fountain, which has become one of the city's symbols.

This was once the haunt of the enlightened bourgeoisie and the place where the local water carriers drew water from the eight lions' mouths sculpted at the base of the fountain.

The fountain was executed in the early 1600s by Genoese artists, who still had a preference for the classical styles of the Renaissance. The base consists of two superimposed white and green marble boxes. The lions' mouths are surrounded by statues symbolizing the four seasons. The original statues were destroyed in the 1795–6 uprisings *(see p164)* and were replaced in 1828.

In the middle, a bearded divinity, known as Giogli, is surrounded by small towers symbolizing the city. On the top of the fountain are two arches which protect the figure of San Gavino.

🏛 Palazzo di Città
Corso Emanuele II 35. **Tel** 079 201 5122. **Open** Nov–Apr: 10am–1pm, 5–8pm Tue–Sat, 10am–1pm Sun. 📷

This Neo-Classical palazzo was built between 1826 and 1829, after the demolition of the pre-existing Municipal House. It was designed by the Piedmontese architect Guiseppe Cominotti, who based the building on the Teatro Carignano in Turin. It features a beautiful small room in the shape of a horse-shoe.

There is an interesting display of local costumes and 19th-century paintings and water-colours illustrating everyday rural and town life, as well as religious and civil events. The Municipal Theatre and the Tourist Board are also housed here.

Hanging on the walls are traditional Sardinian rugs, which resemble abstract paintings with their geometric patterns. There is also fine bobbin lacework and – of interest although not valuable – baskets

📷 Chiesa di Santa Caterina
Via Santa Caterina. **Tel** 079 23 16 92. **Open** pm for Mass.

This church was built at the end of the 16th century for the Jesuits and combines Sardinian Gothic style with Renaissance elements.

In the interior there are paintings by the artist Giovanni Bilevelt.

📷 Piazza d'Italia
This large square is laid out at the edge of the 19th-century quarter of Sassari. It is a well-proportioned public space, surrounded by elegant Neo-Classical buildings and with tall palm trees and well-kept flower beds, guarded by a statue of Vittorio Emanuele II.

One of the finest buildings is the Palazzo della Provincia (provincial government building), built in pure Neo-Classical style. The council chamber on the first floor is open to the public. On the walls are 19th-century paintings depicting important events in the city's political history, such as *The Proclamation of the Sassari Statutes* and *Carlo Maria Angioj Entering Sassari (see p164)*. You can also see the adjacent royal apartments, built in 1884 on the occasion of the King of Sardinia's visit. In summer the courtyard is the venue for concerts and plays.

of dwarf palm wood, terracotta pots and other everyday objects whose design and techniques have been handed down over centuries of tradition. Items on display are for sale.

The entrance to Palazzo di Cittá, Sassari

Sassari's Piazza d'Italia, framed by the Neo-Classical Palazzo della Provincia

The lovely 19th-century Bargone and Crispi arcades on the northwestern side of Piazza d'Italia shelter the city's oldest bars and pastry shops and lead to Piazza Castello.

Entrance to the Museo Nazionale "GA Sanna" in Sassari

🏛 Museo Archeologico Nazionale "GA Sanna"

Via Roma 64. **Tel** 079 27 22 03. **Open** 9am–8pm Tue–Sun. 🅿 🚫 ♿ 🅦 museosannasassari. beniculturali.it

The Sassari archaeological museum was donated to the Italian state by the Sanna family, who built these premises in 1931 to house finds collected by Giovanni Antonio Sanna, an important figure in the island's history and director of the local mine.

Two entire storeys are given over to various periods of Sardinian civilizations, from the Neolithic to the Middle Ages. Arrowheads, nuraghic bronze statuettes, amphoras, furnishings, weapons, tools, ceramics and jewels are on

display in chronological order. On the ground floor, panels illustrate the evolution of Sardinia, and every room has time charts on display.

There are also architectural reconstructions of prehistoric buildings such as dwellings, *domus de janas* (rock-cut tombs) and giants' tombs. In the last hall, among floor plans, sarcophagi and statues there is a reconstructed mosaic floor from a patrician Roman villa in nearby Turris Libisonis (present-day Porto Torres). The mosaic shows lobsters, sea horses, and seals chasing one another in an eternal circle. The next room contains a small art gallery with works by Sardinian artists from the 14th to the 20th centuries.

There is also a traditional crafts section with jewels, costumes, musical instruments and craftsmen's tools, almost all of which are still used in central-northern Sardinia.

🔼 San Pietro in Silki

Via delle Croci. **Tel** 079 21 60 67. **Open** 6:15am–noon, 4–7pm daily.

The Romanesque church of San Pietro in Silki faces a lovely tree-lined square and was most probably named after the medieval quarter built here in the 1100s. Its simple 17th-century façade has a large atrium leading to the Gothic nave with four side chapels. The first of these was dedicated to the Madonna delle Grazie in the second half of the 15th century. It is named for a statue of the Virgin Mary, found inside a column from the square in front of the church. The statue is one of the best examples of Catalan Gothic sculpture in Sardinia.

On the other side of the square, opposite San Pietro, is the Frati Minori monastery, which houses one of the island's richest libraries. The collections consist of over 14,000 volumes, removed from Franciscan monasteries after their closure.

The Romanesque church of San Pietro in Silki, Sassari

The harbour at Castelsardo

㉓ Castelsardo

Road map C2. 5,500. *i* Pro Loco (079 47 15 06). Easter Monday: Lunissanti procession. **W castelsardo turismo.it**

Perched on a volcanic headland, Castelsardo has known a number of name changes in its history. The town was founded in 1102 by the aristocratic Doria family from Genoa, and was originally known as Castelgenovese, a name it kept until 1448, when it became Castellaragonese, after the town's new conquerors. The present name dates from 1776.

The town is dominated by the castle (**Castello**), which now houses a museum with exhibits of traditional basket-weaving. Overlooking the sea is the cathedral of Sant'Antonio Abate.

Local basketwork

The alley-ways of the centre of town are lined with small shops selling all kinds of local handicrafts. Fish-lovers will do well here, as the local cuisine is based on freshly caught fish and lobsters.

On Easter Monday, the traditional **Lunissanti** procession is held in Castelsardo. The streets are lit by flaming torches, and traditional hooded figures form a slow procession, to the sound of three songs, *Lu Stabat*, *Lu Jesu* and *Lu Miserere*. These songs are centuries old, and probably date from before Catalan rule. They have been handed down by word of mouth ever since. The solemn procession, one of the most well-known of Sardinia's Easter festivals, ends at the church of **Santa Maria**.

▦ Castello and Museo dell'Intreccio

Via Marconi. **Tel** 347 111 85 47. **Open** Sep–Jun: 9:30am–1pm, 3–5:30pm daily (to 7:30pm May, Jun & Sep); Jul & Aug: 9am–midnight daily (times vary according to season, call ahead).

Built in the 13th and 14th centuries, this fortress is now occupied by the **Museo dell'Intreccio** (museum of wickerwork). Local baskets are made from traditional materials such as palm, asphodel and cane. From the castle terraces there are fantastic views; on clear days you can see Corsica.

Sant'Antonio Abate in Castelsardo, its bell tower topped by an onion dome

⛪ Cattedrale di Sant'Antonio Abate

Via Seminario. **Open** 8am–6pm daily. Constructed in the 17th century on the site of an existing Romanesque church, the cathedral has a bell tower roofed with majolica tiles. From the tower there is a splendid view of the water below. The cathedral contains fine 16th-century, carved wooden furnishings.

The town of Castelsardo and the castle above

The Roccia dell'Elefante (Elephant Rock) near Castelsardo

ⓘ Santa Maria

Via Vittorio Emanuele. **Open** ask priest for keys.

In the heart of the old town, the upper part of Castelsardo, stands the church of Santa Maria. The building does not have a façade, and entry is gained through the side door. In the interior is a 14th-century crucifix known as the *Cristo Nero* (Black Christ). The church is the focus of the Lunissanti Easter procession, which starts and ends here.

🕳 La Roccia dell'Elefante

To one side of the road near Multeddu, not far from Castelsardo, stands the impressive Roccia dell'Elefante (Elephant Rock). This massive block of dark trachyte rock has been gradually sculpted by the wind into the shape of an elephant with its trunk raised. In ancient times the rock was used as a burial place. At the base you can still see small carved openings for several *domus de janas* (rock-cut tombs).

㉔ Isola Rossa

Road map C1.

The hills of Gallura slope down towards the sea, forming a landscape characterized by rose-coloured crags, sculpted into strange shapes by wind erosion. The small fishing village of Isola Rossa lies on a headland, at the foot of an impressive 16th-century sentinel tower. The village is not an island *(isola)*, but was given its name ("red island") after the small, reddish-coloured rock island out in the bay. Fishing boats are drawn up on the beach below the village after each day's catch is brought in.

The coastline either side of Isola Rossa is worth visiting, especially towards the east, where Monte Tinnari overlooks the sea. To the west, the coast gently slopes to meet the mouth of the Rio Coghina, a short distance from Castelsardo.

Environs

A short distance from Isola Rossa is the small agricultural town of **Trinità d'Agultu**, which developed in the late 19th century around the church of the same name. As is so often the case in Sardinia, the simple country church became a sanctuary and pilgrimage site. As a result, it is also an important trade and commercial centre during the associated religious festivities and pilgrimages.

The fishing fleet at Isola Rossa

The Fishing Industry

The Sardinians are historically a nation of shepherds. Despite this, fishing is still an important activity, even though for centuries it has been carried out almost exclusively by non-Sardinian immigrants: people from the island of Ponza at Castelsardo, and Neapolitans, who founded the village of Isola Rossa in the early 20th century. Nowadays a major source of income in these two places is the cultivation of mussels and shellfish. Tuna fishing, once widespread off the northwest coast, no longer survives in northern Sardinia, the small trawlers having been unable to compete with deep-sea fishing, now practised on an industrial scale.

Craftsman at work making a lobster pot

TRAVELLERS'
NEEDS

WHERE TO STAY

The legendary allure of Sardinia's beaches has resulted in a boom in tourist facilities, especially along the coast, and visitors can now choose from a wide range of hotels and holiday villages. The exclusive and world-famous hotels built on the Costa Smeralda in the early 1960s cater to the wealthy, but less expensive accommodation is also available. Luxury hotels and resorts are common in the south, while the western coast offers plenty of reliable family-run lodgings. On the eastern coast, comfortable and well-equipped tourist villages are easily found, many offering self-catering as an option. The interior has some excellent hotels, especially in the Gennargentu and Barbagia areas, where travellers can also take advantage of organized excursions. For further information, listings and descriptions of hotels, farm holidays and tourist villages, see pages 174–9.

The Club Hotel Torre Moresca at Cala Ginepro, Orosei (see p177)

Grades of Hotel

As in the rest of Italy, hotels in Sardinia are graded using a star-rating system, which runs from one star for minimum comfort to five stars for luxury accommodation. The four-star category offers first-class service without the very high prices of five-star hotels. Three-star lodgings, especially family-run establishments, sometimes offer better value for your money, but in Sardinia this is generally the exception rather than the rule.

Most Sardinian hotels also have a restaurant that is usually open to non-residents as well. The majority of hotels, whatever their category, provide a range of facilities. Along the coast, for example, hotels are likely to offer beach equipment such as umbrellas and deckchairs.

Holiday Villages

Sardinia's wide variety of holiday villages, mostly on or near the coast range from vast establishments with hundreds of rooms and good facilities and service, to smaller places, which may be more luxurious and expensive. The larger holiday villages offer more than one type of lodging within a single site. Guests can often choose between a serviced apartment (residence) or a normal three-or four-star hotel. Some tourist villages offer all-inclusive packages that may even include drinks at the bar. Tourist villages often require guests to take half- or full-board, as do many hotels on the island. In some resorts guests may choose to rent a self-catering apartment or bungalow with the option of other amenities. These services usually include the use of sports facilities and entertainment, such as a disco or nightclub, babysitter, beach facilities, swimming pool and various bars and restaurants. Many holiday villages also offer an excellent range of equipment for water sports.

Renting an apartment in a holiday village is a worthwhile alternative to renting a villa, especially if you plan to be on holiday for less than a month. It allows you to be independent while at the same time giving you access to a range of useful services and facilities. At **Villaggio Cugnana Verde**, for example, there are flats available for up to six people, and a host of activities is provided on site. Other holiday villages include **Park Hotel & Spa Cala di Lepre**, **Baia di Conte Thomson** and more.

Bed and Breakfasts

Staying in a bed and breakfast is an excellent way to save money and interact with the locals. Usually, about three rooms are rented out per apartment or villa, with either a shared or private bathroom, and

Elegant setting at Hotel Colonna San Marco, Porto Rotondo (see p179)

◀ Beautiful terrace with outdoor seating at a restaurant in Sardinia

Plush seating in a guest room at Faro Capo-Spartivento in Baia Chia *(see p176)*

breakfast is provided by the host family. Prices generally start at €25 per room.

Prices

Italian law requires every hotel to place the National Tourist Board price list, with the maximum prices for the current year, behind the door of each room. The prices quoted should never be exceeded. Room prices shown on this list, or quoted by the hotel staff when you book, normally include taxes and service. However, it is advisable to check with staff whether or not breakfast is included in the rate, to avoid misunderstandings.

Hotels on the coast often require guests to take half- or full-board. In low season you could try asking for a bed and breakfast rate, but this is unlikely to be possible during high season. Winter rates are significantly lower than summer rates: in summer prices can easily double. Hotel prices reach their peak in the two middle weeks of August. This is also true of the tourist villages (except that rates here are calculated on a weekly basis).

The location of your hotel will also affect the price. All types of accommodation on the coast are always more expensive than lodgings in the interior. Bear in mind that you may be able to negotiate special rates for groups or for longer stays.

Extras

Generally speaking, guests have to pay separately for drinks consumed with meals, anything taken from the mini-bar in the room, room service as well as telephone calls.

In some cases air-conditioning may be charged as an extra. Glimpses of Sardinia's coast may also be regarded as chargeable and travellers may have to pay extra for rooms that have a sea view. It is always a good idea to verify extras like this when booking or choosing your room. Tipping in hotels is at the visitor's discretion.

Low Season

If you plan to travel to Sardinia in any season other than summer, it is always a good idea to check before-hand on the availability of accommodation. Some hotels are run on a seasonal basis and tend to open around Easter and close in the autumn. The end of the season might depend on unpredictable circumstances such as a sudden turn of bad weather.

Booking and Paying

If you decide to travel in summer, especially in July and August, and want to stay on the coast, book well in advance as the island over-flows with visitors in this period. If you are booking the hotel separately from your travel arrangements, you will almost certainly be asked to pay a deposit. This can be done by credit card or by international money order. Upon arrival, the receptionist will ask for your passport; this is to register travellers with the police – a legal requirement. Guests will be given a receipt at check-out, another legal formality.

Dining room at Mare Monti Miniere, Iglesias *(see p176)*

The swimming pool at Sa Muvara Hotel set amid beautiful surroundings in Aritzo *(see p177)*

Camping

Camping is the most affordable type of accommodation on the island. Sardinia has a number of good camp sites, some of which are located in quiet areas with pleasant views. Most are situated along the coast, sometimes in eucalyptus or pine groves. There are far fewer sites located in the interior. Many have helpful websites, including **La Liccia**, **Baia Blu La Tortuga**, **Sardinia Camping Baia di Conte** and **Isola dei Gabbiani**.

As with Sardinian hotels, camp sites are much in demand in summer. If you have not booked in advance, you'll need to start looking for a place to stay early in the day.

Some camp sites also have a small number of bungalows or chalets with a bathroom and kitchen area. These are often very attractive but be aware that the prices can be steep.

Most camp sites are open from Easter to October. Some may be open for the Christmas period, offering bungalows or camper vans with heating.

Camping outside official sites is forbidden, and camping on the beach is particularly frowned on. Guests need permission to camp on private property (from the owner), and in state forests.

Farm Holidays

Agriturismi – farms or wine estates that offer accommodation – are an excellent way to experience Sardinian customs and local traditions. **Agriturismo Li Scopi**, **Il Giglio** and **Le Querce** are just a few of the many options. The accommodation is often basic, but rooms are usually comfortable and quaint. Farmhouses tend not to be situated in isolated countryside – true

to tradition, at least half the farms are in villages. Local farmers and shepherds often live in villages and travel some distance to work the fields or take their sheep to pasture.

The highest concentration of *agriturismi* is found around Sassari and Oristano, while there are very few in the Cagliari area. Everyone usually eats at the same table, guests and host family alike, so you will probably feel like part of the family by the time you leave. Meals usually include produce from the farm – cheese, meat, vegetables and even honey – cooked according to local tradition. It is an excellent way to explore the specialities of the region. In general, farms offer accommodation by the week on a half- or full-board basis. Many also organize hikes, horseback riding, mountain biking and canoeing.

It is sometimes possible to eat at an *agriturismo* without being a guest there.

Villa Rental

Renting a house for two weeks or a month is an economical solution for those who want to be unconstrained by hotel or guesthouse mealtimes and routines. This is a good option for families with small children. Note that the charge for cleaning is generally the same for a week as for a longer stay.

The local tourist offices are often able to supply lists of

Elegant lobby area at Hotel Le Torri *(see p178)*

private homes available in the area. Travel agents can also arrange this type of accommodation.

Prices are usually quoted on a weekly basis, with a deposit requested. When renting it is advisable to ascertain the exact number of bedrooms as the living room also functions as a bedroom in some houses. Before signing any contract, check if gas, water, electricity and telephone expenses are part of the rent or considered "extras". Make a note of the readings on the meters on arrival if these items are extra.

Adventure Holidays

The great climate and varied scenery of Sardinia make it an ideal location for a sea kayaking or cycling holiday

Organized off-road mountain bike tours, following the paths and tracks of the island, particularly of the inland areas, are becoming common while road-based holidays are more suitable for the independent traveller. **Saddle Skedaddle** organizes a variety of cycling tours with accommodation included (usually *agriturismi* or small hotels). For sea kayaking and paddling tours, **Location Sardinia** offers useful information for planning such a trip.

Recommended Hotels

The hotels listed on pages 176–179 cover a huge variety of accommodation options from camp sites and bed and breakfasts to *agriturismo* lodgings, boutique hotels and luxury retreats. They are listed by price within each area.

Holiday villages are grouped under the resort category. Guests can experience local Sardinian life at an *agriturismo* (farm) while luxury hotels encompass the finest of Sardinia's hotels. The guesthouse category refers to medium-sized hotels that are often family-run and offer simple comforts at affordable prices. Some of these don't offer air conditioning so it is advisable to check in advance

if visiting in the hotter months. There are a couple of historic options, which are hotels housed in old-fashioned quarters or ancient buildings, both rural or urban, usually featuring traditional Sardinian furniture, and stylish boutique hotels, too.

All rooms have private bathrooms unless otherwise indicated. Book in advance if you plan to stay in high season, and note that many hotels close for the winter.

Establishments highlighted as DK Choice offer something extra special. They might have been chosen for their spectacular location, their original style or for their exceptionally high level of luxury and service, or a combination of these.

Traditional stone huts surrounded by beautiful scenery at L'Essenza in Torpe *(see p178)*

DIRECTORY

Holiday Villages

Baia di Conte Thomson
Fertillia (Alghero). **Map** B2.
Tel 079 94 90 00.
W thomson.co.uk

Park Hotel Cala di Lepre & Spa
Località Cala di Lepre, Palau.
Tel 0789 79 00 18.
W hotelcaladilepre.com

Villaggio Cugnana Verde
Cugnana Verde (Olbia).
Map D1 & 2.
Tel 0789 331 94.
W cugnanaverde.net

Camping

Baia Blu La Tortuga
Località Vignola Mare, Aglientu.
Map C1.
Tel 079 60 22 00.
W baiaholiday.com

International Camping
Località Valledoria.
Map D6.
Tel 079 58 40 70.
W campingvalledoria.com

Isola dei Gabbiani
Località Porto Pollo, Palau (Olbia). **Map** D2.
Tel 0789 70 40 19
W isoladeigabbiani.it

La Liccia
Santa Teresa Gallura.
Map C1.
Tel 0789 75 51 90.
W campinglaliccia.com

Sardinia Camping Cala Gonone
Cala Gonone, Dorgali (Nuoro). **Map** D3.
Tel 342 102 8249.
W camping calagonone.com

Farm Holidays

Agriturismo Li Scopi
Località Li Scopi (San Teodoro). **Map** D2.
Tel 338 708 8414.
W agriturismo liscopi.com

Il Giglio
Strada Prov. 9, Massama (Oristano). **Map** B4.
Tel 349 144 7955.
W agriturismo ilgiglio.com

Le Querce
Località Valli di Vatta, Porto Cervo. **Map** D1.
Tel 389 975 5545.
W lequerce.com

Adventure Holidays

Location Sardinia
Tel +44 786 6443377.
W locationsardinia.com

Saddle Skedaddle
Tel +44 191 2651110.
W skedaddle.co.uk

Where to Stay

Cagliari and the South

ARBUS: Hotel Le Dune di Ingurtosu
Resort €€€ Map B5
Via Bau 1 – Fraz. Piscinas di Ingurtosu, 09031
Tel *070 97 71 30*
🔳 ledunepiscinas.com
A beachside hotel with simply furnished rooms. Small fitness and wellness centre.

DK Choice

BAIA CHIA: Faro Capo-Spartivento
Boutique €€€ Map C6
Viale Spartivento, Domus de Maria, 09010
Tel *070 923 01 10*
🔳 farocapospartivento.com
This hotel offers unique accommodation in a lighthouse (dating from 1856) perched on an isolated outcrop above deep waters. With only six suites, seclusion is guaranteed. Facilities are world-class, including impeccable staff, a talented chef and an infinity pool.

CAGLIARI: Aurora
Guesthouse €€ Map C6
Salita Santa Chiara 19, 09124
Tel *070 65 86 25*
🔳 hotelcagliariaurora.it
Centrally located hotel with clean rooms, elegant furnishings and modern decor.

CAGLIARI: Sardegna Hotel
Boutique €€ Map C6
Via Lunigiana 50, 09122
Tel *070 28 62 45*
🔳 sardegnahotelcagliari.it
Spacious rooms, some boasting sea views, and ultra-modern bathrooms. Efficient staff.

CAGLIARI: Sardinia Domus
Historic €€ Map C6
Largo Carlo Felice 26, 09124
Tel *070 65 97 83*
🔳 sardiniadomus.it
A casual and comfortable B&B located in the historic city centre. The staff is friendly and helpful.

CALASETTA: Hotel FJBY
Guesthouse € Map B6
Via Solferino 83, 09011
Tel *0781 884 44*
🔳 hotelfjby.it
Located in the historical city centre close to the beach, this hotel has elegantly styled rooms.

**FLUMINIMAGGIORE:
Perdaba** €
Agriturismo Map B5
Vico III Vittorio Emanuele 15, 09010
Tel *0781 58 05 33*
🔳 agriturismoperdaba.com
This working farm offers basic, clean rooms with garden views. Sheep, pig and cattle are also raised here.

**GONNOSFANADIGA:
Su Murzu e S'Arreposu** €
B&B Map B5
Via Satta 28, 09035
Tel *328 287 23 44*
🔳 murzuearreposu.altervista.org
The rooms at this welcoming B&B are spacious with large windows and a working fireplace.

IGLESIAS: Mare Monti Miniere €
B&B Map B5
Via Trento 10, 09016
Tel *348 331 05 85*
🔳 maremontiminiere-bb.it
A small B&B with friendly hosts and rooms with washing facilities. Strictly non-smoking.

**ISOLA DI SAN PIETRO:
Hotel Hieracon** €€
Boutique Map B6
Corso C. Cavour 62, 09014 Carloforte
Tel *0781 85 40 28*
🔳 hotelhieracon.com
the bright and stylish rooms at this hotel have old-world charm and views of the marina.

**QUARTU SANT'ELENA:
Pini e Mare** €
Camping Map C6
Prov.le per Villasimius, 09045
Tel *347 116 61 40*
🔳 piniemare.com
A fully equipped camp site with single-room and family-style bungalows available.

Price Guide
Price ranges are for a double room per night, inclusive of breakfast, tax and service.

€	under €100
€€	€100 to €250
€€€	over €250

**SANTA MARGHERITA DI PULA:
Hotel Costa dei Fiori** €€
Resort Map C6
SS 195 – km 33, 09010
Tel *070 924 53 33*
🔳 costadeifiori.it
Located close to the sea, this intimate resort has stylish rooms and an infinity pool. Some rooms have Jacuzzis.

SANT'ANTIOCO: Sa Ruscitta €
Agriturismo Map B6
Località Cannai, 09017
Tel *328 761 50 02*
🔳 agriturismosaruscitta.com
Small *agriturismo* with clean, air-conditioned rooms that overlook the hills and olive groves.

The Eastern Coast

ARBATAX: Hotel La Bitta €€
Resort Map D4
Porto Frailis, 08048
Tel *0782 66 70 80*
🔳 hotellabitta.it
Rooms at this beach resort have hand-painted majolica. Some rooms have sea views and deluxe rooms feature Jacuzzis.

CALA GONONE: Cala Gonone Beach Village €€
Resort Map D3
Viale Bue Marino, 08022
Tel *0784 936 93*
🔳 calagononebeachvillage.com
This is a tastefully designed resort catering to families and business travellers. Has a large pool.

Stylish suite at Faro Capo-Spartivento in Baia Chia

DK Choice

DORGALI: Agriturismo Neulè €
Agriturismo **Map** D3
Località Neulè, 08022
Tel *380 728 38 87*
W agriturismoneule.com
Come for an ultimate relaxing
experience at a working farm in
a protected forest area, just steps
from a pristine lake. All lodging
is in the farmhouse where hearty
breakfasts made with local
produce are served.

LOTZORAI: The Lemon House €
B&B **Map** D4
Via Dante 19, 08040
Tel *339 714 64 96*
W peteranne.it
The friendly and well-informed
owners help plan daily activities.
Suitable for sport enthusiasts.

OROSEI: Club Hotel
Torre Moresca €€
Resort **Map** D3
Località Cala Ginepro, 08028
Tel *0784 91 230*
W torremoresca.it
Cheerful hotel a short walk from
the beach. Features a large gym
and pool.

OROSEI: Maria Rosaria €€
Mid-range **Map** D3
Via Grazia Deledda 13, 08028
Tel *0784 986 57*
W hotelmariarosaria.it
This hotel offers clean and spacious
rooms with balconies. The restaurant
serves delicious traditional fare.

POSADA: Maria Caderina
Green Village €€
Resort **Map** D2
Loc. Predarva, 08020
Tel *0784 85 30 70*
W greenvillageposada.com
Quiet location in the countryside
with traditional furnishings. All
rooms have private balconies.

SANTA LUCIA: Villaggio
Camping La Mandragola €
Camping **Map** D2
Viale dei Pini, 08029
Tel *078 481 91 19*
W villaggiomandragola.com
Opt for a tent, camper-van
pitch or bungalow on this site,
set within a pine forest with
direct access to the beach.

SINISCOLA: Camping Selema €€
Camping **Map** D2
Santa Lucia di Siniscola, 08029
Tel *342 814 98 01*
W selemacamping.com
Enjoy full-service beach-front
camping at this site, which is ideal
for nature- and sports-lovers.

TESONIS: Village Tesonis €€
Camping **Map** D4
*Loc. Tesonis, Capo Sferracavallo,
Marina di Tertenia, Ogliastra, 08047*
Tel *0782 57 04 41*
W villaggiotesonisbeach.it
The camp site overlooks three
different beaches and is great for
those who love hiking, fishing
and diving. All pitches have
toilets and hot water.

TORTOLÌ: Hotel Il
Vecchio Mulino €€
Historic **Map** D4
Via Parigi, 08048
Tel *0782 66 40 41*
W hotelilvecchiomulino.it
This hotel features colourful
and rustic rooms with a Spanish
hacienda (ranch) feel and offers
superb value.

VILLAPUTZU:
Agriturismo Marongiu €
B&B **Map** D5
SS 125 – km 72, 09040
Tel *070 997 80 01*
W agriturismomarongiu.it
Stay surrounded by nature in
a tranquil setting. All food comes
directly from the farm and
vegetarian dishes are available.

VILLASIMIUS: Hotel Pullman
Timi Ama €€€
Resort **Map** D6
Viale dei Ginepri, 09049
Tel *070 79 79 70*
W pullman-timiama-sardegna.com
Overlooking the bay, this upscale
spa resort features rooms that
have balconies or terrace offering
sea or garden views. Amenities
include deluxe spa, pool and
tennis courts.

VILLASIMIUS: Hotel
Stella Maris €€€
Luxury **Map** D6
Via dei Cedri 3, 09049
Tel *070 79 71 00*
W stella-maris.com
Lovely rooms at this seaside
resort with a private beach and
ample grounds, make for an
excellent value experience.

Central Sardinia
and Barbagia

ARITZO: Sa Muvara
Hotel €€
Boutique **Map** C4
Viale Kennedy 33, 08031
Tel *0784 62 93 36*
W samuvarahotel.com
Large, elegantly furnished
rooms that are set in beautiful
surroundings. There is also a
mineral water swimming pool.

Unassuming façade of The Lemon House
in Lotzorai

BELVÌ: PhillyRea €
Resort **Map** C4
Viale IV Novembre, 08030
Tel *0784 62 92 00*
W phillyreahotel.it
Enjoy a relaxing stay in the
centre of Sardinia. A veranda
offers panoramic views of the
forest and mountains. Rooms
are clean.

FONNI: Parco Donnortei €
Agriturismo **Map** D3
Via San Antonio n.46, 08023
Tel *0784 585 75*
W agriturismodonnortei.com
The highest hotel in Sardinia,
with bright rooms. Guides
available for hiking tours and
horseback riding.

GAVOI: Sa Posada €
B&B **Map** C3
Viale Repubblica 175, 08020
Tel *0784 531 00*
W saposadagavoi.com
This hotel offers clean rooms
as well as a shared kitchen
for self-catering, though half-
board option is also available
on request.

NUORO: Agriturismo
Testone €
Agriturismo **Map** D3
*Località Testone, Strada
Statale 389, 08100*
Tel *329 411 5168*
W agriturismotestone.com
A traditional converted
farmhouse, where the hosts
serve and sell their own
organic produce.

NUORO: Su Gologone €€€
Hotel **Map** D3
Boutique
Località su Gologone, 08025
Tel *0784 28 75 12*
W sugologone.it
Stunning mountain-side
lodge with luxurious rooms
and rustic decor.

For more information on types of hotels *see page 174*

TONARA: Sa Tzia Crara €
B&B   Map C4
Vico I Kennedy n.8, 08039
Tel *329 161 21 48*
ⓦ satziacrara.it
This small, quaint B&B in the heart of the island offers clean and modern rooms. Pet friendly.

DK Choice

TORPE: L'Essenza €€
B&B   Map D2
Località Cuccu Ezzu
Tel *333 654 01 40*
ⓦ essenzasardegna.com
These four circular stone huts, thatched with tree branches, were once used by shepherds. Brightly painted and decorated in simple, traditional style, they have now also been modernized to include bathrooms and air conditioning. Enchanting views over the valley.

The Western Coast

ALGHERO: Hotel San Francesco €
Historic   Map B2
Via Ambrogio Machin 2, 07041
Tel *079 98 03 30*
ⓦ sanfrancescohotel.com
Small, sober, yet comfortable rooms grouped around a 14th-century cloister; breakfast on a terrace under Gothic arches.

ALGHERO: Hotel Domomea €€
Luxury   Map B2
Via Vittorio Veneto 47, 07041
Tel *079 957 71 66*
ⓦ hoteldomomea.it
The rooms are attractive with modern bathrooms. The rooftop pool is a delightful bonus.

DK Choice

ARBOREA: Hotel Le Torri €
Luxury   Map B4
Via Sardegna 23, 09092
Tel *0783 800 00 31*
ⓦ letorrihotelsardegna.it
In the heart of Arborea this four-star modern hotel has contemporary and spacious rooms, with the option of enjoying a romantic breakfast in bed. Boasts a gym and spa that offers Turkish baths and hydro massages.

BOSA: Hotel Gabbiano €€
Resort   Map B3
Viale Mediterraneo 5, 08013
Tel *0785 37 41 23*
ⓦ hotelalgabbiano.it
A range of comfortable rooms just a few steps from a windswept

bay. In the adjacent villa, apartments are also available.

BOSA: Mannu Hotel €€
Guesthouse   Map B3
Viale Alghero 28, 08013
Tel *078 537 53 06*
ⓦ mannuhotel.it
Spacious, clean rooms with private balconies. The on-site restaurant serves fresh Mediterranean cuisine.

CABRAS: da Pina €
B&B   Map B4
Via Alessandria n.19, 09172
Tel *078 339 12 05*
ⓦ bbdapina.com
Close to the beach, this quaint B&B has bright rooms. Discounts for children aged 12 and under. Pet friendly.

CUGLIERI: Nurapolis €
Camping   Map B3
Via su Paris de Sa Turre, Santa Caterina di Pittinuri, 09073
Tel *0783 52 283*
ⓦ coopsinis.it
This well-equipped campground is just steps from the beach, making it ideal for families and outdoor enthusiasts.

NORBELLO: Nuraghe Ruiu €
Camping   Map C3
Loc. Sant'Ignazio, 09070
Tel *078 589 61 43*
ⓦ nuragheruiu.it
Surrounded by a beautiful forest and rich in wildlife, this campsite offers tent and camper-van pitches, as well as bungalows.

ORISTANO: Eleonora Bed and Breakfast €
B&B   Map B4
Piazza Eleonora d'Arborea 12, 09170
Tel *347 481 79 76*
ⓦ eleonora-bed-and-breakfast.com
Contemporary rooms with parquet flooring. A great starting point to witness one of Sardinia's best festivals – the Sartiglia.

ORISTANO: Hotel Mistral 2 €
Guesthouse   Map B4
Via XX Settembre, 34, 09170
Tel *0783 21 03 89*
ⓦ hotelmistral2oristano.it
This is a modern, no-frills lodging in the heart of the old town. There is a simple outdoor pool.

ORISTANO: Hotel Regina d'Arborea €€
Historic   Map B4
Piazza Eleonora d' Arborea 4, 09170
Tel *0783 30 21 01*
ⓦ hotelreginadarborea.com
This is a charming 19th-century hotel, with seven beautifully themed rooms that are large and elegantly furnished with original furniture of the house.

TRESNURAGHES: La Terrazza €
B&B   Map B3
Via Nuraghe 40, 09079
Tel *339 148 01 10*
ⓦ laterrazzabb.com
Experience Sardinian village life in this 18th-century cottage, with just three bedrooms and a suite.

The North and the Costa Smeralda

AGGIUS: il Muto di Gallura €€
Agriturismo   Map C2
Loc. Fraiga, 097011
Tel *079 62 05 59*
ⓦ mutodigallura.com
This is located in a forest and has two suites. Relaxation area with a Jacuzzi, sauna and Turkish bath.

AGLIENTU: Nuraghe Tuttusoni €
Agriturismo   Map C1
Loc. Portobello di Gallura, 07020
Tel *079 65 68 30*
ⓦ nuraghetuttusoni.it
This is a fabulous family-run *agriturismo* minutes from a sandy shore. There are rooms and villas, both with sea views.

Simply furnished traditional stone hut at L'Essenza in Torpe

BASSACUTENA: Sole e Terra €
Agriturismo Map C1
Loc. Funtana d'Alzi, 07020
Tel 331 584 69 91
w soleeterra.it
A certified organic farm where the main house features a terrace, lounge, library and shop. Pleasant rooms with balconies.

CALA DI VOLPE: Hotel Nibaru €€
Resort Map D1
Loc. Cala di Volpe, 07020
Tel 0789 960 38
w hotelnibaru.it
Serene hotel with a lovely pool, but also close to the beach. Rooms have mountain views.

ISOLA ROSSA: Marinedda Hotel Thalasso & Spa €€€
Luxury Map C1
Via Tanca della Torre, 07038
Tel 0789 79 03 19
w hotelmarinedda.com
A stunning hotel with direct access to the Bay of Marinedda. Full-service spa and an excellent restaurant. Impeccable service.

LA MADDALENA: Camping Maddalena €€
Camping Map D1
Via G.Mary Loc. Moneta, 07024
Tel 078 972 80 51
w campingmaddalena.it
Come for organized camping and three different types of bungalows. Close to the town centre.

DK Choice

LA MADDALENA: La Casitta €€€
Luxury Map D1
Isola di Santa Maria, 07024
Tel 329 370 5621
w lacasitta.com
This intimate resort, located on a private island, offers ultimate luxury in a natural setting and it also has one of the best restaurants in the region. Two magnificent villas offer breathtaking views of the sea and come with a butler, chef and maid. Transfers by boat or by helicopter to the surrounding islands are available. Excellent service.

LURAS: Funtana Abbas €€
Historic Map C1
Loc. San Leonardo, 07020
Tel 345 122 37 37
w funtanaabbas.it
A spectacular hotel set in acres of forest. Spotless, spacious rooms and excellent service.

Serene surroundings at La Casitta in La Maddalena

OLBIA: Hotel Cavour €
Historic Map D2
Via Cavour 22, 07026
Tel 0789 20 40 33
Centrally located hotel with comfortable rooms and traditional Sardinian decor. A good option for families and pet friendly.

OLBIA: Hotel Panorama €€
Luxury Map D2
Via Mazzini 7, 07026
Tel 0789 266 56
w hotelpanoramaolbia.it
An unassuming 4-star hotel with a panoramic roof terrace and attractive rooms. Good value.

PITRIZZA: Hotel Pitrizza €€€
Luxury Map D1
Porto Cervo, 07021
Tel 0789 93 01 11
w pitrizzahotel.com
Grand hotel with super-luxe amenities, grounds and stunning views. Private villas also on offer.

PORTO CERVO: La Murichessa €
B&B Map D1
Loc. Vaddimala, 07021
Tel 339 531 65 32
w lamurichessa.it
Enchanting old-world villa with simple rooms that offer sublime mountain views.

PORTO CERVO: Cervo Hotel €€€
Luxury Map D1
Costa Smeralda Resort, 07021
Tel 0789 93 11 11
w hotelcervocostasmeralda.com
Set in a piazza, this elegant hotel from is part of the Sheraton group, with excellent service. It boasts a private beach and golf course.

PORTO ROTONDO: Villaggio Baia de Bahas €
Apartments Map D1
Località Marana Golfo Di Marinella, 07026
Tel 011 50 47 69
w baiadebahas.com
Spacious and well-equipped apartments with resort facilities and a sandy beach. Pet friendly.

PORTO ROTONDO: Hotel Colonna San Marco €€€
Luxury Map D1
Piazzetta San Marco, 07020
Tel 0789 341 10
w hotelcolonnasanmarco.it
Tastefully furnished hotel with a splendid garden, pool and tennis court. Car or boat rental is available.

SAN PANTALEO: Petra Segreta Resort €€€
Luxury Map D1
Strada Buddeu, 07026
Tel 0789 187 64 41
w petrasegretaresort.com
This resort decorated in a rustic style has first-class facilities and spa services.

SAN TEODORO: La Cinta €€
Camping Map D2
Via del Tirreno, 08020
Tel 078 486 57 77
w campingsanteodoro.it
Close to a beach, this camp site has a market, bar, volleyball court and bowling alley.

SANTA TERESA DI GALLURA: La Coluccia Hotel €€€
Resort Map C1
Via Ulisse, Loc. Conca Verde, 07028
Tel 0789 75 80 06
w hotellacoluccia.com
Sleek and minimalistic, this resort offers exquisite views and a pool. In August, a minimum four-night stay is required.

SASSARI: Hotel Grazia Deledda €
Resort Map B2
Viale Dante 47, 07100
Tel 079 27 12 35
w hotelgraziadeledda.it
This is a large four-star establishment with comfortable and spacious rooms, equipped with modern amenities.

TRINITA D'AGULTU E VIGNOLA: Mediterraneo €
Resort Map C1
Loc. Lu Colbu, 07038
Tel 079 68 98 01
w hotel-mediterraneo.org
Since 1976, this family-run hotel has provided comfortable rooms and excellent service. The food is superb.

VALLEDORIA: Monte Istulargiu €
Agriturismo Map C2
Loc. Monte Istulargiu - Str. Castelsardo
Tel 348 724 04 79
w agriturismomonteistulargiu.com
Located close to the beach, this farm has colourful rooms and apartments that offer garden or sea views. Pet friendly.

For more information on types of hotels see page 174

WHERE TO EAT AND DRINK

Sardinia is an excellent place to explore and appreciate regional variations in cuisine. Fish and seafood fill restaurant menus along the coast, while meat and stuffed pasta are commonly found in the interior. In fact, restaurants that do not serve typical regional dishes are a rarity. The rhythm for mealtimes is Mediterranean, with lunch served at 1–3pm and dinner at 9–10:30pm. In many cases restaurants often stay open until midnight, especially in summer. The restaurants listed on pages 186–9 have been selected from the best that Sardinia can offer across all price ranges.

Unassuming outdoor seating at Luigi Pomata in Cagliari *(see p186)*

Types of Restaurants

In terms of price, cuisine and atmosphere, there is not much difference between a *ristorante* (restaurant) and a trattoria in Sardinia. Even a fairly expensive restaurant may still be decorated in a functional style. Pizzerias are rarely luxurious, but have the advantage of offering decent eating at lower prices. Choose pizzerias with wood-burning ovens for better quality pizzas. An *enoteca* focuses on wine, usually both regional and national, but almost always has a wide array of savoury snacks and dishes. While the traditional regional cuisine offered in many of Sardinia's restaurants is explained on pp182–3, modern Italian cuisine, served usually in more upmarket restaurants, tends to be more creative, with each chef adding his own innovative twist to classic Italian dishes. The island's seafood restaurants feature mainly lobster, squid, tuna, sardines, mussels and clams, and in the fine-dining establishments, generally in or near resort towns, the best of Italian cuisine is exalted and presented as a work of art on your plate.

Prices and Paying

A three-course meal will cost about €25–€50 per person. In top restaurants the bill may add up to €35–€45 but only rarely will it go above €50 (except in the exclusive areas of the Costa Smeralda). In pizzerias a two-course meal with a beer or half-litre of wine will run to €15–€25. The bill often includes a cover charge, usually €1–€3 per person, and service. Although it isn't customary among the locals to tip, it has become almost expected in the more exclusive resorts. Many restaurants accept major credit cards but, just in case, be prepared to pay in cash, especially at bars, cafés or smaller, family-run places.

Fixed-Price Menus

Some restaurants offer a *menù a prezzo fisso* or *menù turistico* (set menus at fixed prices). *Agriturismi (see p174)* prepare a set menu of local specialities daily, usually including regional dishes such as *porceddu*, or suckling pig, which guests would have to order in advance in restaurants. Upmarket places may offer a menu *degustazione* (tasting menu) giving diners the chance to sample five or six house specialities.

Closing Days

Restaurants often close for one day a week – usually Sunday or Monday – except during July and August. Most places also close for one month of annual holidays, usually in winter, except for many restaurants in Cagliari, which are closed in August.

Vegetarian Food

Sardinia is not ideal for strict vegetarians. People who eat fish will not have problems along the coast, although in the interiors the choice may be limited to pasta or soup with fresh bread and cheeses. If you do not see anything suitable on the menu, explain your situation to the waiter. The chef will usually cook you something special – although it may be prepared with meat stock.

Dal Corsaro, one of Cagliari's top restaurants *(see p186)*

The Menu

Restaurants do not always provide a written menu. Instead, a waiter will give a list of the day's dishes at the table and help guests choose. Diners may begin with an *antipasto* (starter) such as sliced sausage, *salumi* or cured meats, grilled vegetables, artichoke hearts or olives. Coastal places offer seafood appetizers such as clams, calamari, cuttlefish, sea anemones and assorted molluscs. This is followed by the *primo* (first course), which may consist of soup, pasta or, occasionally, a rice dish. The *secondo* (second course) will be meat or fish, and may include the famous *porceddu*. Some first courses, such as *pane frattau* (carasau bread in broth) or fregula pasta with clams, make substantial meals. The meal ends with cheese, fruit or dessert, with coffee and perhaps a Sardinian liqueur (*see p185*).

Reservations

Restaurants are often crowded, particularly in the evening and during the summer. It is advisable to book ahead even in the less expensive establishments, or else arrive fairly early to avoid a long wait.

Wine and Drinks

Most restaurants, even those in the medium-price range, will stock a good selection of regional wines and liqueurs. Some may offer non-Sardinian wines. Almost all restaurants also provide a house wine.

Children

Children are welcome in restaurants, especially family-run ones, where staff are more inclined to prepare half-portions or even special dishes for them.

Smoking

Smoking is banned in all public establishments in Italy. Some places may have terraces or outside tables where smoking is permitted.

Bright interiors at Colibrì in Dorgali (*see p187*)

Wheelchair Access

Only a few restaurants in Sardinia are equipped with ramps and adapted toilet facilities for the disabled. Some places have steps, but access is not normally a problem. It is a good idea to call the restaurant beforehand to ensure an easily accessible table and assistance when you arrive.

Food Festivals

The best way to get a taste of the real Sardinia is at one of the frequent *sagre* (food festivals). These pleasant occasions are usually dedicated to one particular dish or product, such as wine, cheese or fish. One of the most interesting is the picturesque tuna festival held around the end of May in Carloforte on the Island of San Pietro, where you can try tuna cooked in a multitude of ways. Fish in general is the theme in September at Cagliari's Sagra del Pesce and also in August when Oristano hosts the Festa del Mare. Another popular festival, Sagra della Castagne e delle Nocciole, dedicated to the harvest of chestnuts and hazelnuts, is held in Aritzo in October, while the following month sees the Sagra delle Olive in Gonnosfanadiga, near Cagliari. Various religious and folk festivals held throughout the year usually have a gastronomic element, often including spit-roast *porceddu* – suckling pig.

Recommended Restaurants

The restaurants listed on pages 186–9 have been selected for their good value, interesting cuisine, excellent location and atmosphere. A range of establishments have been included – from pizzerias and traditional places serving classic Sardinian cuisine to restaurants specializing in seafood and fine-dining spots. Be aware that many restaurants close for a month or more in the off season.

Entries highlighted as DK Choice have been selected in recognition of a special feature – this could be an outstanding level of gourmet cuisine, a panoramic view, excellent value or a combination of these. Most of these places are popular with locals and visitors so be sure to book ahead well in advance.

Ravioli with onions at the Al Tuguri restaurant in historic centre of Alghero (*see p188*)

The Flavours of Sardinia

There is a huge contrast between the extravagant lifestyle of Costa Smeralda and the hard lives of Sardinia's farmers and shepherds that inspired the *cucina povera* – a "poor cooking" style of food. But even the most fashionable restaurants serve versions of these simple tasty dishes, the most famous of which is *porceddu*, traditional spit-roasted suckling pig. Remote from the mainland, rugged and dry, the island has a distinctive cuisine, taking its flavours from the herbs that grow on the hillsides. Other popular ingredients include honey, wild-boar ham and salami, goat's and ewe's cheeses and seafood.

Sardinian herbs

Market vendor offering a wide range of local cheeses

Inland Influences

Centuries of seaborne invasion required Sardinians to make the most of available inland ingredients. Vines and olive trees grow everywhere so families made their own wine and oil. Wild herbs flavoured anything that could go into the pot. Rabbit, hare, game birds and even thrushes were easily caught, and lamb or mutton was usually available. Offal is still used, and local specialities include pigs' trotters, cooked in a piquant sauce, and lambs' feet, which are braised in tomato sauce while their intestines are spit-roasted (*cordula*). *Porceddu* (suckling pig) is spit-roasted over a fire of myrtle and juniper wood and basted until the skin is crisp and the herb-scented meat is tender. Sausages and salami are also made from pork. The meat of the young goats that climb the mountains is cooked with herbs and wine; *capretto al finocchietto* is kid cooked with fennel. Lamb and kid were also roasted by hunters in pits dug in the ground – a technique now reserved for celebrations. Wheat was introduced by the Romans, and bread-making is a local art. Among the many types is the crisp, circular

Fine setting at Il Rifugio in Nuoro *(see p187)*

Sardinian Dishes and Specialities

Many local dishes are unique to the island. Sardinian pastas include little ball-shaped *fregula*; similar to couscous, it is often simmered in lamb stock and flavoured with saffron and Pecorino to make *succu*. It is also served with clams, or in broth as a soup. Ravioli-like *culurgiones* may be filled with cheese and fresh mint and served with a tomato sauce, while semolina *gnocchetti* (dumplings) are delicious served with a hearty meat sauce such as *sugo di cinghiale* (wild boar). *Suppa cuata* is layers of bread, grated cheese, nutmeg and parsley, baked in lamb stock. Pork, beans and vegetables go into *favata*, a hearty winter stew. *Stufato di capretto* is a more extravagant dish – a rich casserole made with kid (young goat), wine, artichokes and saffron. Sometimes eggs are added to make a kind of fricassée.

Fresh green figs

Pesce Spada alla Sardegna is a swordfish steak with a sauce of tomatoes, wine, mint, saffron and chilli.

Tresses of vine-ripened tomatoes hanging on a local produce stall

tuna are grilled with herbs or fried in a semolina-flour batter. Risottos, pasta dishes and fish soups make use of the plentiful squid, cuttlefish, anchovies and shellfish. Octopus, prawns, mussels, clams, scallops and squid are boiled and dressed in oil and vinegar as *antipasti*. *Burrida* is fish marinaded in vinegar with walnuts and parsley, and *bottarga* is the dried and salted roe of grey mullet or tuna, which may be served sliced as an *antipasto* or grated over pasta.

pane carasau, that shepherds would take to work with them. When moistened and topped with a sauce, Pecorino cheese and egg, it is called *pane frattau*. Pecorino is Sardinia's most renowned cheese; soft when young, it hardens with age and is then used grated. *Pecorino pepato* contains peppercorns. Other cheeses include *fiore Sardo* and *dolce Sardo*. Soft ricotta is used in savoury and sweet dishes.

Cosmopolitan Coasts

The Romans, Arabs, Genoese and Spanish who colonized the island brought with them their culinary influences. Saffron, an Eastern import, still adds colour and perfume to numerous savoury and sweet recipes. The west coast has Catalan-influenced dishes that stem from the era of Spanish

rule. *Panadas* are savoury pies filled with meat or cheese and vegetables; the most popular type is stuffed with eel *(panada di anguillas)*. Lobster *alla Catalana*, stewed with vinegar, onion and tomatoes, is a typical dish from Alghero. Mullet, sea bass, bream, swordfish and

Newly harvested olives ready to be taken to the mill for pressing

SARDINIAN SWEETS

Soft almond nougat is a speciality of Tonara. Many Sardinian biscuits and sweets were originally made for religious festivals:

Aranciata or Aranzada Preserved orange peel with honey and nuts.

Caschettes Rose-shaped nut- and honey-filled pastries, given to brides at weddings.

Gianchittos Toasted almond and lemon peel meringues.

Papassinos Walnut, raisin and almond biscuits.

Sebadas Ricotta and citrus peel fritters, covered in honey.

Sos guelfos Balls of almond or hazelnut paste.

Sospiri di Ozieri Iced almond paste and citrus sweets, wrapped in bright paper.

Malloreddus are *gnocchi*-like dumplings served with a fresh tomato sauce and minced sausage meat.

Agnello alla zafferano, saffron- and garlic-scented lamb stew, is shown here served with *fregula* pasta.

Pardulas (or *casadinas*) are fresh cheese pastries that are flavoured with cinnamon, saffron and lemon.

What to Drink in Sardinia

Grapevines first came to Sardinia from the eastern Mediterranean, where the Phoenicians had long cultivated vineyards. The warm climate tends to yield very ripe grapes, which are then turned into strong, deeply coloured wines. Lighter, fruity *novellos* are also worth trying. Good-quality Sardinian wines are widely available in shops, but it also pays to go directly to the suppliers. All types are made, from red *(rosso)*, white *(bianco)* and rosé *(rosato)* to rich dessert wines. Many qualify for the status of *denominazione di origine controllata* (DOC), with guaranteed provenance and quality standards. Sardinian wines are almost always made from a single grape variety. Perhaps the best-known is Vernaccia di Oristano, the first to gain DOC status in Sardinia.

Old winemaking equipment, now largely superseded by modern techniques

Slightly
sparkling Sinis

Vernaccia

Grape harvesting

Recommended Whites

· **Cantina Sociale della Riforma Agraria, Alghero**
Vermentino di Sardegna Aragosta

· **Cantina Sociale Gallura**
Vermentino

· **Tenuta Sella & Mosca, Alghero**
Terre Bianche

White Wines

The white wines of Sardinia go well with fish and seafood dishes, and some are sturdy enough to go with meat dishes such as pork. Nuragus is a widely planted white grape, producing rather neutral, soft and fruity wines. Vermentino is also widely grown and the wines have more complex flavours. Both Vermentino di Sardegna and Vermentino di Gallura, made mostly around Sassari and Nuoro province, tend to be fairly strong. There is also a sparkling version. DOC Vermentino from Cala Viola and Usini is very good. The Campidano area produces the fruity, dry white Semidano.

Red Wines

The best-known red wine is Cannonau, which is usually full-bodied and strong, although some lighter versions are made. Most Cannonau is produced in the province of Nuoro in eastern Sardinia. It goes well with roast meat and game. Another wine to drink with game and mature cheese is Monica di Sardegna, a dry red with intense perfume that should be drunk young. Less common but equally good DOC reds are the light, dry Mandrolisai, Campidano di Terralba and Carignano del Sulcis. Other reds, such as Tanca Farrà di Alghero and Terre Brune del Sulcis, blend Sardinian and imported grape varieties. The most expensive Sardinian red wine is Turriga.

Cannonau grapes

Nieddera rosé and Cannonau

Recommended Reds

· **Azienda Giuseppe Cabras, Nuoro**
Cannonau

· **Tenuta Sella & Mosca, Alghero**
Anghelu Ruju

· **Attilio Contini, Cabras**
Nieddera

Dessert Wines

Sardinia produces a number of sweet dessert wines, both white and red. Besides mature white Vernaccia and sweet red Cannonau, there is Moscato di Sardegna, made from Muscat grapes and bottled at three years old. It is sweet but has good acidity, and an alcoholic content of 15°. Tempio Pausania Muscat tends to be lightly fizzy, while the Cagliari version is strong and sweet. The red Girò di Cagliari and amber-coloured Nasco are also strong and sweet. Two dessert wines made from semi-dried grapes come from the Alghero area: Torbato and the port-like Anghelu Ruju, both produced with Cannonau grapes. The Bosa and Cagliari Malvasia wines are similar to Vernaccia.

Cantina Sociale della Vernaccia at Oristano

Sparkling Vernaccia   Malvasia di Bosa

Vernaccia grapes

Malvasia grapes

Moscato grapes

Harvesting black grapes from Cannonau vines

Recommended Dessert Wines

· *Centro Enologico Sardo, Villacidro*
Malvasia

· *Centro Enologico Sardo, Villacidro*
Moscato Dolce (Muscat)

· *Fratelli Serra, Zeddiani*
Vernaccia

· *Meloni Vini, Selargius*
Malvasia di Cagliari

· *Cantina Sociale Dolianova*
Moscato di Cagliari

Digestivi

The best-known spirit made in Sardinia is *abbardiente* (named from the Spanish *aguardiente*), a *grappa* or eau de vie. Among the best are those made from the strong-tasting Cannonau and the more delicate Malvasia. Grappa here is also called *fil'e ferru* (iron wire), from the wire used to mark hiding places for illegally produced grappa. There is a variety of flavourings used in grappa, such as the combination of wild fennel, juniper and thistle. The most famous liqueur, however, is Mirto, both red and white, made with wild myrtle leaves and berries. The Sardinians' favourite is Zedda Piras.

Cork-covered bottles with characteristic decorative motifs

Where to Eat and Drink

Cagliari and the South

CAGLIARI: Antica Hostaria €€
Traditional **Map** C6
Via Cavour, 09124
Tel 070 66 58 70
Hidden in a winding warren of picturesque backstreets, this surprisingly elegant place serves Sardinian dishes and classic Italian favourites. The ample wine list features local and mainland Italian labels.

DK Choice

CAGLIARI: La Stella Marina di Montecristo €€
Seafood **Map** C6
Via Sardegna 140, 09124
Tel 347 578 89 64 **Closed** Sun
This simple restaurant serves superlative traditional fish dishes at very reasonable prices. The setting is humble, but the atmosphere is warm and welcoming, and the staff courteous. On Thursdays, in addition to seafood, wild game is on offer. The restaurant is very popular so be sure to book ahead.

CAGLIARI: Su Cumbidu €€
Enoteca **Map** C6
Via Napoli 13, 09124
Tel 070 67 07 12
Su Cumbidu means "invitation" in Sardinian dialect and this cozy wine bar, with its attentive service, lives up to its name. Savoury snacks complement a vast selection of local wines.

CAGLIARI: Trattoria Lillicu €€
Seafood **Map** C6
Via Sardegna 78, 09124
Tel 070 65 29 70 **Closed** Breakfast
Old-fashioned trattoria serving rustic, fish-based fare on basic, marble-topped tables. The food is fresh and good, but the prices may seem a bit high considering the simple interior.

CAGLIARI: Dal Corsaro €€€
Fine Dining **Map** C6
Viale Regina Margherita 28, 09124
Tel 070 66 43 18 **Closed** Sun
Sardinian specialities are creatively reinterpreted by the chef at this family-owned, sophisticated restaurant. Archways, mirrors and prettily framed prints enhance the dining experience.

CAGLIARI: Luigi Pomata €€€
Traditional **Map** C6
Viale Regina Margherita 18, 09124
Tel 070 67 20 58 **Closed** Sun
In addition to the tempting seafood dishes, each interpreted with a modern twist on tradition, a sushi bar makes this fun restaurant a well-rounded choice. It is advisable to make reservations in advance.

CALASETTA: Da Pasqualino €€
Traditional **Map** B6
Viale Regina Margherita 85, 09011
Tel 078 18 84 73
Unassuming little trattoria with a relaxed vibe, offering mostly seafood dishes prepared using traditional local recipes. Specialities include tuna dishes and lobster. Good local wines.

CARLOFORTE: Al Tonno di Corsa €€€
Seafood **Map** B6
Via Marconi 47, 09014
Tel 0781 85 51 06
As suggested by the name, tuna is the star of the show at this characterful restaurant with warm and bright rooms set out on two levels. The speciality here is *musciame* or sun-dried tuna.

CARLOFORTE: Da Nicolo €€€
Seafood **Map** B6
Corso Cavour 32, 09014
Tel 0781 85 40 48 **Closed** Winter
Proudly interpreting the local cuisine of the area – a surprising combination of North African, Ligurian and Sardinian flavours – this restaurant serves up unusual dishes, many based on fresh tuna.

PORTOSCUSO: La Vecchia Tonnara €€
Seafood **Map** B6
Viale Corsica 1, 09010
Tel 347 728 53 20
The eating experience at this restaurant is enhanced by the marvellous location overlooking the beach of Portopaglietto. Try the paella and the many fish specialities prepared with the day's catch.

SANT'ANTIOCO: Da Achille €€€
Traditional **Map** B6
Via Nazionale 82, 09017
Tel 0781 831 05
The talented chef at stylish Da Achille expertly prepares excellent Sardinian fare. A touch of Oriental influence livens up the menu. The atmosphere is welcoming.

Price Guide

Price ranges are for a three-course meal for one, including a half-bottle of house wine, cover charge, tax and service.

€	up to €25
€€	€25 to €50
€€€	over €50

TEULADA: Ristorante Sebera €€
Traditional **Map** C6
Via San Francesco 8, 09019
Tel 070 927 08 76
For a hotel restaurant, the atmosphere here is refreshingly charming. The menu items are staples of Sardinian cuisine, and the service is attentive. *Spaghetti ai frutti di mare* (seafood pasta) is a particular favourite.

The Eastern Coast

ARBATAX: Il Faro €€
Traditional **Map** D4
Via Porto Frailis, 08048
Tel 0782 66 74 99
The interior of this seaside restaurant is rather plain, but there are great views from the sunny terrace facing the shore. Simple, time-honoured dishes fill the menu, many based on fish.

BAUNEI: Il Golgo €€
Traditional **Map** D4
Loc. Golgo, 08040
Tel 337 811 828
Rustic and inviting, this restaurant serves authentic local cuisine, such as their speciality, *porceddu*. Sit outside to enjoy the mountain views, or inside by the open fire in cooler weather.

Casual dining space at Luigi Pomata in Cagliari

CALA GONONE: Il Pescatore €€
Seafood   Map D3
Via Lungomare dell'Acqua Dolce 1, 08022
Tel *0784 931 74*
Highlights at this charming seaside spot include swordfish carpaccio and octopus salad. Good local wines.

DORGALI: Colibrì €€
Traditional   Map D3
Via Floris 7, 08022
Tel *0784 960 54*   **Closed** *Sun breakfast*
Sardinian dishes are prepared lovingly using ancient recipes. The wild game is excellent – in particular the *cinghiale* (wild boar) – and the desserts are home-made.

DORGALI: Sa Merula Pizzeria da Lopez €€
Pizzeria   Map D3
Via Kennedy 108, 08022
Tel *0784 92 80 00*
The menu here features tasty pizzas and a range of local dishes such as *pane frattau alla Lopez*, which is dry carasau bread with a four-meat ragú and an egg in the middle, as well as pasta and fish dishes.

OROSEI: Su Barchile €€
Traditional   Map D3
Via Mannu 5, 08028
Tel *0784 988 79*
Located in the heart of the old town, Su Barchile has a versatile seasonal menu featuring varieties of seafood, wild game and vegetarian specialities.

OROSEI: Vigne d'Oro €€
Enoteca   Map D3
Via Nazionale 214, 08028
Tel *0784 98 81 00*
Set amid vineyards and olive groves, this restaurant serves a traditional Sardinian spread with a focus on fish and also offers a good selection of local wines.

POSADA: Da Marco e Caterina €€
Seafood   Map D2
Viale Mario Melis s/n, 08020
Tel *0784 85 45 82*
Cheerful trattoria, run by a husband and wife, that exudes passion for the native cuisine. Tasty dishes have a great balance of traditional and modern flavours.

SANTA MARIA NAVARRESE: Ristorante Nascar €€
Seafood   Map D4
Via Pedras s/n, 08040
Tel *0784 23 13 14*
This romantic place, attached to a small hotel, has a low-lit garden with glass tables and wicker

Beautifully presented food at Ristorante Nascar in Santa Maria Navarrese

armchairs set among the trees. A particular favourite is the *fregula*, a Sardinian version of couscous.

TORTOLÌ: Da Lenin €€
Seafood   Map D4
Via Matteotti 24, 08048
Tel *348 544 55 55*
Despite a relatively simple dining room, this restaurant serves fabulous seafood dishes made with traditional and seasonal recipes. The service is warm and professional.

VILLASIMIUS: Da Barbara €€
Seafood   Map D6
Localita' S.P.76, Solanas, 09049
Tel *070 75 06 30*
It is worth making a short trek to find this family-run gem and dine with the locals. Delicious, traditional fish-based dishes are prepared and served with a smile.

VILLASIMIUS: Il Moro €€
Traditional   Map D6
Loc. Villaggio dei Mandorli, 09049
Tel *070 79 81 80*
A quaint restaurant with an open fireplace and lots of exposed wood. The menu has a wide selection of traditional Sardinian recipes. There is a spacious terrace for outdoor dining.

Central Sardinia and Barbagia

GAVOI: Santa Rughe €€
Traditional   Map C3
Via Carlo Felice 2, 08020
Tel *0784 537 74*   **Closed** *Wed*
Exposed stone walls and wood-beamed ceilings make this rustic place all the more intimate. It serves local specialities such as pasta with wild boar ragù and local salami, plus pizza and delicious pastries.

NUORO: Canne al Vento €€
Traditional   Map D3
Via Giuseppe Biasi 159, 08100
Tel *0784 20 17 62*   **Closed** *Sun*
This simple and homely restaurant is where typical Sardinian recipes meet modern Mediterranean cuisine, and the results are fantastic. The wine list is stellar and the service is warm and attentive.

NUORO: Il Portico €€
Traditional   Map D3
Via Monsignor Bua 13, 08100
Tel *0784 21 76 41*   **Closed** *Wed*
Top-class cuisine at affordable prices is offered here, in the heart of Nuoro's old town. Traditional local dishes including pasta and seafood are given a modern twist.

NUORO: Il Rifugio €€
Traditional   Map D3
Via Antonio Mereu 28, 08100
Tel *0784 23 23 55*
Genteel service in an atmospheric setting. The menu features an ample variety of Sardinian dishes; try one of the specialities featuring sheep's cheese. The pizza is excellent too.

NUORO: Ristorante Tascusi €€
Traditional   Map D3
Via Aspromonte 13, 08100
Tel *0784 37 287*
Sardinian art on the walls echoes the culinary arts of Barbagia on the menu – try the antipasti, the *culurgiones* pasta and *seadas*, a local dessert of cheese pastries topped with honey.

OLIENA: Gicappa €€
Traditional   Map D3
Corso Martin Luther King 2, 08025
Tel *0784 28 80 24*
Local dishes presented with style and detail. An impressive variety of seafood as well as meat dishes, and in the evenings there are inventive pizzas as well.

OLIENA: Su Gologone　€€€
Fine Dining　Map D3
Località su Gologone, 08025
Tel *0784 28 75 12*
Set amid lush, gorgeous gardens
this exquisite restaurant serves
Sardinian cuisine paired with
excellent wines. The *pasticceria*
creates delicate confections.

DK Choice

**ORGOSOLO: Ai Monti del
Gennargentu**　€€
Traditional　Map D3
SS Fonni-Lanusei 22, 08027
Tel *078 440 23 74*　**Closed** *Nov–
Easter*
An elegant restaurant situated
high in the mountains offering
a mouthwatering range of
quality meats, cooked to
perfection over an open fire.
For a truly unique experience,
take a guided excursion into
the wilderness and relish a
traditional lunch of lamb stew,
roast pork, bread and cheese
with local shepherds.

OTTANA: Il Platano　€€
Traditional　Map C3
Via Ghitti 83, 08020
Tel *0784 755 64*
Quality food, especially the fish.
The decor leaves a little to be
desired, but the mountain views
are fantastic. Pizzas also available.

ORGOSOLO: Il Portico　€€
Traditional　Map D3
Via Giovanni XXIII 34, 08027
Tel *078 440 29 29*
Authentic flavours and local
ingredients are the key draws at
this trattoria. Sardinian favourites
as well as plenty of pizzas on offer.

The Western Coast

DK Choice

ALGHERO: Al Tuguri　€€
Seafood　Map B2
Via Maiorca 113, 07041
Tel *079 97 67 72*　**Closed** *Sun*
Booking ahead is advisable
here, as the few tables at
this cozy restaurant,
converted from a centuries-
old house, are very much in
demand. The staff are
welcoming, service is smooth,
and guests can watch their
fish or meat being grilled in
the open kitchen. There's an
excellent wine list, packed with
local vintages.

ALGHERO: Al Vecchio Mulino　€€
Traditional　Map B2
Via Don Deroma 3, 07041
Tel *079 97 72 54*　**Closed** *Mon dinner;
Tue*
In a rustic spot in the centre of
the old town, this place whips up
traditional delights such as fried
sea urchins and Catalan lobster.
Tasty pizzas are also available.

ALGHERO: Il Ghiotto　€€
Enoteca　Map B2
Piazza Civica 23, 07041
Tel *079 97 48 20*
A casual wine bar with interesting
local labels and a vast selection
of tasty dishes, both hot and cold.
Fritto misto (seafood in batter) is
excellent. Outdoor seating on a
charming piazza.

ALGHERO: Trattoria Cavour　€€
Seafood　Map B2
Via Cavour 110, 07041
Tel *079 973 87 62*
This simple trattoria is one of the
best on the island for scrumptious
fish. Squid ink risotto, fish soup
and *fritto misto* (seafood in batter)
are the highlights.

**ALGHERO: Osteria
Barcellonetta**　€€€
Traditional　Map B2
Via Gioberti 31, 07041
Tel *079 97 32 079*
This intimate restaurant exudes
old-style charm. Seafood tops the
menu but you'll also find gnocchi
with a rich wild boar sauce.

**BOSA: Mannu da
Giancarlo e Rita**　€€
Seafood　Map B3
Viale Alghero 28, 08013
Tel *0785 37 53 06*
The freshest ingredients are used at
this stylish restaurant, in a family-run
hotel. Fish dominates the menu but
meat dishes are also abundant. Try
the town speciality, lobster.

ORISTANO: Cocco E Dessi　€€
Traditional　Map B4
Via Tirso 31, 09170
Tel *0783 25 26 48*
This central spot has an elegantly
retro atmosphere and a vast
menu with good vegetarian
choices, pizzas and delicious
desserts. Try *fregula alle arselle*
(local couscous with mussels).

ORISTANO: Craf da Banana　€€
Traditional　Map B4
Via De Castro S. A. 34, 09170
Tel *0783 42 01 82*
Wild game is the house speciality
at this welcoming restaurant,
popular with locals for its homely
cooking. Try the mixed grill for the
widest range of options.

ORISTANO: Da Giovanni　€€
Fine Dining　Map B4
Via Colombo 8 – Torre Grande, 09170
Tel *0783 220 51*　**Closed** *Mon*
An elegant restaurant with an
impeccable reputation. The
talented local chef interprets
traditional Sardinian recipes with
flair. All fish is caught fresh locally.
Superb wine list.

PORTO TORRES: Li Lioni　€€
Traditional　Map B2
Veccia SS131 direzione Sassari, 07046
Tel *079 50 22 86*
Four brothers run this inviting
restaurant with lots of old-world
charm; many dishes are prepared
in a fine wood-burning oven.
Non-carnivores beware: meat
dishes are the speciality here.

STINTINO: Silvestrino　€€€
Seafood　Map B2
Via Sassari 14, 07040
Tel *079 52 30 07*
Located in a small hotel just steps
from the sea, this restaurant serves
authentic local dishes. Seafood is
the main attraction, and the
lobster is particularly good.

Charming interior of Su Gologone in Oliena

The North and the Costa Smeralda

ARZACHENA: Ristorante La Rocca €€€
Seafood **Map** D1
Loc. Pulicinu, 07021
Tel *0789 93 30 11*
A chic restaurant a short walk from the beach, specializing in the freshest crustaceans and shellfish. An impressive selection of wines.

BAIA SARDINIA: Corbezzolo €€€
Seafood **Map** D1
Piazzetta della Fontana, 07021
Tel *0789 998 93*
There are two dining options here: a family-friendly pizzeria on the pedestrianized piazza, or fine seafood in the airy dining room and on terraces over- looking the sea. Great service.

LA MADDALENA: Ristorante La Terrazza €€
Seafood **Map** D1
Via Villa Glori 6, 07024
Tel *0789 73 53 05*
Fish is the speciality at this traditional restaurant. Try fried fish antipasti, grilled fish and carpaccio paired with good wine.

OLBIA: Antica Trattoria Pizzeria €€
Pizzeria **Map** D2
Via Terme, 1, 07026
Tel *0789 240 53*
Fabulous pizzas with a variety of traditional and unusual toppings, including mixed seafood. The decor is simple but quaint.

OLBIA: Vecchia Gallura €€
Traditional **Map** D2
Localita' Scopa (Palau), 07020
Tel *0789 70 81 94*
Located in a stone house covered with ivy, this restaurant is a picturesque spot to sample local cuisine. The set menu of either meat or fish is excellent value.

PORTO CERVO: Hivaoa €€
Pizzeria **Map** D1
Via della Marina, 07021
Tel *0789 914 51*
White tables and fresh linen on a breezy covered terrace. Pizza is just the beginning: excellent seafood and pasta too. The *frutti di mare antipasto* spread is a must.

PORTO CERVO: Cipriani €€€
Fine Dining **Map** D1
Via Rocce Sul Pevero Localita' Golfo Pero, 07020
Tel *0789 941 92* **Closed** *Oct–May*
With its white sofas, chandeliers and luxurious gold accents this restaurant defines glamour.

Glamorous dining at Cipriani in Porto Cervo

The dishes are delectable and original, the wine list is stellar and the house cocktails legendary.

PORTO CERVO: Gianni Pedrinelli €€€
Fine Dining **Map** D1
Loc. Piccolo Pevero, 07021
Tel *0789 924 36* **Closed** *Nov– Feb*
The menu at this restaurant offers mostly meat and game dishes but many seafood options are also available. Do not miss the house speciality, *porcettu allo spiedo* (spit-roast suckling pig). A lovely space with simple, classic furnishings.

PORTO CERVO: Il Pescatore €€€
Seafood **Map** D1
Porto Cervo, 07020
Tel *0789 93 16 24*
One of the oldest restaurants in this exclusive port town, and the only one offering *pied dans l'eau* (right on the water) dining. Heavenly dishes but small portions. Book ahead.

PORTO CERVO: Spinnaker €€€
Seafood **Map** D1
Res. Alba Ruja, Liscia di Vacca, 07020
Tel *0789 912 26*
One of the Costa Smeralda's best-known restaurants, serving innovative fish pasta dishes, such as black ravioli stuffed with salt cod or farfalline with celery and mullet roe. The portions, however, are on the small side.

PORTO ROTONDO: Da Giovannino €€
Fine Dining **Map** D1
Piazza Quadra 10, 07026
Tel *0789 352 80*
Watch out for celebrities at this high-profile restaurant while sampling the excellent Mediterranean cuisine. Highlights include the scampi sushi with lemon juice and the grilled squid.

DK Choice

PORTO ROTONDO: Pedristellas €€
Traditional **Map** D1
Via Monte Ladu 63, 07026
Tel *377 236 92 01*
The name of this extraordinary restaurant, which translates to "rocks and stars", refers to its magnificent rock garden, dotted with old pine trees. The placement of tables and even the meandering garden paths were designed to complement the glorious setting. The menu has an abundance of seafood and meat specialities in the typical Sardinian tradition.

PORTO ROTONDO: Stella di Gallura €€
Traditional **Map** D1
Via Monte Ladu, 07026
Tel *0789 344 02*
A modern, elegant restaurant close to the beach. The menu is filled with typical Sardinian dishes from both land and sea as well as excellent pizzas. Opt for poolside dining.

SASSARI: Il Cenacolo €€
Traditional **Map** B2
Via Ozieri 1, 07100
Tel *079 23 62 51*
A centrally located, elegant place whipping up all of the best regional specialities. Seasonal menu and friendly service.

SASSARI: L'Antica Hostaria €€
Traditional **Map** B2
Via Cavour 55, 07100
Tel *079 20 00 66* **Closed** *Sun*
Charming, slightly old-fashioned restaurant in the modern town. The chef is Sicilian: don't miss his authentic cassata ice-cream. Long list of Sardinian wines.

For more information on types of restaurants *see page 180*

SHOPS AND MARKETS

Sardinia produces a great variety of handicrafts that are hard to find in other regions of Italy. Among these are hand-woven rugs, linen napkins, *pibbiones* (embroidered fabrics) and baskets. Traditional materials and techniques are used for all these products, and while some are still made in the traditional style, others have been adapted to more modern tastes. Crafted goods are often made to a very high standard of design and workmanship, and include coral and filigree pins and brooches, pottery and crockery, and items made from cork and wrought iron.

In the larger towns and tourist resorts, traditional souvenirs are sold, such as ashtrays in the shape of nuraghi, costumed dolls and seashell pictures. Specialities such as pecorino cheese, salted mullet roe, sweets and wine are also worth trying.

Opening Hours

Shops in Sardinia generally open at 9am, close at 1pm for lunch and reopen 4:30–8pm (5–8:30pm or later in summer). Large supermarkets and larger clothes stores are open throughout the day. In the cities most shops close for a few weeks in August, while on the coast they tend to open on a seasonal basis (June to September).

A potter at the wheel producing traditionally shaped vessels

How to Pay

The majority of the larger shops and department stores accept credit cards, but it is advisable to check in advance. The smaller shops and artisan's workshops will generally prefer payment in cash. You must get a receipt *(scontrino)* when you pay; it is required by law and you may be asked to produce it as you leave the shop. It will also be needed should you want to change purchased articles later on.

Department Stores

The main department store in Cagliari is **La Rinascente** in Via Roma. Other large stores are **Upim** and **Oviesse**, which you will also find in other Sardinian towns and cities. Large shopping centres have grown up on the outskirts of towns, with a wide selection of goods on offer, from shoe shops and clothing stores to supermarkets and fast-food restaurants.

Handicrafts

Local handicrafts are on sale all over Sardinia. In the villages, women display their wares, such as baskets, rugs or ceramics, outside their homes.

For half a century, many shops have received the support of *Istituto Sardo Organizzazione Lavoro Artigianale* (**ISOLA**), Sardinian Institute of Handicrafts, which had worked until 2006, to offer quality products from the local craftsmen's cooperatives, including rugs, tablecloths, leather, jewellery, baskets, pottery, carved wood and wrought-iron objects. Though the ISOLA trademark

Local handicrafts for sale in a certified ISOLA shop

no longer exists, the country supports its handicrafts through **Sardegna Artigianato**. The products of these shops carry a special seal of quality guaranteeing their origin and authenticity.

You can find some good bargains at the *Fiera del Tappeto* (Carpet Fair), which is held at Mogoro in late July–August. Handicrafts can also be purchased at holiday farms. Other useful addresses can be found at www.sardegnartigianato.it.

A fish stall in Cagliari's covered market, San Benedetto

Regional Specialities

Gastronomic specialities in Sardinia are sold in the food section of supermarkets as well as in delicatessens and specialist shops or directly from the producers.

The **Mercato Coperto di San Benedetto** in Cagliari is the largest covered market in Italy. It offers an excellent choice of regional delicacies. *Bottarga* (mullet roe) can be bought at **Vaghi**, on Via Bayle, which also sells sea urchin pâté. Salted *bottarga* can be bought from the manufacturer at

A dish of typical Sardinian honey

San Francesco's feast day celebrated at Lula with barbecued *porceddu*

Fratelli Manca in Cabras. Smoked fish is on sale at **Sarda Affumicati** in Buggerru.

Cakes and sweets are also a Sardinian speciality and a fine selection is on offer in several shops, including **Sorelle Piccioni** in Quartu Sant'Elena, **Pasticceria Sarda** in Olbia and **Acciari** at Porto Torres. A visit to a winery (*cantina*) to taste the wines before buying can prove both interesting and good value. It is sometimes possible to taste wines in a wine shop (*enoteca*).

Visit www.sardegnaturismo.it/en/offerta/enogastromia for useful addresses of shops and workshops.

DIRECTORY

Handicrafts

Alghero
Centro Forme
Via Lamarmora 64/66.
Tel 079 97 53 52.
w centroforme-alghero.it

Cagliari
ISOLA Artigianato
Sardo
Via Bacaredda 184.
Tel 070 40 47 91.
w regione.sardegna.it/isola

Olbia
Sardartis srl
SS125, km 313.
Tel 0789 669 33.
w sardartis.it
Cerasarda
Circonvallazione Nord.
Tel 0789 56 73 11.
w cerasarda.it

Oristano
Cooperativa Su
Trobasciu
Via Gramsci 1, Mogoro.
Tel 0783 99 05 81.
w sutrobasciu.com

Porto Cervo
Sardegna Artigianato
Sottopiazza.
Tel 0789 94 428.

Sant'Antioco
Cooperativa
Sant'Antioco Martire
Lungomare Vespucci 30.
Tel 0781 820 85.

Sassari
Sardegna Artigianato
Viale Mancini.
Tel 079 23 01 01.

Regional Specialities

Alghero
Sella & Mosca
I Piani. Tel 079 99 77 00.
w sellaemosca.com

Buggerru
Sarda Affumicati
Località Sa Colombera.
Tel 0781 549 14.
w sardaffumicati.com

Cabras
Fratelli Manca
Via Cima 5. Tel 0783 29 08 48.
w orodicabras.it

Cagliari
Mercato San Benedetto
Via Cocco Ortu. Tel 070 667 56 14.

Olbia
Pasticceria Sarda
Via Vespignani 2.
Tel 0789 502 39.

Ozieri
Pasticceria Artigianale
Ozieri
Via De Gasperi 10.
Tel 079 78 82 80.

Porto Torres
Acciaro
Corso Vittorio Emanuele 36.
Tel 079 51 46 05.

Quartu Sant'Elena
Sorelle Piccioni
Via Marconi 312.
Tel 070 81 01 12.

Sassari
Fratelli Rau
Via Gorizia 7.
Tel 079 29 22 64.

Tonara
Salvatore Pruneddu
Via Porru 5. Tel 0784 638 05.
w pruneddu.com

Wine

Cabras
Azienda Attilio Contini
Via Genova 48.
Tel 0783 29 08 06.
w vinicontini.com

Cagliari
Antica Enoteca
Cagliaritana
Scalette Santa Chiara.
Tel 070 65 56 11.
w enoteca-cagliaritana.it

Jerzu
Jerzu Antichi Poderi
Via Umberto I 1.
Tel 0782 700 28.
w jerzuantichipoderi.it

Olbia
Cantina della vigne di
Piero Mancini
Tel 0789 50 717.
w pieromancini.it

Oristano
Vino Vernaccia
Loc. Rimedio.
Tel 0783 33 383.
w vinovernaccia.com

Quartu Sant'Elena
Cantina Sociale
Via Nazionale,
Maracalagonis.
Tel 070 78 98 65.
w cantinaquartu.com

Sant'Antioco
Cantine Sardus Pater
Via Rinascita 46. Tel 0781 800 274. w cantine
sarduspater.it

Sennori
Tenute Dettori
Tel 079 51 27 72.
w tenutedettori.it

Serdiana
Cantina Argiolas
Via Roma 28/30.
Tel 070 74 06 06.
w argiolas.it

What to Buy in Sardinia

Sardinia offers a great variety of traditional island products and local handicrafts, ranging from handwoven rugs, bedspreads and pillowcases to baskets woven in asphodel, reed or raffia. Some of the finest baskets are made in Flussio and Castelsardo. Other household articles, such as kitchenware and tableware, are made of cork or ceramics, materials which are also used to make large plates, statues and bas-reliefs. Filigree jewellery production is widespread and worn by the women for festivals and weddings; the best is made in Alghero and Bosa.

Gold buttons

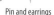

Pin and earrings

Filigree pendant

Jewellery

Traditional Sardinian jewellery, such as earrings, brooches and buttons, often worn with local dress, is made of filigree and coral. Goldsmiths also make bracelets and necklaces in modern designs, including elegant coral spirals.

Cork ice bucket

At Calangianus, in the Gallura region of the Costa Smeralda, cork is used to make numerous household articles such as boxes, umbrella stands, bowls and ice buckets.

Circular amphora

Flower vase

Vases and jugs made to a modern design

Pottery

Sardinian pottery is hand-thrown and glazed with natural colours. The most common articles are vases, plates and jugs and the designs are simple and fluid. Some potters have modified traditional designs to suit modern tastes.

Basket-weaving is an ancient craft that is still widely practised. Baskets are made of straw, raffia, dwarf palm, asphodel, corn sheaves or wicker in delicate, natural colours.

Rug made in Nule

Tapestry from Mogoro

A *pibbiones* rug

Rugs and Tapestries

Among the typical hand-woven articles are woollen rugs, linen bedspreads and napkins, and tapestries. The rugs are made from coloured wool with lively geometric or floral designs. The pibbiones rugs consist of an embroidered raised pattern knitted with small needles on neutral coloured fabric.

Wood carving is an ancient Sardinian tradition. The most common articles produced are chests, kitchen implements, chopping boards and ceremonial masks.

Carved mask

Lacework from Dorgali

Lace-making is a rare craft that requires great skill. At Oliena you can find delicate shawls made of black silk embroidered with bright colours. At Bosa you can still see women making filet lace.

Gastronomic Delicacies

Typical Sardinian products include cakes and cheeses which vary from region to region. Other specialities include jam, wine and liqueurs, such as myrtle (mirto) and lemon (limoncino), salted mullet roe and vegetables in oil.

Typical Sardinian cakes

Salted mullet roe

Myrtle liqueur

Typical Sardinian delicacies

WATER SPORTS

Despite the impressive beauty of its interior, Sardinia's fame is more strongly associated with the sea. The development of the tourist industry means that the island now offers a good range of facilities for water sports, in particular sailing, windsurfing and scuba diving. There are diving centres and sailing schools in almost all the coastal resorts, and many of the holiday villages are well-equipped for water sports. Canoeing is a different matter, since the lack of navigable rivers limits your choice in the interior, and sea canoeing is only practised in a few places along the coast.

Scuba diving in the crystal-clear waters of the Mediterranean

Yachts sailing at an international sailing competition in Porto Cervo

find the Sardinian coast a challenge because of the strong and variable winds. A good source of useful information for a sailing holiday is volume 1A of *Portolano del Mediterraneo* (Mediterranean Pilot's Book), which is published by the Istituto Idrografico della Marina Militare. Another useful publication is the pamphlet *I Porti Turistici della Sardegna* (Sardinian Yacht Harbours), available from all tourist information offices. You need permission from the harbour master to moor in most of Sardinia's harbours.

Sailing

With its marvellous sea and coastline, Sardinia is regarded as a paradise for boating of all kinds, whether your preferred style is a billion-dollar luxury yacht on the Costa Smeralda or a simple dinghy for hire from one of the more affordable centres. The conditions vary considerably and even experienced sailors

Scuba Diving

The coastline offers plenty of opportunities for experienced divers. Among the most famous spots for diving are the coasts of Asinara and Gallura, Capo Caccia, Carloforte, the Golfo di Orosei and the area around the island of Tavolara. Many diving centres – often based at sports shops – organize diving trips.

You can also buy or rent diving equipment and get advice on diving sites.

Windsurfing

Windsurfing equipment is available for hire at almost all the tourist beaches. Some of the sailing centres also offer boards for hire and can organize lessons. The safety rules for sailing also apply to this sport: the winds can be very strong and fickle (especially the mistral), so do not go too far out.

Windsurfing Beaches

The following beaches are the best on the island for windsurfing (see pp22–3).

Bosa Marina
Poetto – Cagliari
Calagrande – Isola di Sant'Antioco
Saline – Isola di Sant'Antioco
Monti d'a Rena – La Maddalena
Porto Massimo – La Maddalena
Porto Taverna – Porto San Paolo Lotzorai
Marinella – Olbia
Porto Istana – Olbia
Torre Grande – Oristano
Porto Pollo – Palau
Capo Testa – Santa Teresa di Gallura
La Cinta – San Teodoro
Putzu Idu – San Vero Milis
Platamona - Sorso
La Pelosa – Stintino

The Centro Velico Caprera sailing school

Canoeing

Although there are very few navigable rivers for canoeing in the interior – and the variable weather makes practising the sport even more difficult – you can canoe in the lakes or along certain stretches of the coast.

Other Sports

There are numerous coves along the Sardinian coasts where you can explore the rocks and the water and observe the varied marine life. Snorkelling is perhaps best left to the experienced: strong winds and currents can easily create difficult and dangerous conditions.

Subaqua fishing with a harpoon and aqualung is not permitted but freshwater fishing is possible in Sardinia's lakes and reservoirs. You will need to obtain a permit to fish in the rivers.

In some holiday villages water-based tours are offered to guests, and some also provide dinghies in which to explore the coastline.

Canoeing along the coast of Sardinia

DIRECTORY

Sailing and Windsurfing Centres

Carloforte Yacht Club
Tel 328 893 4596.
W carloforteyacht
club.org

Centro Velico Caprera – La Maddalena
Localita Punta Coda
Caprera. Tel 02 8645 2191.
W centrovelico
caprera.it

Circolo Nautico Arbatax
W circolonautico
arbatax.it

Circolo Nautico Olbia
Molo Brin 6.
Tel 0789 261 87.
W circolonautico
olbia.it

Circolo Nautico Oristano
Porticciolo Turistico
Torregrande.
Tel 346 031 9129.
W circolonautico
oristano.it

Club Nautico La Maddalena
Via G Cesare 20.
Tel 0789 72 79 85.

Windsurfing Club Cagliari
Marina Piccola.
W windsurfingclub
cagliari.org

Windsurfing Vela Club Portoscuso
Via Marco Polo 1.
Tel 340 123 2144.

Yacht Club Alghero
Tel 079 95 20 74.
W yachtclubalghero.it

Yacht Club Cagliari
Marina Piccola.
Tel 070 37 03 50.
W yachtclubcagliari.it

Yacht Club Costa Smeralda – Porto Cervo
Porto Cervo.
Tel 0789 90 22 00.
W yccs.it

Yacht Club Porto Rotondo
Tel 0789 340 10.
W ycpr.it

Diving Centres

Air Sub Service – Villasimius
Tel 070 79 20 33 or 070 50 68 63 (winter).
W airsub.com

Anthias
Palau. Tel 0789 86 311.
W anthiasdiving.com

Aqua Diving Center Puntaldia
Puntaldia, San Teodoro.
Tel 0784 86 43 90 or 348 511 23 33.

Areamare Diving
Cannigione.
Tel 338 822 11 35.
W areamare.com

Centro Sub Tavolara
Porto San Paolo.
Tel 0789 403 60.
W tavoladiving.it

Isla Diving
Carloforte.
Tel 335 46 25 02.
W isladiving.it

Karibu Diving Center
c/o Hotel Capo Caccia.
Tel 338 953 6383.
W karibu.it

L'Argonauta Diving Center
Cala Gonone.
Tel 0784 930 46 or 347 530 40 97.
W argonauta.it

Orso Diving Club – Poltu Quato
Porto Cervo.
Tel 0789 990 01 or 348 064 1825.
W orsodiving.com

Oyster Sub Diving Center
Palau.
Tel 0789 70 20 70.
W oystersub.com

Proteus Diving Center
Arzachena.
Tel 327 530 53 55.
W lnx.proteusdiving.it

Tanka Village Diving Center – Villasimius
Tel 070 79 54 64 or 338 674 14 74.
W subcentertanka.com

Canoeing

Cardedu Kayak
Cardedu, Ogliastra.
Tel 0782 75 185 or 348 936 9401.
W cardedu-kayak.com

Federazione Italiana Canoa Kayak
Cagliari.
Email crsardegna @
federcanoa.it.
W federcanoa.it

Team Kayak Sardegna
Cagliari.
Tel 335 598 6395.
W teamkayak
sardegna.com

OUTDOOR SPORTS

Neglected for years because attention was focused on tourist development along the coast, the interior landscape of Sardinia offers plenty of opportunity to practise outdoor sports. The countryside can be explored on foot or on horseback – riding centres have made great advances in recent years and are in great demand. Facilities for hiking and rock climbing are good and increasing numbers of mountain climbing routes are in the process of being marked out.

The Su Rei riding centre in Sulcis

Horse Riding

Sardinia is ideally suited for trekking and horse riding. Horses have long been an integral part of the island's culture, as the animal has been part of local life since Phoenician times: many of the religious feast days and festivities include horseback rides and horse races.

The many isolated minor roads, mule tracks and paths, far away from traffic and noise, particularly in the interior, are ideal for pleasant rides, and many are not too difficult for beginners.

There are nearly a hundred Sardinian equestrian clubs and centres, large and small, offering facilities for this sport. Most are equipped to organize lessons and rides for beginners as well as extended treks for experienced riders.

Most of the stables and clubs are located near Cagliari, Nuoro and Oristano, but there has been an increase in the number of holiday farms (see p174) offering horse riding and riding excursions for their guests, whatever their ability. Supramonte, Giara di Gesturi and the Valle della Luna are three of the most interesting and popular destinations for those who love long treks in the Sardinian countryside.

Rock Climbing

In the 1960s the Italian mountaineer Alessandro Gogna published *Mezzogiorno di Pietra* (Midday Stone), which opened up the possibilities for rock climbing in Sardinia. Since those days enthusiasm for the sport has grown considerably, and today the island's most challenging rocks and cliffs are tackled by climbers from all over Italy and Europe. Among the most popular climbing areas are Supramonte (Surtana, l'Aguglia), the cliffs at Iglesiente (Domusnovas), where hand- and foot-holds have been placed, and the Isili area in Nuoro province.

Essential reading for rock climbers who decide to come here is *Pietra di Luna* (Moon Stone) by Maurizio Oviglia, the most up-to-date guide to rock climbing in Sardinia.

Additional information can be obtained at the **Sezione di Cagliari del Club Alpino Italiano**. Programmes are organized by a number of companies, including **Barbagia Insolita** and **Keya**. Climbing lessons are available from **Rock & Sun**.

Walking and Trekking

Wild mountains, hills dotted with prehistoric ruins, forests and maquis vegetation make up most of the terrain in the interior of Sardinia. The countryside is rugged but unspoilt and ideal for walking, hiking and more strenuous treks. However, facilities are few and far between, clearly signposted footpaths are rare and there are very few refuges or stopping places. It is always advisable to carry an up-to-date map and to take plenty of water when walking.

The most rewarding and popular areas are Supramonte, the Gennargentu massif and the Sulcis area (which offers an unusual blend of hiking and industrial archaeology). Some stretches of the steep coastline are more suited to those with climbing experience.

In the Supramonte area experienced mountaineers can even tackle the wild and precipitous Su Gorroppu gorges. The trek takes a couple of days and special rock climbers' equipment is needed in order to make it down the vertical walls of the falls. This

Cliffs at the seaside with facilities for rock climbing

The Selvaggio Blu Route

Its very name – Wild Blue – is the best possible description of this difficult route along the Golfo di Orosei, starting from Santa Maria Navarrese and ending at Cala Luna. The Selvaggio Blu was conceived by Mario Verin and Peppino Cicalò in the late 1980s. The course requires excellent physical condition and preparation (since part of it consists of stretches of rock climbing, some of the descents are achieved by abseiling and you have to walk with a heavy load because of the distance between water supply sources) but the rewards are some of the most spectacular views of the Sardinian coast. The town of Baunei publishes a guide to Selvaggio Blu; for information, or if you are interested in buying the book, call 347 290 3101 (www.selvaggioblu.it).

A stretch of the Selvaggio Blu trail

particular excursion is, therefore, not suitable for beginners. Whether walking or climbing, or a combination of both, make sure you have the best map possible to hand (a good map is published by IGM). You should also carefully calculate the time the tour will take and how much food and water will be needed, as it is possible to walk for kilometres without stumbling across a village.

Caving

The mountains of Sardinia are riddled with dozens of fascinating caves to be explored, some of which have tourist facilities. The temperature inside is likely to be relatively high, more or less the yearly average of the surrounding area. Bear in mind that some of the difficult caves, such as the Golgo abyss (at Su Sterru), the Grotta Verde at Capo Caccia or the Su Palu cave near Orosei, are only open to experienced spelunkers.

Golf Courses

Sardinia has some famous golf courses, including the one at the **Pevero Golf Club** in Porto Cervo, designed by the architect Robert Trent Jones. This 18-hole golf course is internationally known for its tournaments.

Other Sports

The island's sports activites are not confined to the mountains and caves in its interior. More traditional sports such as tennis, football, swimming and five-a-side football can be pursued in the many sports grounds and courts throughout the island.

The golf course at Pevero in Porto Cervo, on the Costa Smeralda

DIRECTORY

Horse Riding

Cooperativa Goloritze
Ogliastra.
Tel 368 702 89 80.
W coopgoloritze.com

Horse Country
Arborea.
Tel 0783 80 500.
W horsecountry.it

Maneggio La Cinta
San Teodoro.
Tel 338 822 8984.
W maneggiolacinta santeodoro.it

La Posada del Cavallo
Posada.
Tel 0784 85 41 16.
W posadacavallo.it

Walking Tours

Barbagia Insolita
Oliena. Tel 0784 28 60 05.
W barbagiainsolita.it

Club Alpino Italiano
Cagliari. Tel 070 66 78 77.
W caicagliari.it

Cooperativa Ghivine
Dorgali. Tel 338 834 1618.
W ghivine.com

Cooperativa Goloritze
Baunei. Tel 368 702 89 80.
W coopgoloritze.com

Cooperativa Turistica Enis
Oliena. Tel 0784 28 83 63.
W coopenis.it

Escursioni in Sardegna
Dorgali. Tel 349 672 7750.
W escursioniin sardegna.com

Esedra Escursioni
Bosa. Tel 0785 743 044.
W esedraescursioni.it

Keya
Orosei. Tel 348 6530 682/683. W keya.eu

Nordic Walking
W nordicwalking sardegna.com

Rock & Sun
Tel (from UK) 0203 390 0351.
W rockandsun.com

Scoprisardegna
Porto Torres.
Tel 328 456 46 82.
W scoprisardegna.com

Zente
Dorgali. Tel 349 666 2264.
W zente.it

Caving

Federazione Speleologica Sarda
Iglesias. Tel 0781 306 64.
W federazione speleologicasarda.it

Società Speleologica Italiana
Via Zamboni 67, Bologna.
Tel 051 53 46 57.
W ssi.speleo.it

Golf Courses

Is Molas Golf Club
Pula. Tel 070 924 10 06.
W ismolas.it

Pevero Golf Club
Porto Cervo. Tel 0789 95 80 00. W golfclub pevero.com

Tanka Golf Club
Villasimius. Tel 342 885 6244. W golftanka.it

SURVIVAL
GUIDE

PRACTICAL INFORMATION

Beaches and the clean blue sea are the principal attractions for visitors to Sardinia, and the coastline, especially in the northeast, gets very crowded from early July to late August. Visiting the island out of season can have its advantages: apart from avoiding the bustling crowds, accommodation and ferries are cheaper in June and September, and the towns and countryside, rich in history, ancient culture, old traditions and spellbinding scenery, are best appreciated when it's not too hot. Government funding for monuments is as slow and insufficient here as anywhere else in Italy, so don't be surprised to see signs such as *chiuso per restauro* (closed for restoration).

Bathers cooling off in the Mediterranean as temperatures soar in summer

When to Go

Sardinia is renowned for its six-month summer, with warm and dry weather and seas warm enough for swimming from May to October. Temperatures reach peaks in late July and August, with up to 42°C (108°F) in the inland areas. This is also when most Italians go on holiday so everywhere is overcrowded, in particular the ferries to and from Olbia and Cagliari, and the seaside hotels and resorts. The most crowded areas are the Costa Smeralda, the beaches near the Golfo di Cagliari and the area around Stintino. The best months to visit the beautiful interior are May, June and September. Spring is particularly delightful, when flowers are in bloom. In winter the cold can be quite intense, especially at higher altitudes.

Visas & Passports

European Union (EU) residents and visitors from the US, Canada, New Zealand and Australia need no visa for a stay of up to three months. Information concerning visas can be obtained in advance at your nearest Italian consulate. Non-EU citizens must carry a valid passport, while for EU citizens a national ID card will suffice. It is advisable to check the requirements before travelling. By law you must carry your ID with you at all times, as it may be needed during a road block.

Travel Safety Information

Visitors can get up-to-date travel safety information from the **Foreign and Commonwealth Office** in the UK, the **State Department** in the US and **Department of Foreign Affairs and Trade** in Australia.

Customs Information

Any customs formalities are completed at the first Italian arrival point (usually the mainland). Non-EU citizens can claim back sales tax (IVA) on purchases costing over €154.94. Consulates can generally provide up-to-date information on customs regulations. Non-EU citizens can bring in either 200 cigarettes or 50 cigars or 1kg of tobacco, 1 litre of spirits, 4 litres of wine and 50 grams of perfume.

Tourist Information

The **Sardegna Turismo** website gives visitors an overview of the region's places of interest and events, and also offers the opportunity to book a hotel and to create an itinerary. Every comune (local town council) of tourist interest has its own tourist information office, often housed in the town hall. Local papers – *L'Unione Sarda*, *La Nuova Sardegna* and *Sardegna Oggi* – are useful sources of information, providing complete day-by-day listings of activities and events, though in Italian.

There are also useful websites aimed at tourists in Sardinia, such as www.sardinia.net, which lists holiday accommodation, events and festivals.

Admission Prices

Entrance fees for museums and archaeological sites vary between €2 and €12. Under-18s and senior citizens are usually allowed in free of charge or pay a reduced fee. Where available, student and teacher reductions can be obtained by showing ISIC cards or other forms of identification.

Opening Hours

Museums and archaeological zones are usually open every day except Monday. However, in winter, some sites close in the afternoon and, in summer, opening hours are extended, sometimes even to late evening hours. Churches in the interior are usually closed in the middle of the day and may only be open for mass. If a church is closed, the parish priest (*parroco*)

A store in Sardinia offering luxury goods

or sexton may open it for you as a special favour for a short visit. A small contribution to church funds will always be welcome in return for assistance.

Shops are open from 8 or 9am to 1pm and from 3:30 or 4pm (in winter) or 5pm (in summer) to 7 or 8pm from Monday to Saturday, with one early closing day during the week.

Traditional rituals, still part of the community year in Sardinia

Festivals

Sardinia's festivals have a very long history and are colourful and unusual affairs. The busiest times of year for seeing traditional festivals are Carnival, Easter and Assumption Day (15 August). Town halls provide information on feast days and festivals, and dates are also given in the information for each town in this guide. For an overview of the main festivals and events in Sardinia, see pages 30–33.

Travellers with Disabilities

Unfortunately, facilities for the disabled are rare, even in the larger towns, and touring can be quite a frustrating experience for wheelchair users. However, conditions are improving and ramps, lifts and modified WCs are becoming increasingly common in stations. Some restaurants will have wheelchair access to the dining room, or at least will do their best to help their disabled guests reach their table, but there may not be access to the WC. Visitors travelling by train can request **RFI** (Italian Railway Network) assistance at many

stations including Cagliari, Sassori, Macomer and Olbia by calling their national phone number or contacting **Trenitalia**'s call centre. For further information, contact the offices of the Sardinian provinces.

Travelling with Children

Sardinia is great for children and locals are very welcoming to families. Restaurants generally welcome children and will prepare simple dishes or smaller portions on request. Kids will enjoy spending time at the beach and running around in the piazzas with local children.

Theme parks are becoming increasingly popular. **Diverland** is a great water park in the south, while **Aquadream** offers aquatic entertainment in the north. Animal fans will enjoy the **Cala Gonone Aquarium** and the paleontological park **Dinosardo**, which explores the world of dinosaurs and fossils.

Travelling on a Budget

Sardinia is not a budget destination, especially when it comes to accommodation, but renting a self-catered apartment and shopping at local supermarkets and markets can help reduce costs. Camp sites abound along the coast and are considered the most basic and cheapest form of accommodation. Eating at an *agriturismo* is a cheaper alternative to the smarter restaurants by the sea and is also a great way to try out the regional flavours.

Responsible Tourism

Sardinians are particularly eco-conscious, especially when it comes to preserving their beaches and their landscape. Staying at a family-run guesthouse or an *agriturismo*, shopping at the local markets and businesses, and visiting rural locations are great ways to support the local economy. Tour operator **Just Sardinia** offers "sustainable vacation" packages and provides advice on how to reduce tourist impact while on the island.

Personal Security and Health

On the whole, Sardinia is a safe place for visitors and only a few precautions are needed for a pleasant stay. Beware of pickpockets in the busy passenger terminals of the ports and in cities. Do not leave valuables in your car if the parking place is unsupervised. In general, rural areas are safer than cities. During the summer, forest fires are a serious problem, so make sure you know the local police or firemen instructions should an emergency arise.

Police

There are many different police forces in Italy. The state police, *polizia*, wear blue uniforms and deal with criminal offences and issue passports to Italian citizens. The military police or *carabinieri* wear red-striped trousers and manage offences ranging from theft to speeding. The *vigili urbani*, or municipal police, wear blue uniforms in winter and white in summer, and issue fines for traffic and parking offences. They can be spotted patrolling the streets and regulating traffic. Their work may overlap with the *polizia stradale's* job; this section of the *polizia* is responsible for traffic violations, mainly in state roads, but also issues fines inside the cities. The *guardia di finanza*, or tax police, wear grey uniforms and deal with tax evasion, customs and drugs.

Crimes should be reported to the police or at a *carabinieri* office, where you will get a signed form required to claim insurance. If your car has been towed away, request the help of the *vigili urbani*.

What to be Aware of

Try not to carry large amounts of cash when travelling. Visitors should be wary of bag

Fire, a constant danger, spreading rapidly across the dry, scrubby vegetation

snatchers who operate in quiet streets of bigger cities, such as Sassari, Olbia and Cagliari. Take proper care of your belongings in a busy market place and on public transport.

It is advisable to stay away from unauthorised taxi drivers operating at airports and train stations as they frequently overcharge.

Generally, travelling on Sardinian roads poses few problems; however, you may be stopped at a *posto di blocco* (police or army road block). Roadblocks are routine and should be no cause for alarm. Officers usually check your ID and the vehicle, and they may also search your car and test your alcohol level. Drinking and driving is forbidden and even a small amount of alcohol can result in the suspension of your licence. Parking is generally safe and car theft is rare, but cars do get broken into, so always bring your valuables along, especially laptops, jewellery and passports. If you have possessions or luggage in the car boot, it is advisable not to open the tailgate in a crowded place before leaving the car unattended.

In an Emergency

For immediate medical attention, contact the First Aid (*Pronto Soccorso*) department of a main hospital such as Giovanni Paolo II in Olbia or San Giovanni di Dio in Cagliari. Alternatively, check the phone directories for a doctor (*dottore*) or a dentist (*dentista*). Emergency care in public hospitals is free for all, including foreigners.

Lost and Stolen Property

In major cities, airport terminals, and bus and train stations usually have their own lost property offices. In small towns, enquire at the ticket offices or at the nearest police station.

To report stolen or lost items, head to the nearest *questura* (police station) or *carabinieri* office. In the case of lost passports, contact your embassy or consulate; for lost credit cards, contact the bank or the issuing company's office.

Hospitals and Pharmacies

In tourist areas, the *Guardia Medica* (emergency treatment centre) gives medical attention to summer visitors. These seasonal surgeries are often closed in low season, so in this case you will have to go to a hospital instead.

Sardinia has a good network of hospitals and casualty departments (*pronto soccorso*). EU nationals are entitled to Italian medical care, but you need to carry an EHIC card, while emergency care is free for all. For minor problems, pharmacists can recommend over-the-counter medication.

Policemen on horseback at the Poetto beach near Cagliari

Pharmacies (*farmacie*) are open from Monday to Friday, 9am–1pm and 4–7pm and Saturday morning. Lists of the night and holiday opening rotas for the local area are posted on the chemist's door.

Travel and Health Insurance

EU visitors should obtain the European Health Insurance Card (EHIC) before travelling. This is available online (www. dh.gov.uk) or at a post office. The card comes with a booklet of advice and information on the procedure for claiming free medical treatment.

When booking air travel tickets, it is best to inquire whether there are waivers pertaining to any medical emergencies. It can be difficult to arrange travel insurance once you reach Sardinia, so it is always advisable to purchase it before you travel.

Fire Hazards

Unfortunately, forest fires are a real problem in Sardinia, especially in the summer. Except for the rare cases of accidental fire that may be caused by a thrown-away cigarette, most fires on the island are started deliberately. In some instances forest and brush are destroyed to make way for more grazing

Fire Prevention Rules

1. Always take care to extinguish cigarettes before discarding them.
2. Never light a fire except in areas where this is explicitly permitted.
3. If you see a fire, you must report it to the local firemen.
4. Do not stop or park your car to watch a fire; you may block the roads and interfere with fire-fighting operations.
5. Pay attention to the wind direction – it is highly dangerous to be down-wind of a fire, as it may spread quite rapidly and catch you unawares.

Livestock often graze on fields near camp sites

or to clear space for new buildings. In an attempt to halt the practice, a law has been passed prohibiting construction in areas destroyed by fire, but even this has not stopped arsonists. In the dry heat of summer, fire spreads rapidly in the undergrowth of the maquis, and the main enemy of the firemen is the wind, which is capable of carrying the fire a long way in a very short time. Fire-fighting is carried out by the local fire brigades as well as the state forest rangers, volunteers and specially equipped fire-fighting planes positioned in key areas of the island.

Minor Hazards

In the summer, whether you are on the beach or inland, be wary of too much sun, as it may cause serious burns and sunstroke. If it is windy, you may not be aware you are burning.

If a storm breaks and you need to take shelter, do not head for isolated trees or rocky peaks, which may attract lightning.

Although you cannot simply camp wherever you like, you can make private arrangements with landowners to pitch your tent away from official camp sites. Make sure you take away all your rubbish and do not light fires.

Bear in mind that grazing in the open countryside is still quite common in Sardinia; pigs, sheep, cows and horses may well decide to see whether campers have anything good to eat in their tents. Avoid sheepdogs, as they are

trained to chase away any potential intruders.

While walking or trekking in the countryside you may come across gates or fences barring your way. If possible, ask whether you can go through. Having done so, remember to close the gate so that animals are unable to escape. If you plan a lengthy hike, make sure you carry enough water with you, as villages may be few and far between. Lastly, there are no poisonous snakes on the island.

Banking and Local Currency

Most establishments accept major credit cards. Those paying with a credit card may be asked to show identification proofs, such as passport or driver's licence. Banks are the best place to exchange foreign currency, but opening hours are limited. You'll find foreign exchange machines or *bureaux de change* at airports and some train stations. ATMs, known as *bancomat*, are widespread and accept major cards with a PIN number.

An automatic cash dispenser in Orgósolo

Banks and Bureaux de Change

Bank opening hours are roughly 8:30am–1:30pm and 3–4:30pm from Monday to Friday. All banks close at weekends and on public holidays. Banking hours are slightly erratic, so it's advisable to arrive with some local currency. *Bureaux de change* are found in airports, stations and tourist areas and have longer opening hours, sometimes until late evening, but charge higher commissions.

ATMs

Automatic cash dispenser (*bancomat*) can be found wherever there is a bank and are easy to find both in all the larger towns and smaller villages. To avoid complications, check which cards the ATM accepts before inserting your cards. Costs for cash withdrawals will be set by your bank. Bear in mind that ATMs may run out of notes during weekends or before a major holiday. Before travelling, make sure you inform your bank of your trip to Italy, to prevent your card from getting blocked due to "unusual activity".

Credit and Debit Cards

Credit cards, once regarded with suspicion in Sardinia, are now accepted without any question by hotels, restaurants and shops, especially those in the tourist areas. All the major credit cards are accepted, the most popular cards being **Visa** and **MasterCard**. Only the more expensive establishments will take **American Express**. Travelling with more than one credit (and debit) card is recommended in case one is not accepted. Some restaurants, cafés and shops require a minimum expenditure to accept a credit card payment. Always make sure you have cash in case your card is not accepted.

Currency

The euro (€) is the common currency of the European Union. It went into general circulation on 1 January 2002, originally for 12 participating countries, of which Italy was one.

Euro Bank Notes

Euro bank notes have seven denominations. The €5 note (grey in colour) is the smallest, followed by the €10 note (pink), €20 note (blue), €50 note (orange), €100 note (green), €200 note (yellow) and €500 note (purple). All the notes show the stars of the European Union.

5 euros

10 euros

20 euros

50 euros

Euro Bank Coins

The euro has eight coin denominations: €1 and €2; 50 cents, 20 cents, 10 cents, 5 cents, 2 cents and 1 cent. The €2 and €1 coins are silver and gold in colour. The 50-, 20- and 10-cent coins are gold. The 5-, 2- and 1-cent coins are bronze.

5 cents   10 cents   20 cents   1 euro   2 euro

Communications and Media

Communication in Sardinia is generally efficient, especially in the coastal areas, where many places now offer Wi-Fi connection. The inland towns and villages are more isolated, and cell phone reception may sometimes be a problem. The postal service is slow, but couriers provide a fast, reliable alternative. Foreign-language newspapers and magazines can be bought in the bigger towns (usually at the train stations) and in the tourist areas. State-run and privately owned television stations exist, but only satellite TV and radio stations, available in some hotels, broadcast foreign-language programmes.

Pubic Telephones and Mobile Phones

The Italian national telephone company, **Telecom Italia**, dismantled the last remaining public telephone booths in 2014, so it's best to rely on your mobile phone, either by setting up a roaming agreement with your provider at home, or by purchasing a local SIM card. **TIM** and **Vodafone** are the main providers in Sardinia.

International and Local Telephone Calls

A cheap and efficient way to make an international call is to buy an international calling card, which can be purchased at tobacconists and newsstands. Rates are slightly higher when using it to call a mobile phone. Check with your hotel before using a card from your room, as extra charges may be applied. To make a local call, always dial the area code preceded by 0, even if you are calling a number in the same town. The 0 before the local area code needs to be dialled after the country code when calling from abroad. Mobile phone numbers always start with a 3, and are not preceded by a 0.

Internet

The Internet is widely available, particularly in urban areas. Telecom Italia provides Internet services in the country's major train stations and public phone centres. Privately operated Internet points can be found in most towns. **Internet Train** has three branches, in Cagliari, Quartu

Sant'Elena and Villasimius; simply buy a charged magnetic card, which can be used across the network. There are Wi-Fi hotspots across Sardinia, and many of them are free.

Postal Services

Small post offices are open from 8am to 1:15pm, while larger offices open until 6:45pm or 7pm (1:15pm on Saturday). For English-language information on post office services, visit the **Poste Italiane** website. Letters can take between four days and two weeks to arrive. For a more reliable option, use *posta raccomandata* (recorded delivery). Anything of value should be sent by *assicurata* (insured post). For urgent communications, use **DHL** or **Fedex**, or try the state couriers, Postacelere and Paccocelere, which are based at all the main post offices.

Newspapers and Magazines

The leading local papers are *L'Unione Sarda*, *La Nuova Sardegna* and *Sardegna Oggi*, and they provide useful information and event listings, but are only in Italian. English-language

The newsstand of L'Unione Sarda in Cagliari

magazines and papers are sold in the major towns and in main tourist areas.

Television and Radio

Television channels include the state-owned RAI and Mediaset. There are also many local channels. Most foreign programmes are dubbed into Italian. Satellite channels, such as BBC World News, Sky, and CNN, show news and sports programmes in English but are only available in hotels that have satellite TV. There are three national radio stations.

DIRECTORY

Country Codes

To call Italy from these countries, dial the code and then the number.

Australia
Tel 00 1139.

Canada
Tel 011 39.

United Kingdom
Tel 00 39.

United States
Tel 011 39.

Public Telephones and Mobile Phones

Telecom Italia
w telecomitalia.com

TIM
Via Fratelli Kennedy 9E, Alghero.
Via Roma 84, Cagliari.
w tim.it

Vodafone
Piazza Garibaldi 16, Cagliari.
Centro Commerciale Auchan,
SS 125, Olbia.
w vodafone.it

Internet

Internet Train
w internettrain.it

Postal Services

DHL
Tel 199 199345. w dhl.it

Fedex
Tel 199 151 119. w fedex.com

Poste Italiane
w poste.it

TRAVEL INFORMATION

Sardinia is served by Europe's major airlines, including British Airways, the Sardinian Meridiana and the Italian carrier, Alitalia. Low-cost flights are available from Ryanair and easyJet. In addition, many charter flights operate in summer, often with low fares or as part of a package deal. During summer there are also more direct flights available. If no direct flights or suitable connections are available, Alitalia and Meridiana provide regular domestic flights from Italy's mainland cities throughout the year. The island is also served by an excellent network of ferries from ports on the Italian mainland. Slower ferries offer a long crossing, with berths for overnight trips, whereas the faster and more expensive ferry lines can almost halve the travelling time. During the peak summer season of July and August it is not easy to find places on passenger and, in particular, car ferries, so make sure to book your place well in advance.

Arriving by Air

The main airports in Sardinia are Cagliari's **Elmas** airport, Alghero's **Fertilia** airport and the **Olbia-Costa Smeralda** airport. These are not far from their respective city centres and offer taxi services as well as public transport into town. In Alghero, for example, a bus runs according to the flight timetable, linking the airport to the city centre (call 079 95 04 58 for details). In the summer there is also a coach service from Olbia-Costa Smeralda airport to the towns on the Costa Smeralda.

   Alitalia and the Sardinian airline **Meridiana** serve Cagliari and Olbia from a number of Italian cities, providing links to major European capitals. Meridiana also flies daily from Gatwick to Cagliari via Florence. **British Airways** flies

Alitalia airbus taxing into the Elmas airport

from London Heathrow to Cagliari. Low-cost airline **Ryanair** serves Alghero direct from London Stansted, East Midlands and Liverpool airports, while **easyJet** serves Olbia from London Gatwick and Cagliari from London Luton.

   Long-haul passengers will almost inevitably have to change in an Italian mainland or other European city. If you are travelling from the United States, American, United Airlines and Delta offer direct flights to Rome or Milan where you can get a connection to one of the island's airports. Canadian Airlines flies from Canada and Qantas flies from Australia. Alitalia also has a regular service between these countries and Rome.

Passenger waiting area, Olbia-Costa Smeralda airport

A Tirrenia line car ferry

Tickets and Fares

If you are based in the UK, Ryanair and easyJet usually provide the cheapest flights. However, it is also worth scouring the small ads of newspapers as well as airline aggregator websites such as skyscanner.co.uk for cut-price charters and discounted scheduled flights. Fares vary greatly during the year, but the most expensive periods are summer, Christmas and Easter holidays. Meridiana offers low-season economy flights.

For intercontinental flights the most economical option is to take a budget flight to London, Berlin or Barcelona and get a Ryanair or easyJet flight from there to the island.

Arriving by Sea

Sardinia is easily reached by ferry from Italy's mainland ports which are accessible by train. The crossing can be long (16 hours from Naples to Cagliari, 7 hours between Civitavecchia and Olbia), although the more expensive ferry lines offer a faster service. For overnight crossings, passengers can book a cabin. Ferry services leave from Civitavecchia, Fiumicino, Naples, Genoa, Livorno, Palermo and Trapani. They dock at Sardinia's tourist ports of Arbatax, Cagliari, Olbia, Golfo Aranci, Palau and Porto Torres. **Corsica Sardinia Ferries'** fast service connects Livorno and Civitavecchia with Golfo Aranci in just over four hours. **Tirrenia** offers a similar service from La Spezia and Civitavecchia to Olbia (a four- to five-hour trip). There are also ferries from Bonifacio in Corsica, bound for Santa Teresa di Gallura and between Palau and Porto Vecchio in Corsica during the high season. **Moby** sails from mainland Italy to the Sardinian port of Olbia and between Bonifacio (Corsica) and Santa Teresa di Gallura.

Package Holidays

Most travel agencies, both in Italy and abroad, offer holidays to Sardinia. The sea and coast are the greatest attractions, but there are also options for holidays in the interior. Many holiday villages provide a wide range of entertainment and sports facilities, including diving and windsurfing, sailing lessons and horseback riding.

A Moby ferry

Getting Around Sardinia

Many of Sardinia's roads are characterized by an interminable number of curves and tight bends: annoying if you are in a hurry, but pleasant if you're on holiday and can take time to enjoy the scenery. With the exception of a few major roads, such as the SS131, which connects the four corners of the island, the roads wind their way over hills and across plains so that, even though the traffic outside the towns is light, always calculate plenty of time when planning a tour. The empty roads, on the other hand, are perfect for cyclists.

Bikers cycling down a dirt track in Cagliari

Travelling by Car

Given the inefficient public transport system, and the spectacular natural scenery, travelling by car is the best way to become acquainted with the island.

It is important, however, to be aware of the issues that may occur. Minor roads will often be blocked by flocks of sheep, adding to your travel time. Road signs are not always clear and may be missing just when you need them most. Should this occur, the best thing to do is to ask someone on the way – Sardinians will happily help. Another potential problem is petrol, as there are not many filling stations in the interior. Lastly, you will often find yourself forced to take difficult dirt roads, particularly when looking for an out-of-the-way church or archaeological site.

Always carry a good, up-to-date road map. One of the best is published by the Touring Club Italiano, to a scale of 1: 200.000. Keep your vehicle and identity documents (including driving licence) with you in the car at all times, since the police often do spot checks. In case

of breakdown, contact the **ACI Breakdown Service**.

Green Travel

Sardinians rely heavily on their cars for travelling owing to the lack of an efficient and fast public transport system between smaller towns and cities. However, in big cities such as Cagliari, car-sharing schemes are becoming increasingly popular. These are aimed mainly at residents rather than tourists. Bicycle tourism is also popular throughout the island and the website www.piste-ciclabili.com, provides a map of bike lanes and bike-friendly itineraries for

pleasant excursions. Although the bus systems in towns and cities are rather busy and chaotic, they are always a better and more eco-friendly options than driving in city centres.

Parking

In winter, parking at the beach is normally free. In summer, car park attendants charge by the hour, half a day, or a full day. The Costa Smeralda has the highest charges. Cagliari's Poetto beach always has free parking.

Renting a Car

Most international car rental companies, such as **Avis**, **Europcar**, **Hertz** and **Maggiore**, are represented in Sardinia, with offices in the main port towns (Olbia, Cagliari, Porto Torres) and in the airports of Cagliari Elmas, Olbia-Costa Smeralda and Alghero Fertilia. Hertz offers discounts for those who fly with Meridiana and Ryanair.

A number of holiday companies offer fly-drive deals.

Rules of the Road

The speed limits are 50 km/h (30 mph) in town and 90 km/h (55 mph) on major roads. Seat belts are required, and motor cyclists, moped riders and passengers must wear helmets.

Boat Hire

In many ports it is possible to charter yachts, from one day to one week. The prices may include a crew or simply the use of the boat. Hiring a boat enables

A car on a single-track road travelling through the Sardinian countryside

The narrow-gauge train known as the *trenino verde*

Cycling and Mountain Biking

The quiet roads along the coast or the stunning countryside in the interior are ideal for long trips by bicycle. If you prefer more arduous exercise, the steeper mountain roads are suitable for mountain bikes. Tourist offices will have suggestions for local bicycle routes and several associations exist with information about off-road tours by mountain bike. Cyclists should wear high-visibility clothing.

Travelling by Train

Sardinia has an efficient – if sometimes slow – railway service. There are several daily departures from Cagliari to Sassari, Porto Torres and Olbia, and the journey takes between 3 and 4 hours. Most journeys necessitate a change of train at Oziere-Chilivani.

Local trains running between Cagliari, Iglesias and Carbonia depart regularly, as do trains between Alghero and Sassari. Fares are surprisingly cheap: €18 one-way between Cagliari and Olbia.

A train ride in true late-19th-century style, such as

you to see the island away from the busy resorts. For information, make enquiries with the harbour authorities or boat owners.

on the Mandas–Sòrgono route (see p113), is an enjoyable and relaxing way to see the island's stunning scenery, which has fascinated travellers for many centuries. In spring and summer, the **Azienda Regionale Sarda Trasporti** (ARST) organizes train services from Mandas to Sorgono, Seui and Arbatax on the *trenino verde* (see pp96–7). "Vintage" wagons dating from 1913 are pulled by steam locomotives from the 1930s.

Travelling by Coach

The Azienda Regionale Sarda Trasporti (ARST) network covers most towns, cities and resorts in Sardinia. In order to meet the needs of the ever-growing number of visitors, ARST has issued a special tourist pass (biglietto turistico), available to non-residents only, between 1 June and 30 September. The pass allows you to travel on all ARST coaches, and can be purchased for a period of 7 (€45), 14 (€70), 21 (€100) or 28 (€130) days.

Other bus companies operate within specific towns or provinces. Tickets are sold in newspaper kiosks and at tobacconists, as well as bus stations. For more information, contact the local tourist office.

DIRECTORY

Travelling by Car

ACI Breakdown Service
Tel 803116.

Renting a Car

Avis
Tel 199 100 133.
W avisautonoleggio.it

Europcar
Tel 199 30 70 30.
W europcar.it

Hertz
Tel 070 24 00 37.
W hertz.it

Maggiore
Tel 199 15 120.
W maggiore.it

Cycling and Mountain Biking

Cicloexpress
Alghero.
Tel 079 98 69 50.
W cicloexpress.com

Dolcevita Bike Tours
Pula.
Tel 070 920 98 85.
W dolcevitabiketours.com

Federazione Ciclista Italiana
Tel 070 66 32 43.
W federciclismo.it/sardegna

Mountain Bike Club Taxus Baccata
Gonnasfanadiga.
Tel 070 979 98 64.
W taxusbaccata.it

Sardinia Cycling
Quartu Sant'Elena.
W sardiniacycling.com

Travelling by Train

ARST Information Offices
Tel 800 86 50 42.
W arst.sardegna.it

Trenitalia
Tel 892 021, 199 30 30 60
(disabled users).
W trenitalia.com

General Index

Phrase Book

In an Emergency

Help!	Aiuto!	eye-**yoo**-toh
Stop!	Ferma!	fair-**mah**
Call a doctor.	Chiama un medico	kee-**ah**-mah oon **meh**-dee-koh
Call an ambulance.	Chiama un' ambulanza	kee-**ah**-mah oon am-boo-lan-tsa
Call the police.	Chiama la polizia	kee-**ah**-mah lah pol-ee-tsee-ah
Call the fire brigade.	Chiama i pompieri	kee-**ah**-mah ee pom-pee-**air**-ee
Where is the telephone?	Dov'è il telefono?	dov-eh eel teh-**leh**-foh-noh?
The nearest hospital?	L'ospedale più vicino?	loss-peh-**dah**-leh pee-oo vee-**chee**-noh?

Communication Essentials

Yes/No	Sì/No	see/noh
Please	Per favore	pair fah-**vor**-eh
Thank you	Grazie	**grah**-tsee-eh
Excuse me	Mi scusi	mee **skoo**-zee
Hello	Buon giorno	bwon **jor**-noh
Goodbye	Arrivederci	ah-ree-veh-**dair**-chee
Good evening	Buona sera	**bwon**-ah **sair**-ah
morning	la mattina	lah mah-**tee**-nah
afternoon	il pomeriggio	eel poh-meh-**ree**-joh
evening	la sera	lah **sair**-ah
yesterday	ieri	ee-**air**-ee
today	oggi	**oh**-jee
tomorrow	domani	doh-**mah**-nee
here	qui	kwee
there	la	lah
What?	Quale?	**kwah**-leh?
When?	Quando?	**kwan**-doh?
Why?	Perchè?	pair-**keh**?
Where?	Dove?	**doh**-veh?

Useful Phrases

How are you?	Come sta?	**koh**-meh stah?
Very well, thank you.	Molto bene, grazie.	**moll**-toh **beh**-neh grah-tsee-eh
Pleased to meet you.	Piacere di conoscerla.	pee-ah-**chair**-eh dee coh-noh-shair-lah
See you later.	A più tardi.	ah pee-**oo tar**-dee
That's fine.	Va bene.	va **beh**-neh
Where is/are...?	Dov'è/Dove sono...?	dov-eh/dov-eh **soh** noh?
How long does it take to get to...?	Quanto tempo ci vuole per andare a...?	**kwan**-toh **tem**-poh chee voo-**oh**-leh pair an-**dar**-eh ah...?
How do I get to...?	Come faccio per arrivare a...?	**koh**-meh **fah**-choh pair arri-**var**-eh ah...?
Do you speak English?	Parla inglese?	**par**-lah een-**gleh**-zeh?
I don't understand.	Non capisco.	non ka-**pee**-skoh
Could you speak more slowly, please?	Può parlare più lentamente, per favore?	pwoh par-lah-reh pee-**oo** len-ta-**men**-teh pair fah-**vor**-eh?
I'm sorry.	Mi dispiace.	mee dee-spee-**ah**-cheh

Useful Words

big	grande	**gran**-deh
small	piccolo	**pee**-koh-loh
hot	caldo	**kal**-doh
cold	freddo	**fred**-doh
good	buono	**bwoh**-noh
bad	cattivo	kat-**tee**-voh
enough	basta	**bas**-tah
well	bene	**beh**-neh
open	aperto	ah-**pair**-toh
closed	chiuso	kee-**oo**-zoh
left	a sinistra	ah see-**nee**-strah
right	a destra	ah **dess**-trah
straight on	sempre dritto	**sem**-preh **dree**-toh
near	vicino	vee-**chee**-noh
far	lontano	lon-**tah**-noh
up	su	soo
down	giù	joo
early	presto	**press**-toh
late	tardi	**tar**-dee
entrance	entrata	en-**trah**-tah
exit	uscita	oo-**shee**-ta
toilet	il gabinetto	eel gab-hee-**net**-toh
free, unoccupied	libero	**lee**-bair-oh
free, no charge	gratuito	grah-**too**-ee-toh

Making a Telephone Call

I'd like to place a long-distance call.	Vorrei fare una interurbana.	vor-**ray far**-eh oona in-tair-oor-**bah**-nah
I'd like to make a reverse-charge call.	Vorrei fare una telefonata a carico del destinatario.	vor-**ray far**-eh oona teh-leh-fon-**ah**-tah ah **kar**-ee-koh dell dess-tee-nah-**tar**-ree-oh
I'll try again later.	Ritelefono più tardi.	ree-teh-**leh**-foh-noh pee-oo **tar**-dee
Can I leave a message?	Posso lasciare un messaggio?	**poss**-oh lash-**ah**-reh oon mess-**sah**-joh?
Hold on.	Un attimo, per favore	oon **ah**-tee-moh, pair fah-**vor**-eh
Could you speak up a little please?	Può parlare più forte, per favore?	pwoh par-**lah**-reh pee-oo for-teh, pair fah-**vor**-eh?
local call	telefonata locale	te-leh-fon-**ah**-tah loh-cah-leh

Shopping

How much does this cost?	Quant'è, per favore?	kwan-**teh** pair fah-**vor**-eh?
I would like...	Vorrei...	vor-**ray**
Do you have...?	Avete...?	ah-**veh**-teh...?
I'm just looking.	Sto soltanto guardando.	stoh sol-**tan**-toh gwar-dan-doh
Do you take credit cards?	Accettate carte di credito?	ah-chet-**tah**-teh **kar**-teh dee **creh**-dee-toh?
What time do you open/close?	A che ora apre/chiude?	ah keh **or**-ah **ah**-preh/kee-oo-deh?
this one	questo	**kweh**-stoh
that one	quello	**kwell**-oh
expensive	caro	**kar**-oh
cheap	a buon prezzo	ah bwon **pret**-soh
size, clothes	la taglia	lah **tah**-lee-ah
size, shoes	il numero	eel **noo**-mair-oh
white	bianco	bee-**ang**-koh
black	nero	**neh**-roh
red	rosso	**ross**-oh
yellow	giallo	**jal**-loh
green	verde	**vair**-deh
blue	blu	bloo

Types of Shop

antique dealer	l'antiquario	lan-tee-**kwah**-ree-oh
bakery	il forno/il panificio	eel forn-oh/eel pan-ee-**fee**-choh
bank	la banca	lah **bang**-kah
bookshop	la libreria	lah lee-breh-**ree**-ah
butcher	la macelleria	lah mah-chell-eh-ree-ah
cake shop	la pasticceria	lah pas-tee-chair-ee-ah
chemist	la farmacia	lah far-mah-**chee**-ah
delicatessen	la salumeria	lah sah-loo-meh-**ree**-ah
department store	il grande magazzino	eel **grah**-deh mag-gad-**zee**-noh
fishmonger	il pescivendolo	eel pesh-ee-**ven**-doh-loh
florist	il fioraio	eel fee-or-**eye**-oh
greengrocer	il fruttivendolo	eel froo-tee-**ven**-doh-loh
grocery	alimentari	ah-lee-men-**tah**-ree
hairdresser	il parrucchiere	eel par-roo-kee-**air**-eh
ice cream parlour	la gelateria	lah jel-lah-tair-**ree**-ah
market	il mercato	eel mair-**kah**-toh
newsstand	l'edicola	leh-**dee**-koh-lah
post office	l'ufficio postale	loo-fee-choh pos-**tah**-leh
shoe shop	il negozio di scarpe	eel neh-**goh**-tsioh dee skar-peh
supermarket	il supermercato	eel su-pair-mair-**kah**-toh
tobacconist	il tabaccaio	eel tah-bak-**eye**-oh
travel agency	l'agenzia di viaggi	lah-jen-**tsee**-ah dee vee-**ad**-jee

Sightseeing

art gallery	la pinacoteca	lah peena-koh-**teh**-kah
bus stop	la fermata dell'autobus	lah fair-**mah**-tah dell **ow**-toh-booss
church	la chiesa	lah kee-**eh**-zah
	la basilica	lah bah-**seel**-i-kah
closed for holidays	chiuso per le ferie	kee-oo-zoh pair leh **fair**-ee-eh
garden	il giardino	eel jar-**dee**-no
library	la biblioteca	lah beeb-lee-oh-**teh**-kah
museum	il museo	eel moo-**zeh**-oh
railway station	la stazione	lah stah-tsee-**oh**-neh
tourist information	l'ufficio di turismo	loo-**fee**-choh dee too-**ree**-smoh

Numbers

1	uno	**oo**-noh
2	due	**doo**-eh
3	tre	treh
4	quattro	**kwat**-roh
5	cinque	**ching**-kweh
6	sei	**say**-ee
7	sette	**set**-teh
8	otto	**ot**-toh
9	nove	**noh**-veh
10	dieci	dee-**eh**-chee
11	undici	**oon**-dee-chee
12	dodici	**doh**-dee-chee
13	tredici	**tray**-dee-chee
14	quattordici	kwat-**tor**-dee-chee
15	quindici	**kwin**-dee-chee
16	sedici	**say**-dee-chee
17	diciassette	dee-chah-**set**-teh
18	diciotto	dee-**chot**-toh
19	diciannove	dee-chah-**noh**-veh
20	venti	**ven**-tee
30	trenta	**tren**-tah
40	quaranta	kwah-**ran**-tah
50	cinquanta	ching-**kwan**-tah
60	sessanta	sess-**an**-tah
70	settanta	set-**tan**-tah
80	ottanta	ot-**tan**-tah
90	novanta	noh-**van**-tah
100 .	cento	**chen**-toh
1,000	mille	**mee**-leh
2,000	duemila	**doo**-eh **mee**-lah
5,000	cinquemila	**ching**-kweh **mee**-lah
1,000,000	un milione	oon meel-**yoh**-neh

Time, Days, Months, Seasons

one minute	un minuto	oon mee-**noo**-toh
one hour	un'ora	oon or-ah
half an hour	mezz'ora	medz-**or**-ah
a day	un giorno	oon **jor**-noh
a week	una settimana	oona set-tee-**mah**-nah
Monday	lunedí	loo-neh-**dee**
Tuesday	martedí	mar-teh-**dee**
Wednesday	mercoledí	mair-koh-leh-**dee**
Thursday	giovedí	joh-veh-**dee**
Friday	venerdí	ven-air-**dee**
Saturday	sabato	**sah**-bah-toh
Sunday	domenica	doh-**meh**-nee-kah
January	gennaio	jen-**nah**-yo
February	febbraio	feb-**bra**-yo
March	marzo	**mar**-tzo
April	aprile	a-**pree**-leh
May	maggio	**mah**-jo
June	giugno	**joo**-nyo
July	luglio	**loo**-lyo
August	agosto	ag-**os**-toh
September	settembre	set-**tem**-bre
October	ottobre	ot-**toh**-bre
November	novembre	no-**vem**-bre
December	dicembre	dee-**chem**-bre
Spring	primavera	pree-mah-**veh**-ra
Summer	estate	es-**tah**-te
Autumn	autunno	ow-**toon**-noh
Winter	inverno	een-**vair**-no
Christmas	Natale	nah-**tah**-le
Christmas Eve	la Vigilia di Natale	vee-**jee**-lya dee nah-**tah**-le
Good Friday	Venerdí Santo	ven-air-**dee** san-toh
Easter	Pasqua	**pas**-kwa
New Year	Capodanno	kah-poh-**dan**-noh
New Year's Eve	San Silvestro	san seel-**ves**-tro
Whitsun	Pentecoste	pente-**kos**-te

Travelling

adult	l'adulto	ad-**ool**-toh
airport	l'aeroporto	a-air-oh-**por**-toh
baggage claim	il ritiro bagagli	ree-**tee**-roh bah-**gal**-yee
boarding card	la carta d'imbarco	**kar**-tah deem-**bar**-koh
boat	la barca	**bar**-kah
booking office	la biglietteria	beel-yet-teh-**ree**-ah
bus	l'autobus	**ow**-toh-booss
bus stop	la fermata dell'autobus	fer-**mah**-tah del-**ow**-toh-booss
check-in desk	l'accettazione	achet-ah-**tzyoh**-neh
luggage	i bagagli	bah-**gal**-yee
child (male)	il bambino	bam-**bee**-noh
child (female)	la bambina	bam-**bee**-nah
coach (bus)	la corriera	kor-ee-**air**-ah
connection	la coincidenza	ko-een-chee-**den**-tza

couchette	la cuccetta	koo-**chet**-tah
customs	la dogana	doh-**gah**-nah
delay	ritardo	ree-**tar**-doh
domestic	nazionale	natz-yoh-**nah**-leh
exit gate	l'uscita	oo-**shee**-tah
fare	la tariffa	tah-**reef**-fah
ferry	il traghetto	trah-**get**-toh
first class	prima classe	pree-**mah klas**-seh
flight	il volo	**voh**-loh
left luggage	il deposito bagagli	deh-**poh**-zee-toh bah-**gal**-yee
lost property	l'ufficio oggetti smarriti	oof-**fee**-cho **ojet**-tee zmar-**ree**-tee
luggage trolley	il carrello	kar-**rel**-loh
non-smoking	non fumatori	**noh**-n foo-mah-**toh**-ree
passport	il passaporto	pas-sah-**por**-toh
platform	il binario	bee-**nah**-ree-o
railway	la ferrovia	fer-roh-**vee**-a
reservation	la prenotazione	pre-noh-**tatz**-yoh-neh
return ticket	andata e ritorno	an-**dah**-tah ay ree-**tor**-no
seat	il posto	**poss**-toh
second class	seconda classe	sek-**on**-da **klas**-seh
single ticket	solo andata	**soh**-loh an-**dah**-tah
smoking	fumatori	foo-mah-**toh**-ree
station	la stazione	statz-**yoh**-neh
supplement	il supplemento	soop-leh-**men**-toh
taxi	il taxi	**tak**-si
ticket	il biglietto	beel-**yet**-to
timetable	l'orario	oh-**rah**-ry-oh
train	il treno	**treh**-no
underground	la metropolitana	met-roh-poh-lee-**tah**-nah

Motoring

Fill her up	il pieno	eel **pyeh**-noh
Do you do repairs?	Effettua riparazioni?	ef-**fet**-tua ree-paratz-**yoh**-nee?
I'd like to hire a car	Vorrei noleggiare una macchina	vor-**ray** noh-ledg-**ah**-re oona **mah**-keena
automatic	con il cambio automatico	kon eel **kam**-bee-oh ow-toh-**mah**-tee-oh
boot	il portabagagli	porta-bah-**gal**-yee
car	l'automobile, la macchina	ow-toh-**moh**-bee-leh, **mah**-kee-nah
car ferry	il traghetto	trah-**geh**-to
diesel oil	gasolio	gaz-**oh**-lyo
garage (repairs)	Il meccanico	mek-**ah**-neeko
four-star petrol	benzina super	ben-**dze**-na **soo**-per
licence	la patente	pah-**ten**-teh
motorbike	la motocicletta	moh-toh-chee-**kleh**-ta
motorway	l'autostrada	ow-toh-**strah**-da
petrol	la benzina	ben-**dzeena**
petrol station	la stazione di servizio	statz-**yoh**-neh dee sair-**veetz**-yo
ring road	raccordo anulare	rak-**or**-do an-oo-**lah**-re
road	la strada	**strah**-da
traffic lights	il semaforo	sem-**ah**-foh-roh
unleaded petrol	benzina senza piombo	ben-**dzeena** sen-dza peeom-**boh**

Signs you may see on the Road

accendere i fari	ach-**en**-deh-reh ee **fah**-ree	headlights on
caduta massi	kah-**doo**-tah **mah**-see	falling rocks
divieto di accesso	dee-**vyeh**-toh dee ach-**eh**-so	no entry
divieto di sosta	dee-**vyeh**-toh dee **sos**-tah	no stopping
dogana	dog-**ah**-nah	customs
escluso residenti	es-**kloo**-so reh-zi-**den**-ti	residents only
ghiaccio	**gyah**-cho	ice
lavori in corso	lah-**voh**-ree een kor-so	roadworks
nebbia	**neb**-bya	fog
parcheggio a pagamento	par-**kej**-yo a pah-gah-**men**-toh	paying car park
parcheggio custodito	par-**kej**-yo koo-toh-**dee**-toh	car park with attendant
pedaggio	peh-**daj**-oh	toll
pericolo	peh-**ree**-koh-loh	danger
rallentare	rah-lehn-**tah**-reh	reduce speed
senso unico	**sen**-tzo oo-nee-ko	one way
uscita camion	oo-**shee**-tah **kah**-myon	works exit
zona pedonale	**dzoh**-na peh-doh-**nah**-leh	pedestrian area

Staying in a Hotel

Do you have any vacant rooms?	Avete camere libere?	ah-**veh**-teh **kah**-mair-eh **lee**-bair-eh?
double room	una camera doppia	oona **kah**-mair-ah **doh**-pee-ah
with double bed	con letto matrimoniale	kon **let**-toh mah-tree-moh-nee-**ah**-leh
twin room	una camera con due letti	oona **kah**-mair-ah kon **doo**-eh **let**-tee
single room	una camera singola	oona **kah**-mair-ah **sing**-goh-lah
room with a bath, shower	una camera con bagno, con doccia	oona **kah**-mair-ah kon **ban**-yoh, kon **dot**-chah
I have a reservation.	Ho fatto una prenotazione.	oh **fat**-toh oona preh-noh-tah-tsee-**oh**-neh
balcony	balcone	bal-**coh**-neh
breakfast	prima colazione	**pree**-ma coh-lah-**tzyoh**-neh
key	la chiave	lah kee-**ah**-veh
porter	il facchino	eel fak-**kee**-noh
room service	servizio in camera	ser-**vitz**-yoh een **cah**-meh-rah

Eating Out

Have you got a table for…?	Avete un tavolo per…?	ah-**veh**-teh oon **tah**-voh-loh pair…?
I'd like to reserve a table.	Vorrei riservare un tavolo.	vor-**ray** ree-sair-**vah**-reh oon **tah**-voh-loh
the bill, please.	il conto, per favore.	**kon**-toh pair fah-**vor**-eh
I am a vegetarian.	Sono vegetariano/a.	**soh**-noh veh-jeh-tar-ee-**ah**-noh/nah
beer	la birra	**bee**-rah
bread	il pane	**pah**-neh
bottle	la bottiglia	bot-**teel**-yah
breakfast	la prima colazione	**pree**-mah koh-lah-tsee-**oh**-neh
butter	il burro	**boor**-roh
carafe	la caraffa	kah-**raff**-fah
child's portion	una porzione per bambini	portz-**yoh**-neh pair bam-**bee**-nee
coffee	il caffè	kaf-**feh**
cover charge	il coperto	**koh**-pair-toh
cup	la tazza	**tat**-zah
dessert	il dessert	des-**ser**
dinner	la cena	**cheh**-nah
dish of the day	il piatto del giorno	pee-**ah**-toh dell **jor**-no
first course	il primo	**pree**-moh
fixed price menu	il menù a prezzo fisso	meh-**noo** ah **pret**-soh **fee**-soh
fork	la forchetta	for-**ket**-tah
glass	il bicchiere	bee-kee-**air**-eh
half-litre	da mezzo litro	da **met**-zoh **lee**-troh
knife	il coltello	kol-**tel**-loh
litre	un litro	**lee**-troh
lunch	il pranzo	**pran**-tsoh
main course	il secondo	seh-**kon**-doh
medium (meat)	al punto	al **poon**-toh
menu	il menù	meh-**noo**
milk	il latte	**lat**-teh
pepper	il pepe	**peh**-peh
plate	il piatto	p-**yat**-toh
rare (meat)	al sangue	al **sang**-gweh
receipt (in bars) (in restaurants)	lo scontrino la ricevuta	skon-**tree**-noh ree-cheh-**voo**-tah
restaurant	il ristorante	rees-toh-**ran**-teh
salad	l'insalata	een-sah-**lah**-tah
salt	il sale	**sah**-leh
sandwich	il panino	pan-**ee**-noh
serviette	il tovagliolo	toh-val-**yoh**-loh
snack	lo spuntino	spoon-**tee**-noh
soup	la minestra	mee-**nes**-trah
spoon	il cucchiaio	koo-kee-**eye**-oh
starter	l'antipasto	an-tee-**pas**-toh
sugar	lo zucchero	dzoo-keh-roh
tea	il tè	teh
teaspoon	il cucchiaino	kook-yah-**ee**-noh
tip	la mancia	**man**-cha
vegetables	il contorno	eel kon-**tor**-noh
waitress	la cameriera	kah-mair-ee-**air**-ah
waiter	il cameriere	kah-mair-ee-**air**-eh
water	l'acqua	**ak**-wah
fizzy/still	gassata/naturale	gah-**zah**-tah/ nah-too-**rah**-leh
well done (meat)	ben cotto	ben **kot**-toh
wine	il vino	**vee**-noh
wine list	la lista dei vini	**lee**-stah day **vee**-nee

Menu Decoder

abbacchio	ab-**ak**-yoh	spring lamb
acciughe	ach-**oo**-geh	anchovies
aceto	ach-**eh**-toh	vinegar
acqua minerale gassata/ naturale	ah-kwah mee-nair-**ah**-leh gah-**zah**-tah/ nah-too-**rah**-leh	mineral water fizzy/still
aglio	**al**-ee-oh	garlic
agnello	ah-**niell**-oh	lamb
al forno	al **for**-noh	baked
alla griglia	ah-lah **greel**-yah	grilled
albicocche	al-bee-**kok**-eh	apricots
ananas	**an**-an-ass	pineapple
anatra	**an**-at-rah	duck
anguria	an-**goo**-rya	water melon
antipasti	ahn-ti-**pas**-ti	starters
aperitivo	apeh-ree-**tee**-voh	aperitif
aragosta	ara-**goss**-tah	lobster
arancia	ah-**ran**-cha	orange
aringa	ah-**reen**-gah	herring
arrosto	ar-**ross**-toh	roast
asparagi	as-**pah**-rah-ji	asparagus
baccalà	bak-al-**la**	dried cod
basilico	bas-**ee**-lee-ko	basil
besciamella	besh-ah-**mel**-ah	white sauce
birra	**beer**-rah	beer
bistecca	bees-**tek**-ka	steak
bottarga	bot-**ahr**-gah	salted mullet roe
branzino	bran-**zee**-no	sea bass
brasato	bra-**sah**-toh	braised beef
bresaola	breh-**sah**-oh-lah	slices of cold, wind-dried beef with oil and lemon
brioche	bri-**osh**	type of croissant
brodo	**broh**-doh	clear broth
budino	boo-**dee**-noh	pudding
burro	**boor**-oh	butter
caffè	kah-**feh**	espresso coffee
caffè corretto	kah-**feh** koh-**reh**-toh	espresso coffee with a dash of liqueur
caffè lungo	kah-**feh** loon-goh	weak espresso coffee
caffè macchiato	kah-**feh** mak-**yah**-toh	espresso coffee with a dash of milk
caffè ristretto	kah-**feh** ree-**streh**-toh	strong espresso coffee
caffelatte	kah-**feh-lah**-teh	half coffee, half milk
calamari	kah-lah-**mah**-ree	squid
calzone	kal-**zoh**-neh	folded pizza filled with tomato and mozzarella
camomilla	kah-moh-**mee**-lah	camomile tea
cannella	kan-**el**-ah	cinnamon
cannelloni	kan-neh-**loh**-neo	stuffed pasta tubes
cappuccino	kap-oo-**chee**-noh	coffee with foaming milk
carciofi	kar-**choh**-fee	artichokes
carne	**kar**-neh	meat
carote	kar-**roh**-teh	carrots
castagne	kas-**tan**-yeh	chestnuts
cavolfiore	kavol-**fyoh**-reh	cauliflower
cavolo	**kah**-voh-loh	cabbage
cefalo	che-fah-loh	grey mullet
cernia	**cher**-nya	grouper (fish)
ciambella	cham-**bella**	ring-shaped cake
cicoria	chih-**kor**-ya	chicory
ciliege	chil-**yej**-eh	cherries
cioccolata	choc-oh-**lah**-tah	chocolate
cipolle	chih-**poh**-leh	onions
coniglio	kon-**ee**-lyo	rabbit
contorni	kon-**tor**-nee	vegetables
coperto	kop-**er**-toh	cover charge
coppa	**koh**-pah	cured pork, sliced finely and eaten cold
cordula	kor-doo-lah	Sardinian spit-roasted plaited lamb entrails
cotoletta	kot-oh-**let**-ta	pork or lamb chop
cozze	**kot**-zeh	mussels
crema	**kreh**-mah	custard dessert
crespella	kres-pel-lah	savoury pancake
crostata di frutta	kros-**tah**-tah dee **froo**-tah	fruit tart
datteri	**dat**-eh-ree	dates
digestivo	dee-jes-**tee**-voh	digestive liqueur
dolci	**dol**-chi	desserts, cakes
espresso	es-**pres**-soh	strong black coffee
fagiano	fah-**jah**-noh	pheasant
fagioli	fah-**joh**-lee	beans
fagiolini	fah-joh-**lee**-nee	long, green beans
fegato	**feh**-gah-toh	liver
fettuccine	feh-too-**chee**-neh	ribbon-shaped pasta
fichi	**fee**-kee	figs
filetto	fee-**leh**-toh	fillet (of beef)
finocchio	fee-**noh**-kyo	fennel
formaggio	for-**maj**-yo	cheese
fragole	**frah**-goh-leh	strawberries
frappé	frap-**eh**	whisked fruit or milk drink with ice
fregula	**freh**-goo-lah	small, granular pasta
frittata	free-**tah**-tah	type of omelette
fritto	**free**-toh	deep fried
fritto misto	**free**-toh **mees**-toh	seafood in batter
frittura di pesce	free-**too**-rah dee **pesh**-eh	variety of fried fish
frutta	**froo**-tah	fruit
frutta secca	**froo**-tah sek-kah	dried fruit
frutti di mare	**froo**-tee dee **mah**-reh	seafood

funghi	**foon**-g-ee	mushrooms
gamberetti	gam-beh-**reh**-tee	shrimps
gamberi	**gam**-beh-ree	prawns
gamberoni	gam-beh-**roh**-nee	king prawns
gelato	gel-**ah**-toh	ice cream
gnocchi	**nyok**-ee	small flour and potato dumplings
gorgonzola	gor-gon-**zoh**-lah	strong, soft blue cheese
granchio	**gran**-kyo	crab
granita	gra-**nee**-tah	drink with crushed ice
grissini	gree-**see**-nee	thin, crisp breadsticks
insalata	een-sah-**lah**-tah	salad
involtini	een-vol-**tee**-nee	meat rolls stuffed with ham and herbs
lamponi	lam-**poh**-nee	raspberries
latte	**lah**-teh	milk
lattuga	lah-**too**-gah	lettuce
leggero	leh-**jeh**-roh	light
legumi	leh-**goo**-mee	pulses
lenticchie	len-**teek**-yeh	lentils
lesso	**less**-oh	boiled
lepre	**leh**-preh	hare
limone	lee-**moh**-neh	lemon
lingua	**leen**-gwa	tongue
macedonia di frutta	mach-eh-**doh**-nya dee **froo**-tah	fruit salad
maiale	mah-**yah**-leh	pork
mandarino	man-dah-**ree**-noh	mandarin
mandorla	**man**-dor-lah	almond
manzo	**man**-dzo	beef
mascarpone	mah-skar-**poh**-neh	soft, sweet cheese
mela	**meh**-lah	apple
melanzane	meh-lan-**zah**-neh	aubergines
melone	meh-**loh**-neh	melon
menta	**men**-tah	mint
merluzzo	mer-**loo**-tzoh	cod
minestrone	mee-nes-**troh**-neh	thick vegetable soup
mirtilli	meer-**tee**-lee	bilberries
more	**mor**-eh	blackberries
nasello	nah-**seh**-loh	hake
nocciole	noch-**oh**-leh	hazelnuts
noce moscata	**noh**-che mos-**kah**-tah	nutmeg
noci	**noh**-chi	walnuts
olio	**oh**-lyo	oil
orata	oh-**rah**-tah	gilthead bream
origano	oh-**ree**-gah-noh	oregano
ossobuco	os-oh-**boo**-ko	stewed shin of veal
ostriche	**os**-tree-keh	oysters
pane carasau	**pah**-neh cah-rah-**sahw**	bread crisp, circular bread
panino	pah-**nee**-noh	filled roll
panna	pah-**nah**	cream
parmigiana di melanzane	par-mee-**jah**-nah dee meh-lan-zah-neh	aubergine, tomato, mozzarella and parmesan bake
parmigiano	par-mee-**jah**-noh	parmesan cheese
pasticcio	pas-**tich**-oh	pasta and meat bake
patate	pah-**tah**-teh	potatoes
pecorino	peh-coh-**ree**-noh	strong, hard ewe's milk cheese
penne	peh-**neh**	pasta quills
pepe	**peh**-peh	pepper (spice)
peperoncino	peh-peh-**ron**-chee-noh	cayenne pepper
peperoni	peh-peh-**roh**-nee	peppers
pera	**peh**-rah	pear
pesca	**pes**-kah	peach
pesce	**pesh**-eh	fish
piselli	pee-**seh**-lee	peas
polenta	poh-**len**-tah	boiled cornmeal with meat or vegetables
pollo	**poh**-loh	chicken
polpette	pol-**peh**-teh	meatballs
polpettone	pol-**peh**-toh-neh	meatloaf
pomodori	poh-moh-**doh**-ree	tomatoes
pompelmo	pom-**pel**-moh	grapefruit
porceddu	por-**ched**-doo	roast suckling pig
porri	**poh**-ree	leeks
prezzemolo	pretz-**eh**-moh-loh	parsley
primi piatti	**pree**-mee **pyah**-tee	first courses
prosciutto cotto/crudo	pro-**shoo**-toh **kot**-toh/**kroo**-doh	ham cooked/cured
prugne	**proo**-nyeh	plums
radicchio	rah-**deek**-yo	red chicory
ragù	rah-**goo**	mince and tomato sauce
ravanelli	rah-vah-**neh**-lee	radishes
ravioli	rah-vee-**oh**-lee	square-shaped egg pasta filled with meat
razza	**rah**-tzah	skate
ricotta	ree-**kot**-tah	white, soft cheese
ripieno	**ree**-pyeh-noh	stuffed
riso	**ree**-soh	rice
risotto	ree-**soh**-toh	rice cooked in stock
rognone	ron-**yoh**-neh	kidney
rosato	roh-**sah**-toh	rosé wine
rosolato	roh-soh-**lah**-toh	fried
rosmarino	ros-mah-**ree**-noh	rosemary
salame	sah-**lah**-meh	salami
sale	**sah**-leh	salt
salsa	**sal**-sah	sauce
salsiccia	sal-**see**-cha	sausage
salvia	**sal**-vya	sage
scaloppine	skah-loh-**pee**-neh	veal escalopes
seadas	say-**ah**-dahs	sweet cheese and lemon fritters
secco	**seh**-koh	dry

secondi piatti	seh-**kon**-dee **pyat**-ee	main courses
sedano	**seh**-dah-noh	celery
selvaggina	sel-vah-**jee**-nah	game
semifreddo	seh-mee-**freh**-doh	ice cream and sponge dessert
senape	**seh**-nah-peh	mustard
seppie	**sep**-pee-eh	cuttlefish
servizio compreso	ser-**vitz**-yo com-**preh**-soh	service charge included
servizio escluso	ser-**vitz**-yo es-**cloo**-so	service charge not included
sogliola	**sol**-yoh-lah	sole
sorbetto	sor-**bet**-oh	sorbet
speck	sp-**ek**	cured, smoked ham
spezzatino	spetz-ah-**tee**-noh	stew
spiedini	spyeh-**dee**-nee	meat or fish on a spit
spinaci	spee-**nah**-chee	spinach
spremuta	spreh-**moo**-tah	freshly squeezed juice
spumante	spoo-**man**-teh	sparkling wine
stufato	stoo-**fah**-toh	casserole
tacchino	tak-**ee**-noh	turkey
tagliatelle	tah-lyah-**teh**-leh	flat strips of egg pasta
tartine	tar-**tee**-neh	small sandwiches
tartufo	tar-**too**-foh	ice cream covered in cocoa
tè teh	teh	tea
tiramisù	tee-rah-mee-**soo**	dessert of coffee-soaked sponge, Marsala and mascarpone
tisana	tee-**zah**-nah	herbal tea
tonno	toh-**noh**	tuna
torta	**tor**-tah	tart, cake
torta salata	**tor**-tah sah-**lah**-tah	savoury flan
tortellini	tor-teh-**lee**-nee	stuffed pasta shapes
triglia	**tree**-lya	red mullet
trippa	tree-**pah**	tripe
trota	**troh**-tah	trout
uova	oo-**wo**-va	eggs
uova sode	oo-**wo**-va **soh**-deh	hard-boiled eggs
uva	**oo**-va	grapes
verdura	ver-**doo**-rah	vegetables
vino	**vee**-noh	wine
vino bianco	**vee**-noh **byan**-ko	white wine
vino da dessert	**vee**-noh dah deh-**ser**	dessert wine
vino da pasto	**vee**-noh dah **pas**-toh	table wine
vino da tavola	**vee**-noh dah **tah**-voh-lah	table wine
vino rosso	**vee**-noh **ros**-soh	red wine
vitello	vee-**tel**-loh	veal
vongole	**von**-goh-leh	clams
zafferano	zah-fair-**ah**-noh	saffron
zucca	**dzoo**-kah	pumpkin
zucchero	**dzoo**-kair-oh	sugar
zucchine	dzoo-**kee**-neh	courgettes
zuppa	dzoo-**pah**	soup
zuppa inglese	dzoo-**pah** een-**gleh**-seh	trifle

Acknowledgments

Dorling Kindersley would like to thank the following organizations and people whose contributions have made the preparation of this book possible:

Special Assistance

Agriturismo di Lucia Sotgiu, Agriturismo Sa Perda Marcada, Hertz, Claire Littlejohn, Hotel Mediterraneo, Greca Mattan, Meridiana, Anna Chiara Montefusco, Filomena Rosato, Anna Sacripanti, Terranostra Sardegna.

Design and Editorial

Additional Picture Research Ellen Root
Revisions and Relaunch Team Louise Abbott, Beverley Ager, Gillian Allen, Robert Andrews, Jennifer Avventura, Claire Baranowski, Uma Bhattacharya, Emma Bird, Samantha Borland, Antonugo Cerletti, Michelle Clark, Michelle Crane, Cooling Brown, Felicity Crowe, Vivien Crump, Dipika Dasgupta, Fay Franklin, Anna Freiberger, Camilla Gersh, Vinod Harish, Mohammad Hassan, Elinor Hodgson, Annette Jacobs, Jasneet Kaur, Rupanki Kaushik, Rahul Kumar, Vincent Kurien, Leena Lane, Sarah Lane, Georgina Matthews, Alison McGill, Daniel Mosseri, George Nimmo, Tiffany Parks, Helen Peters, Piero Pirosu, Gillian Price, Lee Redmond, Zoe Ross, Azeem Siddiqui, Rituraj Singh, Tarini Singh, Ellie Smith, Susana Smith, Tiziana Tuveri, Sylvia Tombesi-Walton, Helen Townsend, Conrad van Dyk, Nikhil Verma, Ingrid Vienings, Catherine Waring.

Additional Photography

Nigel Hicks, Ian O'Leary, Rough Guides/Roger Mapp

Picture Credits

Key: a = above; b = below; c = centre; f = far; l = left; r = right; t = top.

All the photographs were taken by the photographic agency Overseas S.r.l., except for the following:

123RF.com: Stefano Garau 206cra.

Alamy Images, London: Arco Images 14tc; Claudio H. Artman 10c, 96cl; Marco Casiragh 179tc; Authors Image/Mickael David 182cl; CuboImages srl/Marco Casiraghi 150cla, 203tr; Renato Granieri 32c; Robert Harding Picture Library Ltd/J Lightfoot 13tr; Yadid Levy 188br; Enrico Spanu 187tr; Specialpictures.nl 206bj; Tim E White 123t; **Alamy Stock Photo:** CHROMORANGE/Lothar Hinz 166br; Cultura Creative (RF) 208cla; Hemis 105br; imageBROKER 34; Pavel Kocur 147tl; Massimo Piacentino 135bl; REDA &CO srl 75tr; M. Sobreira 205bc; Mauro Spanu 31cla, 128bl; **Fabio De Angelis, Milan:** 36tr, 36cra, 147bl, 192c, 193cr; **Fabrizio Ardito, Rome:** 28tr, 28br, 29cr, 36cr, 37bl, 37br, 41t, 63bl, 87b, 89bl, 89cr, 100b, 103cr, 108tr, 108bc, 109tl, 110tl, 110cr, 110b, 112c, 115tl, 115cr, 120tr, 120cl, 123cl, 124tc, 125t, 128tl, 128c, 129tl, 154tl, 154b, 155tr, 155cr, 155br, 155cla, 156tl, 157tl, 159cr, 160tr, 160c, 160b, 161tl, 161cr, 161b, 162tr, 162c, 162cb, 163tl, 163b, 168cr, 169tl, 169crb; **AWL Images:** Francesco Iacobelli 200br.

Fabio Braibanti, Milan: 150br, 190cl, 193bl, 193tr, 193crb.

Cipriani Porto Cervo 189tr; **Colibri:** 181tr; **Corbis:** David Fleetham 23br, 87cr; Owen Franken 183c; Michelle Garrett 183tl.

Il Dagherrotipo: Marco Melodia 13bl; **Dreamstime.com:** Alkan2011 50–51, 52clb, 64bl, 142, 148tl; Byvalet 198–9; Ana Del Castillo 10bl, 14br 131t; Cenzo 105c; Jeanne Coppens 12t; Simon Dannhauer 145tr; Famed01 30br, 114tl, 195cra; Inna Felker

170–71; Marta Fernandez 53br; Frhojdysz 194tr; Filip Fuxa 208br; Neptune Grotto 14bl; Ilfede 53tr, 194cla; Elisa Locci 10cr, 15tr; Lpd82 49bl; Marmo81 15bl; Patrizio Martorana 99b; Fabio Medda 21b, 97cr; Milosk50 55b; MNStudio 168b; Neneo 49cra; Alessio Orrù 134t; Pressurepics 27bl; Denise Serra 101tr; Simba3003 197cla; Nico Smit 75tl; Radim Štrobl 82br, 86bl; Unclejo978 19b; **L'Essenza:** 175cr, 178br; **European Commission:** 203b.

Faro Capo-Spartivento: 173t, 176br; **Foto Carfagna + Associati, Rome:** 137br.

Cristina Gambaro, Milan: 29b, 74cl, 74c, 95cr, 112tl, 113cl; **Getty Images:** Riccardo Deiana Photography 2–3; DEA/S. MONTANARI 98; Massimo Di Nonno 107tl; Peppos 132cr; DEA/A. VERGANI 158tl.

Robert Harding Picture Library: Bruno Morandi 18; **Hotel Colonna San Marco:** 172br; **Hotel Le Torri:** 174bl.

Ilisso edizioni, Nuoro: 163cra, 163crb; **iStockphoto.com:** Elisalocci 196bc.

The Lemon House: 177tr.

Antonio Mannu, Sassari: 36bl, 45br, 47cr, 52tr, 56cl, 76tl, 106clb, 117b, 121tl, 121cra, 121crb, 122cl, 122bl, 123cl, 125tl, 130tr, 130cr, 130bl, 131cr, 132tl, 138cl, 138br, 139tl, 140t, 140bl, 158br, 158bl, 161cr, 161br, 164cl, 164br, 167br, 167cl, 167t, 191tr; **Mare Monti Miniere:** 173br; **Moby Lines Ferry, Italy:** 207cr.

Pevero Golf Club: 197cr; **Photoshot:** 102br, Cuboimages/ Enrico Spanu 64tr, Frank Sorge 196cla, Wothe, K. 204tr; **Luigi Pomata:** 180cla, 186br.

Alfio Elio Quattrocchi, Cagliari: 26tr, 46cl, 57tr, 66b, 110tr, 113cr, 149tl, 153tl, 169br, 192bl, 193br.

Raccolta Delle Stampe Achille Bertarelli, Milan: 35b, 40, 41c, 41bl, 42b; **Francine Reculez, Milan:** 182, 183, 193bc; **Rex by Shutterstock:** Canadian Press 148br; **Il Rifugio:** 182crb.

Sa Muvara Hotel: 174t; **Sardegna Turismo:** 143b; **Superstock:** DeAgostini 8–9; Ana del Castillo/age fotostock 54; Peter Eberts/ age fotostock, age fotostock/Danuta Hyniewska 159br, Hemis.fr/ MONTICO Lionel 84bc, Mauritius/Klaus Scholz 133b.

Trenino Verde: 33crb, 97bl, 113cla, 209cl; Tirrenia Di Navagazione S.P.A, Italy: 207tl; Al Tuguri: 181br.

Ufficio Stampa Del Comune Di Cagliari: Enzo Pinna 49crb.

Yacht Club Costa Smeralda: 153br

Front Endpaper:
Dreamstime.com: Alkan2011 Lbc, Ltl; **Getty Images:** Andy Christiani Rtr; DEA/S. MONTANARI Ltr; **Superstock:** Ana del Castillo/age fotostock Rbc.

Cover
Front and Spine – **Alamy Stock Photo:** Jan Wlodarczyk
All other images © Dorling Kindersley. For further information see: **www.dkimages.com**

Special Editions of DK Travel Guides

DK Travel Guides can be purchased in bulk quantities at discounted prices for use in promotions or as premiums. We are also able to offer special editions and personalized jackets, corporate imprints, and excerpts from all of our books, tailored specifically to meet your own needs.

To find out more, please contact:

in the US **specialsales@dk.com**

in the UK **travelguides@uk.dk.com**

in Canada **specialmarkets@dk.com**

in Australia **penguincorporatesales@ penguinrandomhouse.com.au**

Road Map
of Sardinia